Sir Walte

THE

DISCOVERY

OF THE

LARGE, RICH, AND BEAUTIFUL

EMPIRE OF GUIANA

WITH A RELATION OF

THE GREAT AND GOLDEN CITY OF MANOA

EDITED

WITH COPIOUS EXPLANATORY NOTES AND A BIOGRAPHICAL MEMOIR

BY

SIR ROBERT H. SCHOMBURGK

Elibron Classics
www.elibron.com

Elibron Classics series.

ISBN 1-4021-9584-2 (paperback)
ISBN 1-4021-4783-X (hardcover)

This Elibron Classics Replica Edition is an unabridged facsimile of the edition published in 1848 edition by the Hakluyt Society, London.

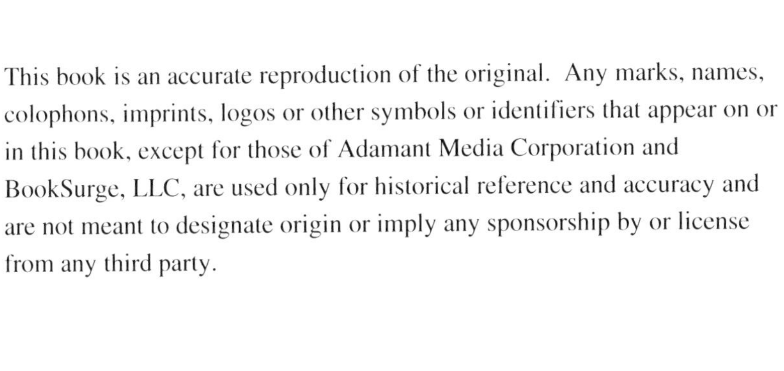

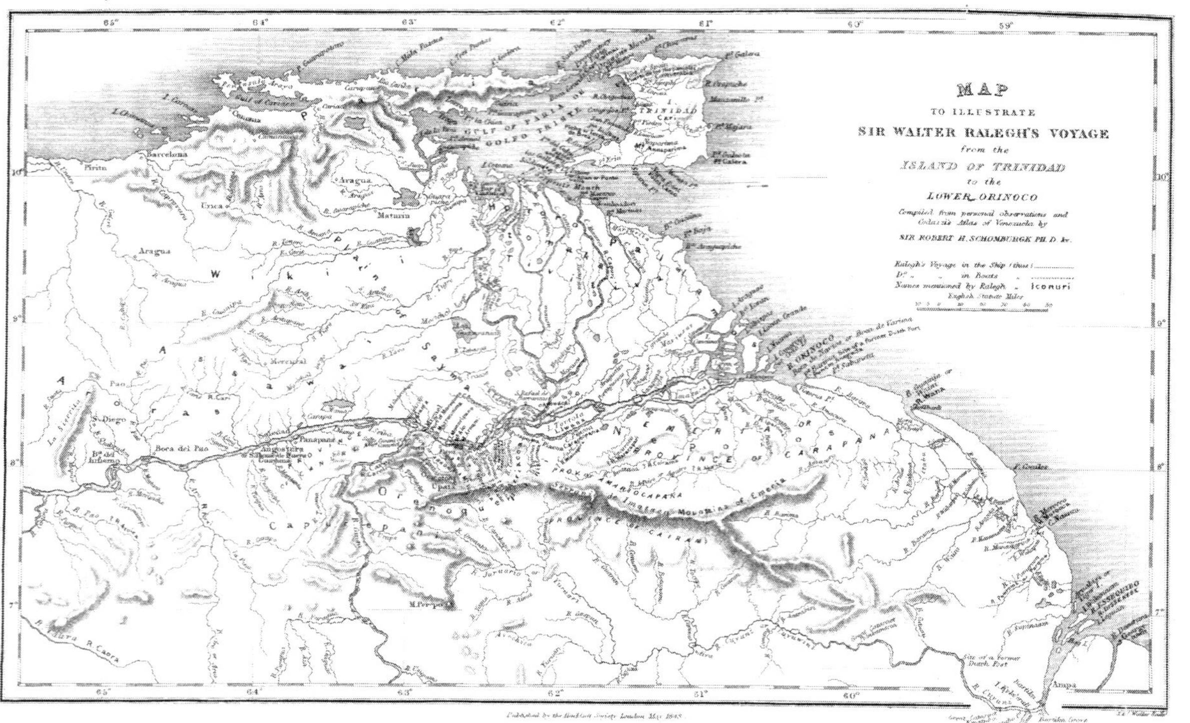
MAP
TO ILLUSTRATE
SIR WALTER RALEGH'S VOYAGE
from the
ISLAND OF TRINIDAD
to the
LOWER ORINOCO
Compiled from personal observations and
Codazzi's Atlas of Venezuela by
SIR ROBERT H. SCHOMBURGK PH. D. &c.
Ralegh's Voyage in the Ship (thus)
D° in Boats
Names mentioned by Ralegh Iconuri
English Statute Miles
TRINIDAD
GULF OF PARIA
GOLFO TRISTE
ORINOCO
Barcelona
Piritu
Cumana
Maturin
Aragua
Angostura
Boca del Pao
Panapana
PROVINCE OF CARAPANA
Published by the Hakluyt Society London May 1848

WORKS ISSUED BY

The Hakluyt Society.

THE DISCOVERY OF

THE EMPIRE OF GUIANA,

BY

SIR WALTER RALEGH, KNIGHT.

M.DCCC.XLVIII.

THE

DISCOVERY

OF THE

LARGE, RICH, AND BEAUTIFUL

EMPIRE OF GUIANA,

WITH A RELATION OF

THE GREAT AND GOLDEN CITY OF MANOA

(WHICH THE SPANIARDS CALL EL DORADO), ETC.

PERFORMED IN THE YEAR 1595,

BY

SIR W. RALEGH, KNT.,

CAPTAIN OF HER MAJESTY'S GUARD, LORD WARDEN OF THE STANNARIES, AND HER HIGHNESS'S LIEUTENANT-GENERAL OF THE COUNTY OF CORNWALL.

REPRINTED FROM THE EDITION OF 1596,

WITH SOME

UNPUBLISHED DOCUMENTS RELATIVE TO THAT COUNTRY.

EDITED,

WITH COPIOUS EXPLANATORY NOTES AND A BIOGRAPHICAL MEMOIR,

BY

SIR ROBERT H. SCHOMBURGK, PH.D.,

KNIGHT OF THE ROYAL PRUSSIAN ORDER OF THE RED EAGLE, OF THE ROYAL SAXON ORDER OF MERIT, OF THE FRENCH ORDER OF THE LEGION OF HONOUR, ETC.

LONDON:

PRINTED FOR THE HAKLUYT SOCIETY.

M.DCCC.XLVIII.

LONDON:

PRINTED BY RICHARD AND JOHN E. TAYLOR,

RED LION COURT, FLEET STREET.

THE HAKLUYT SOCIETY.

Council.

SIR RODERICK IMPEY MURCHISON, G.C.St.S., F.R.S., Corr. Mem. Inst. Fr., Hon. Mem. Imp. Acad. Sc. St. Petersburg, &c. &c., PRESIDENT.

VICE-ADMIRAL SIR CHARLES MALCOLM, KNT.
THE REV. H. H. MILMAN, M.A.
} VICE-PRESIDENTS.

CHARLES T. BEKE, ESQ., PH.D., F.S.A.
CAPT. C. R. D. BETHUNE, R.N., C.B.
CAPT. F. P. BLACKWOOD, R.N.
MAJ.-GEN. J. BRIGGS, F.R.S.
BOLTON CORNEY, ESQ., M.R.S.L.
SIR HENRY ELLIS, K.H., F.R.S.
JOHN FORSTER, ESQ.
J. E. GRAY, ESQ., F.R.S.
JOHN WINTER JONES, ESQ.
R. H. MAJOR, ESQ.
R. MONCKTON MILNES, ESQ., M.P.
CHARLES NEWTON, ESQ.
REV. G. C. RENOUARD, M.A.
W. B. RYE, ESQ.
SIR ROBERT SCHOMBURGK, PH.D., K.R.E., K.S.M.
ANDREW SMITH, ESQ., M.D.
SIR GEORGE T. STAUNTON, BART., M.P., F.R.S.

WILLIAM DESBOROUGH COOLEY, ESQ., F.R.G.S., HON. SEC.

EDITOR'S PREFACE.

How frequently are we reminded of the pleasures of former days by an accidental word, the perusal of a passage in a book, or by the view of a place associated in thought with past enjoyments! Scenes are then recalled to mind which had seemingly faded from the memory. Such was my case as I recently perused Sir Walter Ralegh's 'Discoverie of Guiana.' Every page, nay almost every sentence, awakened past recollections, and I felt in imagination transported once more into the midst of the stupendous scenery of the Tropics. As Her Majesty's Commissioner to survey the boundaries of British Guiana, I explored in 1841 that wondrous delta of the Orinoco: on that occasion I encamped at Punta Barima, visited the Amacura and Aratura, and traversed at a later period the regions which Keymis describes as the site of the gorgeous capital of El Dorado, with the sea-like lake, enlivened by its multitude of canoes; what wonder therefore that I should read Ralegh's descriptions, expressed with such force and elegance, with the greatest delight?

When requested by the Council of the Hakluyt Society to edit a reprint of Sir Walter Ralegh's 'Discoverie of Guiana,' although a task more agreeable to my feelings could scarcely have been suggested, yet I hesitated, from a feeling of the difficulty for a foreigner to impart to the required notes and explanations the fluency and correctness of style which such a work deserves. These objections were overruled, and encouraged by the lenience with which some of my former labours have been judged, I commenced this work of love.

The text of the 'Discoverie of Guiana' is here reproduced from the edition of 1596, without any alterations in the ancient orthography or the various spellings of proper names. The original text has invariably been adhered to, except where a typographical error was evident. The work is accompanied by copious notes, the places and circumstances to which the author alludes being identified or explained from the Spanish and other historians, not only of that period but likewise of our own time. The manners and customs of the natives, the description of scenery and phænomena of nature, have been so extensively commented on in the notes, that I almost fear incurring the reproach of having overburdened the text. My chief object was to prove, from circumstances which fell within my own experience, the general correctness of Ralegh's descriptions, and to exculpate him from ungenerous reproaches.

The existence of two interesting documents in the British Museum, which have not before been published, rendered it desirable to seize the present opportunity of bringing them before the public. Of these documents, which were productions of Ralegh at two remarkable periods of his life, the first is entitled "Of the Voyage for Guiana," and was probably penned in the year 1596; the other is his autograph journal of that voyage, the ultimate result of which was his death on the scaffold. An interval of more than twenty years lies between these two documents; and it appeared to me that, to publish them without filling up the intermediate chasm by a rapid sketch of the chief incidents of Ralegh's life during that period, would be like attempting to illustrate the geological structure of an extensive district by specimens of the rocks composing its mere extremities.

I assume the reader to be acquainted with the chief

events of Ralegh's life; but as the connecting links of those events may have escaped his memory, the Introduction will be welcome. The biographical sketch accompanying the 'Discoverie of Guiana,' and the two Documents just mentioned, form together a complete though succinct account, in the compilation of which I have spared no pains or research.

In the composition of the biographical sketch, I have brought into view Ralegh's merits as the founder of the British colonial empire, and have devoted more space to this subject than I had originally intended; it however appeared to me of paramount importance, in forming an opinion of the motives of this remarkable man. I do not deny that I am strongly biased in favour of Ralegh, but this partiality has not blinded me to his numerous failings; on the contrary, it has induced me to judge his character with more strictness than I should have done if not conscious of such a leaning.

It remains only to say a few words on the Map which accompanies this Work. Where pages of letter-press are required to explain the configuration of a coast, the course of a river or the situation of a place, a single glance at a map will convey to the mind's eye relative local positions, however complex, better than any verbal description. It was gratifying to find that my proposition to illustrate Sir Walter Ralegh's journey up the Orinoco by a Map met with the approbation of the Council of the Hakluyt Society. This map is laid down in a great measure from personal observations made during eight years' rambles through Guiana; the northern part of it has been chiefly constructed from Colonel Codazzi's Atlas of Venezuela. Where I have been able to identify the places, rivers and islands mentioned in Ralegh's narrative, by inspecting ancient maps or otherwise, the name used by Ralegh has been added to the present one, in a style of printing which renders its discrimination easy.

R. H. S.

Surbiton, Surrey,
May, 1848.

INTRODUCTION.

The reign of Queen Elizabeth presents one of the most interesting periods in the history of England. If we contemplate the master-spirits of that time, distinguished in literature, in enterprize, or in the new projects of colonization, as heroes or as politicians, we must acknowledge that the close of the sixteenth century offers the brightest examples, singly and collectively. The age of Shakespeare and Spenser, in itself of an interest unparalleled in literature, exhibits at the same time statesmen like the Cecils and Walsingham, heroes like Essex, Drake, and Howard, who triumphantly established the claim of England to be the mistress of the ocean; and Spain, who had hitherto aspired to that distinction, was humbled by the victories of the English fleets under their command. It was during this period that England founded her first colonies in America; indeed the discoveries which each successive year brought to light, render that reign remarkably distinguished for maritime expeditions and colonization. From whatever side we view this pleasing picture of England's fame, one man stands forth conspicuous alike as a soldier, a navigator, and an author; and who, after having during this eventful æra attained a dazzling height of fame, was fated to lose his head in the succeeding reign upon the scaffold: that man was Sir Walter Ralegh.

Ralegh's name is one of the most renowned in history, and his melancholy fate has imparted to it a strong and peculiar interest. Although we cannot deny that as the founder of colonies, as the introducer or disseminator of two important articles of subsistence and luxury, as the promoter of commerce, as an active partaker in the glorious actions which led to the destruction of the Spanish Armada, the capture of Cadiz and the storming of Fayal, as an improver of naval architecture, but above all as the author of that remarkable work the 'History of the World,' his name would have been handed down to posterity with honour, yet his failings would have partially overshadowed his fame, did he not also appear as a martyr, and the political victim of a pusillanimous prince.

Sir Walter was the fourth and youngest son of Walter Ralegh[1], Esq. of Fardel, by his third wife

[1] Cayley says, "Few names vary so much in the manner of writing it." We have seen it written in thirteen different ways, namely Ralegh, Raleghe, Raleigh, Rawleigh, Rawlie, Rawley, Rawly, Rauleigh, Raleighe, Rale, Real, Reali, Ralego. His original letters in the Harleian Collection, and his MS. Journal of his Second Voyage, prove that Sir Walter himself wrote Ralegh. In the Commission for his second journey to Guiana it is written in Rymer's 'Fœdera' Rawleigh, while the Commission is headed, "De Commissione Speciali dilecto Waltero Rawley Militi concernente Voiagium Guianianum." Sir Arthur Georges in a letter to Sir Robert Cecil writes it Rawly. In the copy of Sir Walter's arraignment, Sir

Catharine, daughter of Sir Philip Champernon of Modbury, and relict of Otho Gilbert of Compton in Devon[1]. The biographers of Ralegh generally admit that he was born in 1552, at a farm called Hayes in the parish of Budleigh in Devonshire, of which his father possessed the remainder of an eighty years' lease. We are entirely unacquainted with Ralegh's childhood; Hooker and Lord Bacon agree that he studied at the University of Oxford, and Anthony Wood records in his 'Athenæ Oxonienses,' that Ralegh "became Commoner of Oriel College in or about the year 1568, when his kinsman C. Champernon studied there; and his natural parts being strangely advanced by academical learning, under the care of an excellent tutor, he became the ornament of the juniors, and was worthily esteemed a proficient in oratory and philosophy." Young Ralegh did not remain long at the University, for we find him already in 1569 among the gentlemen volunteers[2] who were to assist

Thomas Overbury writes the name Rawleigh. In the scarce pamphlet, 'Newes of Sir Walter Rauleigh,' it is spelt in the manner just mentioned. Fray Simon calls him "Real o Reali," Gili "Ralego." King James in his Declaration writes the name Raleigh, which orthography Sir Walter's son Carew seems to have adopted. Sir Robert Naunton and Lord Bacon write Rawleigh. We have adopted the orthography of Sir Walter himself.

[1] Sir Walter was therefore a brother by the mother's side of Sir John, Sir Humphry, and Sir Adrian Gilbert, all eminent men during Queen Elizabeth's reign. Sir Humphry published in 1576 a Discourse on the Practicability of a North-west passage to China.

[2] Queen Elizabeth permitted Henry Champernon, a relative by marriage to the Earl of Montgomery, to conduct a troop of volunteers, consisting of one hundred gentlemen, to the assistance of the persecuted Protestants. On their standard was the motto, "Finem det mihi virtus,"—Let valour decide the contest. Amongst their number were Philip Butshid, Francis Barcley, and Walter Ralegh. (Camden, Ann. Eliz. Ann. 1569.)

the Protestants in France. During this struggle for religious liberty he had an ample field for acquiring experience in the art of war, and in the knowledge of men and manners, of which he appears to have availed himself materially, as may be observed in the observations on the conduct and characters of the great generals and their exploits during the campaign, which are recorded in his 'History of the World'[1]. After a sojourn of about six years in France, he returned to England in 1575, and appears to have had chambers in the Middle Temple; but there seems to be no foundation for Wood's assertion, that he followed the profession of the law; on the contrary, he solemnly declared on his arraignment, in a reply to the Attorney-General, that he had never "read a word of the law, or statutes, before he was a prisoner in the Tower[2]." We are rather inclined to suppose that the two years he spent in leisure at that period were devoted to his own improvement, and the acquirement of the Spanish language, which opened to him a knowledge of the writings of the Spanish historians on America. It is asserted by one of his earliest biographers, Benjamin Shirley, that only five hours out of the twenty-four were given to sleep, and that he voluntarily shared in the duties of the common soldier and sailor. In his succeeding maritime expeditions he had always a box of books on board,

[1] History of the World, book iv. cap. 2. sect. 16; book v. cap. 2. sect. 3 and 8.

[2] Theobald's Memoirs of Sir W. Raleigh, p. 5. State Trials, vol. i. fol. 180.

and several hours in the course of the day were employed in study. In 1577 Walter Ralegh accompanied Sir John Norris, with Sir Robert Stewart, Colonels North, Cavendish, Morgan and others, to the Netherlands, to serve under the Prince of Orange against the Spaniards; and it is probable that he was present at the battle of Rimenant, where the English forces under Sir John Norris greatly distinguished themselves[1].

On his return from the Netherlands he found his half-brother, Sir Humphry Gilbert, engaged in fitting out a maritime expedition, having received a patent from Queen Elizabeth, for planting and forming settlements in certain northern parts of America, unpossessed by any prince with whom she was in alliance. Ralegh engaged in this adventure, and it appears that, although the expedition proved unsuccessful, his active mind was thenceforth especially directed to maritime enterprize and discovery. Dissension arising amongst the volunteers, who refused to embark, Sir Humphry prosecuted his adventure with only a few followers, among whom was Ralegh. The ships sailed early in 1579, and returned to port after various disasters, and with the loss of one of the vessels in an engagement with the Spaniards, during which, as Oldys asserts, Ralegh was exposed to great danger.

The rebellion in Ireland of 1580 afforded him an opportunity of resuming his sword, having received a captain's commission under Lord Arthur Grey, who

[1] Birch's Life of Sir W. Ralegh, vol. i. p. iv.

was appointed shortly after his arrival Lord Deputy of Ireland. We shall pass over this war, during which the most dreadful cruelties were committed. Ralegh distinguished himself under the Earl of Ormonde, and is several times mentioned in the Chronicles of Holinshed, afterwards continued by John Hooker, who dedicated to Sir Walter his translation and continuation of the Chronicles of Ireland. Ralegh's name is unfortunately connected with that merciless massacre of the Spaniards who fought in aid of the Irish rebels. They had fortified themselves at Smerwick in Kerry, where they were besieged by Lord Deputy Grey. After a siege of five days they surrendered at discretion, and the greater part of the garrison was put to the sword; the execution of this order fell to Captains Ralegh and Mackworth. It does not appear that Sir Walter was much pleased with his sojourn in Ireland. In a letter to the Earl of Leicester, Elizabeth's favourite, by whom he appears to have been patronized at that early period, he expresses his dissatisfaction with the service in this "common-wealth, or rather common-woe," and that were it not for recommending himself to notice, he would "disdain it as much as to keep sheep[1]." There is however a pleasing fact connected with his Irish campaign: Edmund Spenser, the poet, was secretary to Lord Grey, and the friendship which existed between Ralegh and Spenser was probably formed during this period. Ralegh himself possessed great talent for poetry; and although he considered the

[1] Cayley's Life of Sir W. Ralegh, 4to, London 1805, vol. i. p. 25.

exercise of this merely in the light of a recreation, the contemporary criticisms of Puttenham declare, "for ditty and amorous ode, Sir Walter Ralegh's vein most lofty, insolent and passionate[1]."

The authenticity of some of the poems ascribed to him has been questioned, and we have to regret that no collection was made during his lifetime or shortly after his death[2]. As we shall not recur again to Ralegh in the character of a poet (except to quote "his epitaph," written the evening before the closing scene of his life), we would here allude to his visit, during a temporary banishment from court, to Spenser, then residing at Kilcolman, an ancient castle of the Desmonds, which meeting Spenser so beautifully describes in his 'Collin Clout.' This pastoral is dedicated to Ralegh as "the Shepherd of the Ocean[3]," and in it the poet gratefully records his introduction

[1] One of the finest and most sublime poems is, "Go, Soul, the body's guest:" Sir Egerton Brydges observes, "Though the date ascribed to this poem is demonstrably wrong, I know no other author so capable of writing it as Raleigh. What must be the taste of the reader who can peruse these lines without sympathy, without feeling a swell and exultation of his heart?" It is asserted by Mrs. Thomson, in her Memoirs of Sir Walter Ralegh, that these lines were found in a MS. collection of his poems dated 1596, which would remove all doubts respecting the authorship. Sir Egerton observes of Ralegh's beautiful poem, known as 'his Pilgrimage,' that "it contains a mixture of bold and sublime passages, such as the aspiring and indignant soul of Ralegh was likely to utter. The first stanza, in which the imagery drawn from a pilgrim is vividly depicted, fills the mind with a wild interest."

[2] Within our own times Sir Egerton Brydges has published "The Poems of Sir Walter Raleigh, now first collected, with a Biographical and Critical Introduction. Printed at the private press of Lee Priory, 1813."

[3] Spenser likewise committed the first three books of his 'Fairy Queen' to the press under the encouragement of Ralegh.

and recommendation to the Queen by the former after his restoration to favour :—

> "The Shepherd of the Ocean, quoth he,
> Unto that goddess' grace me first enhanc'd,
> And to mine oaten pipe inclin'd her ear."

Ralegh returned from his campaign in Ireland in 1581. He was then twenty-nine years of age, handsome, and of a graceful address. The fame of his exploits had gone before him, and it is supposed that the Earl of Leicester, by whom he was patronized, afforded him an opportunity of appearing at court in the course of the following year. Without doubting the well-known anecdote of his gallantry to the Queen, in throwing his cloak on the ground for her Majesty to walk over, we should rather ascribe his first introduction at court to the influence of the Earl of Leicester; and in this we are confirmed by the letter which Ralegh wrote to the powerful favourite when still in Ireland; however this may be, an opportunity occurred soon after his return to display to the Queen the powers of his mind. Some difference had arisen during the Munster rebellion between Lord Grey and Ralegh, which was brought before the Council Board and discussed in the Queen's presence, "where," says Sir Robert Naunton, "what advantage he [Ralegh] had in the case in controversy I know not, but he had much the better in the manner of telling his tale; insomuch as the Queen and the Lords took no slight mark of the man and his parts, for from thence he came to be known, and to have access to the Lords; and then we are not to doubt how such a man would comply to progression; and whether or no my Lord of Leicester had then cast in a good word for him to the Queen, which would have done him no harm, I do not determine; but true it is, he had gotten the Queen's ear in a trice, and she began to be taken with his election, and loved to hear his reasons to her demands. And the truth is, she took him for a kind of oracle, which nettled them all; yea, those that he relied on began to take this his sudden favour for an alarm, and to be sensible for their own supplantation, and to project his[1]."

Formed by nature in the finest mould, Ralegh also possessed an assemblage of brilliant qualities, a ready wit, and high mental endowments. These among other causes doubtless contributed to his rapid advance in the favour of Queen Elizabeth; and in the course of a few years after his introduction at court, he was knighted, made Lord Warden of the Stannaries, Captain of the Guard, and Lieutenant-General of the county of Cornwall[2]; he moreover received a grant of twelve thousand acres of the forfeited lands of the Earls of Desmond, and the lucrative patent for licensing the vendors of wine throughout the kingdom. These preferments exposed him to envy at court, and even his former patron, the Earl of Leicester, began to be jealous of the rising favourite, and exerted his influence to undermine Ralegh's career. Sir Henry

[1] Fragmenta Regalia, 1641, p. 35.

[2] The Queen bestowed this dignity upon him in the early part of 1587, consequently about five years after he was first noticed by Her Majesty.

Wotton, the author of 'Reliquiæ Wottonianæ,' and secretary to the Earl of Essex, conjectures that Leicester brought forward the dawning talents of his son-in-law, the young Earl of Essex, to oppose Sir Walter's growing influence with the Queen. But as our object is to view Ralegh chiefly as the father of American colonization and a promoter of commerce and navigation, we must leave him to pursue his career at court, noticing merely such incidents as affected or were closely connected with his maritime enterprizes.

Sir Humphry Gilbert had been obliged, in consequence of the failure of his enterprize in 1579, to delay any further attempt to take possession of the territories in North America which he intended to colonize; but as his patent was dated the 11th of June, 1578, granting him six years for the execution of his design, he undertook in 1583 another voyage to Newfoundland in person, to keep it in force.

Ralegh, tired of the inactive life at court, probably contemplated accompanying his brother, and built for that purpose a vessel of two hundred tons burthen, which he called the Bark Ralegh[1]: although he did not execute his project, his bark, which had cost him two thousand pounds[2], formed part of the fleet which sailed under Gilbert's command from Plymouth on the 11th of June, 1583. The Queen sent through Ralegh's hands a golden token to Sir Humphry, "an anchor guided by a lady," to be worn at his breast,

[1] Birch, vol. i. p. xi.

[2] Birch's Memoirs of Queen Elizabeth, vol. i. p. 34.

and she commanded him, as Ralegh writes to Sir Humphry, that he should leave his picture with Sir Walter[1].

Scarcely had the little fleet been two days out at sea, when on account of a contagious disease the Bark Ralegh returned to Plymouth in distress[2]. Sir Humphry took possession of Newfoundland in right of the English crown; but on his return two of his vessels were lost, in one of which, the Squirrel, he himself perished; the vessel (one of only ten tons) foundered at midnight on the 9th of September, 1583[3].

Let us here pause, and passing over the period which has elapsed between the year 1583 and our own time, cast a glance on the present condition of Great Britain as compared with that early period. Though Sir Humphry Gilbert received the first patent for the settlement of colonies, he was cut off in his career ere he could execute his design, and the Spaniards and Portuguese were at that time almost entirely in possession of the New World. How different is the case now! Great Britain's territorial possessions in Europe, girded by the ocean, occupy a surface of one hundred and twenty-one thousand square miles, whilst in point of territorial extent she is only

[1] Cayley's Life of Sir W. Ralegh, vol. i. p. 31.

[2] Sir H. Gilbert seems to have been ignorant that sickness was the cause of this desertion; he writes to Sir George Peckham after his arrival in Newfoundland: "On the 13th the Bark Raleigh ran from me, in fair and clear weather, having a large wind. I pray you solicit my brother Raleigh to make them an example to all knaves." (Purchas' Collect. vol. iii. p. 808.)

[3] Hakluyt, vol. iii. pp. 149, 165.

the sixth among the European powers, even Spain surpassing her: nevertheless she occupies the first position in point of national greatness, founded upon her valuable and extensive dominions in all quarters of the globe. In the East her sway extends over nearly one hundred and twenty-five millions of human beings; in the West she rules a population of two millions and a half; and in Africa and Australia she numbers half a million subjects. How striking a picture of her grandeur is contained in the remark, that the sun never sets upon her empire! The origin of this superiority is to be ascribed to the valour of those intrepid men who, towards the end of the sixteenth century, wrung from Spain the supremacy on the ocean; it is founded upon the enterprize and prowess of the maritime discoverers who distinguished the Elizabethan age, but above all upon the establishment and extent of the British colonies, those grand sources of national wealth. In perusing the pages of England's colonial history, we are struck with the beneficial results which originated from these enterprizes. What was in the commencement merely the offspring of a spirit of adventure, was gradually converted into a regular system: new articles of use and luxury were introduced, new fields of labour were opened, the productions of distant regions became articles of necessity, and vast tracts of land before uncultivated and sparely inhabited, now offered means of employment to a redundant European population, who brought with them not only the language and civilization, but likewise the customs and wants, of their own country. The activity of man's industry is ceaseless; new branches of commerce were gradually and successively developed, enlarging the intercourse with the mother-country, increasing her demand for colonial produce, and consequently augmenting her mercantile navy. "Thus the productions of new regions operate to increase the activity and to multiply the commercial relations of the old; this gives new life, extending even to the interior of the more civilized countries, and multiplies the objects of traffic; industry produces riches, and riches reproduce industry; and thus commerce at length becomes the foundation and the cement of the whole social edifice[1]." Some politicians have been of opinion, "that as the Roman empire was the greatest the world ever saw, so it chiefly owed its grandeur to its colonies."

The first English vessels which visited the West Indies after their discovery were two ships of war, under Sebastian Cabot and Sir Thomas Pert. This was between 1516 and 1517: two years afterwards the first English trading vessel arrived in Porto Rico[2], being sent by the King, as the commander asserted, to ascertain the state of those islands, of which there was so much talk in Europe. Captain John Hawkins followed in 1565, and Captain Francis Drake in 1572, but neither attempted to form a settlement;

[1] Maxims of F. von Gentz, in his 'State of Europe before and after the French Revolution.'

[2] According to Oviedo, 'Historia General de las Indias' (Sevilla, 1535), this occurred in 1527. (Oviedo, l. 19. cap. 13.)

this was reserved for Sir Walter Ralegh, to whom belongs the honour of being the founder of England's colonial empire.

Unfortunately a thirst for gold was the only inducement which during the first half of the sixteenth century incited the Spanish conquerors to settle in the New World, and to this idol the lives of millions of human beings were sacrificed. Nor can we deny that many of the early English maritime adventurers were actuated by merely similar motives. The conquest of the rich cities of Quito and Cusco spread such a lustre over the newly discovered regions, that the popular imagination connected with America the idea of an abundance of gold and precious stones; and the acquisition of spices, the beautiful dye-woods and other produce of the country, had not sufficient attraction to induce them to encounter danger and privation.

The treatises of Gilbert, Peckham, Captain Carlisle[1] and others, prove that there were men who had more enlarged views than the mere discovery of gold-mines, and who endeavoured to awaken their countrymen to the advantages which settlements in the New World might have upon commerce and navigation. Their arguments however produced little effect; the illusory

[1] The production of the latter was published in 1583; it consists of eight leaves in 4to, and is entitled, "A Discourse upon the Intended Voyage to the hethermoste parts of America, written by Captaine Carleill for the better inducement to satisfie such merchauntes, as in disburseing their money, do demaunde forwith a present return of gaine; albeit their saied particular disbursements are in such slender sommes as are not worth the speaking of."

hopes of gold were the sole allurement. We must keep this circumstance in mind when judging of Ralegh's character, in connection with the representations he made of the commercial resources of Guiana. The ill-success of his half-brother had little or no effect in damping Ralegh's ardour for such undertakings; on the contrary, his mind appears to have been now entirely directed to the pursuit of maritime discovery, and his knowledge of foreign languages enabled him to study the Spanish accounts respecting the conquests of the New World. On examining the relation of their voyages, he found that they had not extended beyond the Gulf of Mexico. Having coasted along the Mexican Gulf, they came out by what has since been called the Gulf of Florida; and by standing away to the east, to make the coast of Spain, a long extent of country stretching northward remained unexplored. This coast appeared to Ralegh's enterprizing genius a rich field for colonization, and having drawn up a proposition to that effect, he laid it before the Queen and her Council, who approved of it, and her Majesty granted him her letters patent, "to discover, search, find out and view such remote heathen and barbarous lands, countries and territories, not actually possessed of any Christian prince, nor inhabited by Christian people[1]." This document is dated the 25th of March, 1584; and on the 7th of April following two vessels, fitted out at the cost of himself and some associates, sailed under the command of Captains

[1] Hakluyt's Voyages, vol. iii. p. 243.

Philip Amidas and Arthur Barlow from the west of England[1]. Navigation was still in its infancy, and no direct course was attempted; they passed the Canaries, sailed round the West Indies, and on the 4th of July arrived on the coast of North Carolina. After having sailed along the shore about one hundred and twenty miles, they cast anchor at the island of Wocokon, of which they took possession in right of the Queen and for the use of Ralegh. They afterwards went ashore on the continent called Wingandacoa, over which a king reigned named Wingina. They maintained an amicable intercourse with the Indians, but made no settlement, and returned to England about the middle of September. Captains Amidas and Barlow drew up a favourable report of the fertility of the soil and the healthiness of the climate[2], which Ralegh laid before the Queen, who was so much pleased with it, that she conferred upon the new territory the name of Virginia, the discovery being made in the reign of a virgin Queen[3].

About two months after the return of this expedition, Ralegh was chosen one of the knights of the shire for the county of Devon, Sir William Courtenay being the other. During this session the bill confirming his patent for the discovery of foreign coun-

[1] Oldys says that these two vessels were equipped at Ralegh's own expense, while others assert that Sir Richard Grenville and Mr. William Sanderson had a share in the undertaking.

[2] It is printed in Hakluyt's Voyages, vol. iii. p. 246.

[3] The Virginians assert that the colony received its name "because it still seemed to retain the virgin purity and plenty of the first creation, and the people their primitive innocence." (Oldmixon's British Empire in America, vol. i. p. 211.)

tries was read a first time, on the 14th of December, 1584; it passed, but not without opposition and some amendments.

The favourable report of their discovery given by Amidas and Barlow induced Ralegh to prosecute vigorously his design of planting a colony in Virginia. Early in 1585 seven sail were fully equipped, having on board a party of about one hundred men under the orders of Mr. Ralph Lane; and the command of this fleet was given to Ralegh's cousin Sir Richard Grenville. In their company was Thomas Hariot, one of the most celebrated early English mathematicians and astronomers[1], who was commissioned to make the survey, and to report upon the capabilities of the new colony. The squadron sailed from Plymouth on the 9th of April, 1585, and came to anchor at Wocokon on the coast of North Carolina on the 26th of June. The adventurers landed at several places in order to examine the country, and in August following fixed upon a site for a settlement at the island of Roanoak. Sir Richard Grenville weighed anchor and set sail for England on the 25th of August[2]. The misconduct of the colonists and the hostility of the natives after Sir Richard's departure caused the Governor, Mr. Lane, much uneasiness; and as the settlers neglected the cultivation of articles of food, they were reduced to great distress. Ralegh meanwhile fitted out in 1586 at his own charge

[1] Descartes is accused of having drawn from Hariot's 'Artis Analyticæ Praxis,' Londini, 1631, all his pretended discoveries in algebra.

[2] Hakluyt's Voyages, vol. iii. p. 255.

a ship of one hundred tons, freighted with plentiful supplies for the relief of the colony; but before she arrived, Sir Francis Drake visited Virginia on his return from St. Domingo and Carthagena, and the colonists, despairing of relief, solicited him to take them on board, and the settlement was broken up. It has been asserted by Theobald and others, that Sir Walter Ralegh himself accompanied this vessel which he sent for the relief of the young colony: such may have been his intention, as Captain Smith states in the first book of his 'General History of Virginia;' but we have so many proofs that Sir Walter did not leave England in that year, that we are surprized how such an erroneous statement has found credence up to the present day. Soon after the departure of this vessel Sir Richard Grenville sailed with three ships, fitted out and provisioned by the Company; but not meeting any of the colonists in Roanoak, he landed fifteen men to retain possession of the country, and returned to Europe.

The following year Sir Walter Ralegh sent out another expedition, consisting of one hundred and fifty men under the command of Mr. John White, with twelve assistants, whom he incorporated under the name of "Governor and Assistants of the City of Ralegh in Virginia[1]." White left Plymouth with three ships on the 8th of May, 1587, and arrived at Hatorask on the 23rd of July. The colonists were afterwards landed at Roanoak, where they learned that the fifteen men left by Sir Richard Grenville had nearly all been

[1] Hakluyt's Voyages, vol. iii. p. 280.

massacred, and the few who escaped had fled into the interior. The designs of Sir Walter respecting Virginia were again defeated; differences arose among the settlers, and the cruelties committed towards the Indians had prevented any amicable intercourse. They were therefore apprehensive of want, and urged the Governor to return for fresh supplies and new powers and instructions[1]. The arrival of Governor White in England could not have happened at a more unfortunate moment. The whole nation was engrossed with the apprehended invasion of the Spanish Armada; he therefore experienced great delays in fitting out only two pinnaces with supplies, while the fleet which was preparing to convey assistance on a larger scale under Sir Richard Grenville at Bideford, received an injunction not to proceed to sea, all armed vessels being required for the defence of the country. The two small pinnaces sailed, with fifteen planters and the desired supplies, on the 22nd of April, 1588; but one having been taken near Madeira by two armed vessels from Rochelle, and stripped, they both ultimately returned to England without accomplishing their purpose, and the poor colonists were left to their fate.

Sir Walter had spent forty thousand pounds upon his colonial enterprize, and the experience which he had acquired at such a price, taught him the difficulties that stood in the way of the accomplishment

[1] Governor White left on the 27th of August, 1587; at that time the colony consisted of eighty-nine men, seventeen women, and eleven children. (Hakluyt, vol. iii. pp. 286, 287.)

of so great a design by a single individual. He resolved therefore to assign his patent, and the right of continuing the plantation in Virginia, to a company of merchants, reserving to himself a fifth part of all the gold and silver ore raised. The legal document to this effect is dated the 7th of March, 1589.

White made another attempt to relieve the unfortunate planters in the year 1589. He arrived at Roanoak on the 15th of August, and found that the English were removed to Croatan, an island twenty leagues to the south. He set sail for it, but a dreadful storm obliged the fleet to bear up for Europe. This was the last effort made by the patentees for the rescue of the settlers, nor does it seem that their fate raised the slightest commiseration in the government of their own country. It was however not so with Ralegh, who, notwithstanding the transfer of his rights to a Company, upon whom the duty consequently devolved of assisting the colonists, continued to take the greatest interest in their fate. His intention of going to their relief, after his return from Guiana in 1595, was prevented by the severity of weather which forced him from the coast[1]: we learn however from Purchas that he made several other attempts, and one as late as 1602: "Samuel Mace of Weymouth, a very sufficient mariner, who had been in Virginia twice before, was employed thither by Sir Walter Ralegh, to find those people which were left there in 1587, to whose succour he

[1] See page 6 of the present edition.

hath sent five several times, at his own charges[1]." Captain Gosnold sailed the same year from Dartmouth, and was the first who entered the Chesapeake Bay. Though the voyage was undertaken for the purpose of trade, he would doubtless, had he received any information of the English being still alive, have come to their assistance. The Indians seeing the unfortunate settlers forsaken by their countrymen, fell upon and destroyed them; and the celebrated chieftain Powhattan confessed to Captain Smith, "that he had been at the murder of the colony, and showed him certain articles which had been theirs[2]."

We have reviewed chronologically the events connected with the first attempts at establishing a British colony in America; and although they proved unfortunate, and nearly twenty years elapsed before any permanent settlement could be effected in Virginia, the honour of having led "the ancient and heroical work of plantations" belongs to Ralegh; for by drawing public attention to this part of the hemisphere, his project may be considered as the forerunner of the subsequent settlement of New England.

Thomas Hariot, after his return with Governor Lane in 1588, published a report, which is remarkable for the large views it contains in regard to the extension of industry and commerce. "It is one of the earliest, if not the very first extensive specimen in the language, of a statistical survey; for such it was, inasfar as there were materials in the country

[1] Purchas' Pilgrims, vol. iv. p. 1653.

[2] Purchas, vol. iv. p. 1728. See likewise Edinb. Review, No. cxliii. p. 15.

described for such a production[1]." Hariot's treatise, in connection with Sir William Alexander's 'Encouragement to Colonies,' Captain Smith's various accounts of Virginia, and numerous other publications of less importance, attracted general attention to the desirableness of following up more energetically the settlement of colonies. It has been observed by Southey, that it is not the least remarkable circumstance, that, although all Ralegh's colonial enterprizes were unfortunate, they should incidentally have produced consequences of great benefit to this country. It is stated that, on the return of Governor Lane, tobacco was for the first time brought to England, and that Ralegh introduced the custom of smoking. As an article of commerce, but chiefly as affording a large revenue, since an impost was laid upon it in 1614, its introduction is of great importance[2]. But

[1] Edinb. Review, No. cxliii. p. 11. The title of this remarkable and now very rare production gives some general idea of its contents. It is :— "A Briefe and true report of the new found land of Virginia: of the commodities there found and to be raysed, as well marchantable, as others for victuall, buildind and other necessarie use for those that are and shall be planters there : and of the nature and manners of the naturall inhabitants : discovered by the English Colony there seated by Sir Richard Greinville, Knight, in the yeere 1585, which remained under the government of Rafe Lane esq. one of her Majesties equieres, during the space of twelve moneths. At the special charge and direction of the honorable Sir Walther Raleigh, Knight; directed to the adventurers, favourers and wellwillers of the action, for the inhabiting and planting there, by Thomas Hariot: servant to the above named Sir Walther, a member of the Colony, and there employed in discovering; 4to London 1588." The Latin edition forms the first part of De Bry's Great Voyages.

[2] It appears that soon after the introduction of smoking, a proclamation was issued against it, and bitter complaints were made of "this immitation of the manners of savage people." It was feared, says Camden, that by the practice of smoking tobacco, "Anglorum corpora in barbarorum

of still greater interest is the cultivation of the potato, which, according to Gough, Sir W. Ralegh first planted on his estate of Youghal near Cork, from whence it was soon after carried into Lancashire. When this plant was first introduced as a delicacy on the tables of the rich, it was little imagined that two centuries later it would become an article of food of such vital importance, that the failure of its cultivation in two successive years would entail misery upon the land where it was first planted in the British islands[1].

It must not be assumed that Ralegh's prosecution of his Virginian scheme with such energy and perseverance prevented his attention to other maritime adventures. Adrian Gilbert of Sandridge, his half-brother, was not deterred by the unfortunate issue of his brother Humphry's project from prosecuting similar enterprizes; and having obtained a patent, he instituted a partnership under the name of "The

degenerasse videantur." (Ann. Elizab. 1585.) The Star Chamber ordered in 1614 the duty to be 6*s*. 10*d*. per pound. An Act to lay an impost on the importation was passed in 1684. The quantity consumed in England in 1791 was nine millions and a half of pounds, and in 1845 twenty-six millions three hundred thousand pounds, and the gross amount of the duty derived from it during that year, four millions two hundred thousand pounds sterling.

[1] It has been asserted that Sir John Hawkins brought the first potatoes from Santa Fé as early as 1563. We are only acquainted with his voyage from Guinea to San Domingo that year, having on board the first cargo of human merchandise carried in an English vessel. He visited however Santa Fé in the 'Jesus' in 1565. Others ascribe this introduction to Sir Francis Drake in 1586. The importance of the potato as a food-plant may be learned from the circumstance, that a field planted with potatoes will furnish twice as much food as it would do if cultivated with wheat.

Colleagues of the Fellowship for the Discovery of the North-west Passage." Sir Walter joined the enterprize, the conduct of which was entrusted to Captain Davis; and from this voyage resulted the discovery of the Strait which bears Captain Davis's name. Ralegh shared likewise in the voyage undertaken in 1586 by the Earl of Cumberland to the South Seas: and his fine pinnace, the Dorothy, joined the fleet at Plymouth. The expedition however proved abortive, as they reached only the forty-fourth degree of south latitude, when they returned with some small prizes. Much greater success attended a privateering expedition to the Azores in 1586, with two pinnaces, fitted out at Ralegh's expense and commanded by Captains John Whiddon and John Evesham. Among the prizes taken during this cruise was one with the Governor of the island of St. Michael on board, and in another was Don Pedro de Sarmiento, Governor of the Straits of Magellan, one of the most eminent navigators of Spain[1].

Ralegh's fame now extended beyond the confines of England; he was known not only as the promoter of maritime discovery and the founder of colonies, but likewise as a patron of science in general. Hakluyt, who published his first work, 'Divers Voyages touching the Discoverie of America,' in 1582, seems to have early sought the acquaintance of Ralegh, and

[1] It has been asserted that Don Pedro was a near relative of Don Diego Sarmiento de Acuña (afterwards Count de Gondomar), and that the future Spanish ambassador had, in consequence of the captivity of Don Pedro, already taken at that period a dislike to Ralegh. This appears to have been merely a matter of conjecture.

acknowledges him, in his preface to 'The Principal Navigations,' as one of those benefactors "from whom he had received his chief light into the western navigations." Previous to the publication of this work, Hakluyt had sent the manuscript of a voyage performed by René Laudonnière and three other Frenchmen in Florida, to M. Martin Bassanière of Paris, who published it in 1586 with a dedication to Ralegh. At the desire of Admiral Coligny, Laudonnière was accompanied in his voyages by Jacque Morgue, a skilful painter. This artist afterwards came to London, and was chiefly aided by Ralegh in the expense of publishing his sketches and descriptions. Hakluyt translated Laudonnière's Voyage, and dedicated it likewise to Ralegh: the translation was first published in 1587 in a separate form, and afterwards inserted in the third volume of his 'Navigations.' Sir Walter also procured for Hakluyt the manuscript of a voyage made in 1541 to the Red Sea by Estevan de Gama, the Portuguese Viceroy of the Indies, which was written by Joaõ de Castro, one of his principal commanders, and was dedicated in 1542 by the latter to his patron the Infant Don Luiz[1].

[1] In speaking of this voyage in his History of the World (Book ii. chap. iii. sect. 8), Ralegh observes, "which discourse I gave to Mr. Hakluyt." An abridged translation appeared in Purchas (vol. ii. ch. 6), who says that Ralegh bought the original for £60. It is most probable that the MS. in the Cottonian Collection (Brit. Mus. Bibl. Cotton. Tib. D. IX.) is the identical one purchased by Ralegh, as Sir Robert Cotton seems to have been a zealous collector of all relics which had reference to Ralegh. It was greatly injured during the fire at Sir R. B. Cotton's in 1731. The late Dr. Carvalho, who filled a Professor's Chair in the University of Coimbra, and sojourned for some time afterwards in London, transcribed

It is supposed that about this period Ralegh wrote two of his treatises upon military operations. The Queen had appointed him, in 1586, Seneschal of the Duchies of Cornwall and Exeter, and Lord Warden of the Stannaries in Devonshire and Cornwall; and in the beginning of the following year he received another mark of her Majesty's favour, being advanced to the post of Captain of her Guard and Lieutenant-General of Cornwall. The eventful year of 1588, when Philip's navy, vast and unrivalled on the ocean, threatened to annihilate the power of England, saw Ralegh in the field and on the ocean. He had been nominated in the preceding November one of the Council of War, to consider the most effectual means for maintaining the security of the nation. Some considered the kingdom strong enough to resist the landing of any hostile troops, and hence it was argued that there was no necessity for any great defensive naval preparations. This opinion was strongly opposed by the first minister, and likewise by Ralegh, who demonstrated that no conclusions should be drawn from France or other European countries in the possession of many fortified places, "whereas the ramparts of England consist only of a body of men." There is a difference, he says, between an invasion by land and one by sea, where the choice of the place of debarkation remains with the enemy; and he arrives at the conclusion

this MS. in 1828, and published it in Paris in 1833. While we give every praise to his public spirit for rescuing this remarkable voyage from oblivion, we cannot admit the claim of a literary *trouvaille*, as the manuscript is described with sufficient precision in the Cottonian Catalogue. (See Athenæum, February 14th and 21st, 1846.)

that such an attempt could not be successfully resisted on the West of England without a fleet. The plan which Ralegh drew up on this occasion was based on a practical acquaintance with the comparative advantages of a land and naval force, an experience that resulted from his campaigns in France, the Low Countries and Ireland, which Shirley calls "the military academies of those times." But from whence he received his knowledge of maritime affairs is a riddle, as, with the exception of the smart action in which he shared with his half-brother Sir Humphry Gilbert in 1579, we are not aware that he had any opportunity up to that period of acquiring practical experience in naval tactics. Sir Walter Ralegh's proposition was however adopted, and a fleet was equipped, the command of which was given to Lord Howard of Effingham.

After having raised and disciplined the militia of Cornwall, Ralegh joined the fleet in July 1588 with a squadron of volunteers, and took an active part in the several engagements which led to the destruction of the Spanish Armada. It was probably in acknowledgement of these services that the Queen nominated him Gentleman of her Privy Chamber. When the expedition for the support of Don Antonio, King of Portugal, was resolved upon, Ralegh accompanied that prince, in April 1589, with Sir Francis Drake and Sir John Norris, and on his return was honoured by his sovereign, as well as the other commanders, with a gold chain.

The elaborate report which Ralegh published in defence of the conduct of his friend Sir Richard Grenville, who lost his life in the expedition under Lord Thomas Howard in 1591 for intercepting the Spanish Plate fleet at the Azores, "breathes a spirit of loyalty and patriotism truly admirable." It was, we believe, the first essay which Ralegh printed[1], and the scene where the enemy's numerous fleet surrounded the ship of the admiral, who continued the fight, although mortally wounded, till all the ammunition was spent, and then commanded the master gunner to sink her—which was only prevented by the interference of the survivors of the crew—"presents a view of perhaps the most astonishing naval conflict ever delineated by any pen[2]."

The love of enterprize which so eminently distinguished Ralegh, suggested the plan of attacking the Spaniards in the West Indies, particularly at Panama, with a view of meeting the Plate fleet. He endeavoured to engage his friends and others in this adventure, and thirteen vessels were fully equipped for service. The scheme, having been laid before the Queen, appeared to her so feasible, that she added two men-of-war, the Garland and the Foresight, to the expedition, and gave Ralegh a commission as General

[1] It is entitled, "A report of the truth of the fight about the isles of Azores this last summer, betwixt the Revenge, one of Her Majesty's ships commanded by Sir Richard Grenville, and an Armada of the King of Spain." 4to, 1591. It was afterwards reprinted in Hakluyt's Voyages in 1599 (vol. ii. part 2. p. 169).

[2] Edinburgh Review, No. cxliii. p. 17.

of the Fleet, the post of Lieutenant-General being conferred upon Sir John Burgh. Owing to contrary winds, and the want of due arrangements, the fleet was detained until May 1592. From a letter which Ralegh wrote at that period from Chatham to Sir Robert Cecil, it appears that the Queen had repented allowing him to depart. This letter, which is printed in Murdin's State Papers, and has since been reprinted by Cayley, gives us the first decided proof of Ralegh's duplicity; he deceived those who had trusted him, and there is but too much probability that he likewise deceived the Queen, and wounded her in that most vulnerable point her self-love. We extract the following paragraph in explanation:—"I have promised her Majesty," writes Ralegh to Cecil, "that if I can persuade the companies to follow Sir Martin Frobisher, I will without fail return, and bring them but into the sea, but some fifty or threescore leagues, for which purpose my Lord Admiral hath lent me the 'Disdain'; which to do, her Majesty many times with great grace bid me remember, and sent me the same message by Will. Killgrewe, which, God willing, if I can persuade the companies, I mean to perform, though I dare not to acknown thereof to any creature. . . . . . I mean not to come away, as they say I will for fear of a marriage, and I know not what. If any such thing were, I would have imparted it to yourself before any man living; and therefore I pray, believe it not, and I beseech you to suppress what you can any such malicious report. For I protest before God, there is none on the face of the earth that I would be fastened unto[1]."

Now there is every probability that while he wrote these words, as we shall presently see, he was already privately married, or contemplated marriage.

Sir Walter sailed with the fleet on the 6th of May, 1592, but was overtaken the day following by Sir Martin Frobisher, with letters from the Queen recalling him. He notwithstanding continued his course, but meeting a storm off Cape Finisterre, on the 11th of May, which scattered the fleet, he considered the season too far advanced for an expedition to Panama, and resolved to obey the Queen's orders. He divided the fleet into two squadrons, and gave the command of one to Sir Martin Frobisher[2] and the other to Sir John Burgh. This expedition resulted in the capture of the 'Madre de Dios,' one of the largest ships of Portugal, and the richest prize ever brought to England. The 'Madre de Dios' arrived in Dartmouth on the 7th of September, at a period when Sir Walter was atoning in the Tower for his gallant intrigues. The beautiful Elizabeth, daughter of Sir Nicholas Throgmorton, and one of the Maids of Honour to the Queen, had made such an impression upon Sir Walter's heart, that he forgot the ardent devotion which he had led Queen Elizabeth to believe he cherished for

[1] Cayley's Life of Ralegh, vol. i. p. 120.

[2] Among Sloane's MSS. (No. 43, fol. 33) is a short relation of "A voyage undertaken by Sir Walter Rawleigh, but himself returning left the charge thereof to Sir Martin Frobisher. Anno 1592."

her. It is asserted by some of Ralegh's biographers, that when the consequences of his intercourse with Elizabeth Throgmorton betrayed the intrigue, he was already privately married to her, and that the Queen considered Ralegh's conduct as both personally and politically offensive;—personally, as having broken that faith which she exacted from her favourites; and politically, as interfering with her prerogative, which rendered her permission for the marriage of one of her Maids of Honour necessary. According to others, Ralegh did not marry her until after the discovery of their intrigue[1]. Be this as it may, the offending couple were imprisoned in the Tower, and Ralegh was deprived of those offices which gave him free access to the Queen. It is asserted by Oldys that Walter, the eldest son of Ralegh, was born in 1594, consequently two years after the marriage. There is unfortunately much want of information respecting the private life of Sir Walter. We recollect having seen it stated somewhere, that doubts were expressed of Elizabeth Throgmorton's having been his first wife. A passage in a very remarkable letter which Sir Walter wrote at a later period, when imprisoned in the Tower on account of the Cobham treason, renders it evident that, besides his son Walter, he had a daughter—Carew was not then born. His misfortune produced such a despondency before his trial, that he resolved upon committing suicide; and pre-

[1] Camden says, "Walterus Raleghus, Regii Satellitii præfectus, honoraria Reginæ virgine vitiata (quam postea in uxorem duxit)," etc. Ann. Elizab. 1595.

vious to this attempt upon his life, to which we shall have occasion to allude again hereafter, he wrote a letter to Lady Ralegh, in which occurs the following passage :—

"To witness that thou didst love me once, take care that thou marry not to please sense, but to avoid poverty and to preserve thy child. That thou didst also love me living witness it to others ; to my poor daughter to whom I have given nothing, for his sake who will be cruel to himself to preserve thee. Be charitable to her, and teach thy son to love her for his father's sake[1]."

From the expressions which Sir Walter uses, we cannot doubt that this daughter was not the offspring of his marriage with Elizabeth Throgmorton, as he so pointedly calls his son, in addressing Lady Ralegh, "thy child," while the girl is styled "my daughter ;" but the last sentence is still more conclusive, as the mother would not have required an appeal to her feelings on behalf of her own child. If therefore Sir Walter was not previously married, the daughter here alluded to was illegitimate, which, judging from this letter, seems more doubtful than the supposition of his having been a widower when he married Elizabeth Throgmorton.

Sir Edward Stafford writes to Anthony Bacon, on the 30th of July, 1592, "If you have anything to do with Sir Walter Ralegh, or any love to make to Mrs. Throckmorton at the Tower, tomorrow you may

[1] The Court of King James the First, by Dr. Godfrey Goodman, Bishop of Gloucester, vol. ii. p. 95.

speak with them, if the countermand come not to-night, as some think will not be, and particularly he that hath charge to send them thither." Ralegh was not released until late in September; the fair prisoner no doubt much earlier.

It was during this confinement that Sir Walter "acted Orlando Furioso," as Sir Arthur Georges expresses himself; because the Lieutenant of the Ordnance at the Tower, Sir George Carew, in whose charge he was, would not permit him, on the occasion of Queen Elizabeth's paying a visit at Sir George Carye's, to leave the Tower in disguise, "to ease his mind but with a sight of the Queen, or else he protested his heart would break." Equally fulsome was a letter which Ralegh wrote to Sir Robert Cecil (no doubt for the purpose of being laid before the Queen), in which he represents himself as cast into the depth of misery, "from being deprived of the light of seeing her[1]." It has been observed, that "Ralegh was bred in a school where scruples as to the means of gratification were not yet taught," and hence we find so many lamentable blemishes in his moral character. His proceedings in the Tower affixed to it a stain which after years could not entirely remove.

After his release from the Tower, Ralegh remained only two days in London, and then proceeded to the west of England, to look after his share in the rich prize the 'Madre de Dios.' For some time he was not allowed to approach the court, but her Majesty's

[1] The letter is reprinted from the Burleigh State Papers in Cayley's Life of Sir W. Raleigh, vol. i. p. 126.

displeasure seems at length to have relented, when he exerted himself in Parliament on behalf of the Crown, on the question of subsidies to the Queen; and he soon regained her favour so far, that on occasion of the manor of Sherborne in Dorsetshire being alienated from the see of Salisbury, and falling to the Crown, Ralegh solicited and obtained it. Shortly afterwards he retired to Sherborne, where he commenced various improvements,—"So that," says Coker, (the author of the Survey of Dorsetshire,) "whether you consider the pleasantness of the seat, the goodness of the soil, or the delicacies belonging unto it, it was unparalleled by any in these parts."

During this period of exile from court, he matured a project which seems to have occupied his mind for some time. The voyages of discovery, performed by the Spaniards during the sixteenth century, had made him acquainted with vague reports of the existence of a rich and splendid city in the interior of the unexplored parts of South America, abounding in gold, and to which they gave the name of El Dorado. Various expeditions had been undertaken from the year 1535 until Ralegh's time, and prosecuted with zeal, by individuals who enjoyed the greatest reputation at that stirring period. In their execution no regard was paid to the sacrifice of life, or to the enormous cost attending these adventures[1]. These rumours reawakened the ardour for maritime enterprize and discovery, which Ralegh's life at court and his ambitious

[1] Southey says that these expeditions "have cost Spain more than all the treasures she has received from her South American possessions."

projects had for a while suppressed, but which under the disfavour of the Queen, and his temporary banishment from court, revived. He now availed himself of all the information he could procure from books, or orally from persons who had been in the New World, and ultimately resolved in 1594 on sending Captain Whiddon, an old officer who had commanded one of his pinnaces during the cruise to the Azores in 1586, to the West Indies, to examine the coast and collect information. For this purpose Ralegh drew up certain instructions, with which Whiddon departed; and his report being favourable, Ralegh determined upon his first voyage to Guiana.

It is difficult to judge of the motives which first induced Ralegh to take this step. We are told by Naunton that "he found his favour declining and falling into a recess;" and his imagination probably suggested the discovery and conquest of a second empire of the Incas, or the plunder of another Temple of the Sun, which would not only invest him with the fame that his restless ambition coveted, but restore him to full favour at court, and fill his exchequer from

> "Yet unspoil'd
> Guiana, whose great city Geryon's sons
> Call El Dorado."

The vast tracts of land still unknown in the interior of South America, could not fail to possess other regions where, even in the absence of that alluring idol gold, England might establish a colony of greater importance to her dominions than Mexico or Peru was to Spain. The mania for discovering auriferous regions was not confined to Spain; it spread equally over England and Germany; and such was the influence of this seducing picture, first sketched by rumour, and then coloured by imagination, that the more victims it drew into its vortex, the more were found to embark in plans for its attainment. We cannot now discern, through the veil which the lapse of centuries has spread over the events of those days, whether Ralegh fully shared in the common belief; he however possessed too much sagacity, with the failure of his Virginian project still fresh upon his mind, to suppose that any anticipated advantages from the settlement of a colony for the production of sugar, ginger, tobacco and other merchandize, would tempt adventurers to share in the danger and expense. He therefore devised his famous voyage in search of El Dorado, and after his return published the work, a new edition of which is now presented to the reader. Wonderful and surprising as the various events and actions in Ralegh's life had hitherto been, his 'Discoverie of Guiana' may be said to have formed their climax; but although it conferred upon him greater fame than any of his former exploits, the statements which he advanced in it reflected more doubt upon his veracity "than all the other questionable acts of his varied life put together."

The reader of Hume's History of England may recollect that Ralegh's narrative is branded as being full of the grossest and most palpable lies,—an ungenerous and inconsiderate remark, which most probably refers to Ralegh's statements respecting El Dorado, the existence of the Amazons, the tribe without heads, and the auriferous rocks in Guiana. We shall anticipate the chronological order of events by examining here two or three of these statements. Our desire is that the reader should peruse the pages of this work, without considering Ralegh as the gratuitous inventor of statements, which we, with the advantage that two centuries and a half have given us, now regard with a smile.

The marvellous discoveries and narratives of the first conquerors of America had prepared the minds of the credulous for the greatest wonders, and disposed them to admit the accounts given of a still more recently discovered country, called El Dorado, the gold-covered capital of which was built upon a vast lake, surrounded by mountains so impregnated with precious metals, that they shone with a dazzling splendour. This picture excited the cupidity of thousands, and led them to encounter dangers, privations, and a waste of human life unparalleled in the history of enterprize. But it was not Ralegh's publication which spread this illusion; the fable already existed in the early part of the sixteenth century, when large expeditions in search of El Dorado were directed to the eastern part of the Andes. We are informed by Oviedo, that in 1539 Gonzalo Pizarro sought a great prince, of whom report related that he was covered with powdered gold, so that from head to foot he resembled a golden figure worked by the hands of a skilful artist. In lieu of El Dorado, Pizarro discovered the province of the Cinnamon-trees of America (*Nec-*

tandra cinnamomoides Nees.). One of the most distinguished adventurers in search of El Dorado was Philip von Huten (erroneously called Philip de Urre), or Uten, as he is named by Herrera, who set out on his expedition in 1541, and whose narrative excited great attention. The name El Dorado was not originally used to designate any particular region, but a custom, which, as related by the Indians, was in itself sufficiently remarkable. Father Gumilla observes that, according to the histories of Terra firma and New Granada, the fable had its origin on the coast of Carthagena and Santa Martha, whence it passed to Bogota. A rumour was spread through those regions, of a sovereign prince, who lived in a country which abounded in gold, and who on public occasions appeared with his body sprinkled over with gold-dust; hence the name El Dorado was given to him, meaning in Spanish 'the gilded' or 'golden,' which was afterwards applied to the whole region. According to others, it denoted a religious custom, practised by the sect of Bochica or Idacanzas. The chief priest, "before he performed his sacrifice, caused powder of gold to be stuck upon his hands and face after they had been smeared with grease[1]."

When after fruitless searches in New Granada the locality of the fable was transferred to Guiana, the whole province was designated by the name of El Dorado; but the lake or laguna, surrounded by auriferous mountains, continued a necessary accompani-

[1] Humboldt's Personal Narrative, vol. v. p. 814.

ment to the shifting fable. Whether its locality was placed on the eastern descent of the Andes, between the Uaupes and Caqueta, tributaries of the Rio Negro, or between the Essequibo and River Parima (Rio Branco), the lake remained connected with it. When therefore the attention of adventurers was, at the close of the sixteenth century, attracted to Guiana as the spot where El Dorado was situated, the name of the river Parima, and the inundations of the flat country and savannahs through which the rivers Parima, Takutu, and Rupununi take their course, gave rise to the fable of the White Sea, or Laguna del Parima, or Dorado. Ralegh, after his return from his first voyage, was undecided where to place the locality of this lake; he conceived the water to be saltish, and called it another Caspian Sea[1]. Hondius constructed his 'Nieuwe Caerte van het goudreyke landt Guiana' after Ralegh's and Keymis's return, and was the first geographer who introduced the imperial city of Manoa upon the Laguna Parima, Rupununi, or Dorado. He made the lake two hundred leagues long and forty broad, and assigned to its locality the isthmus between the Rupununi and Rio Branco. This inland sea was bounded by the latitudes of 2° north and 1° 45′ south, and was larger than the Caspian Sea.

Captain Keymis, who accompanied Ralegh on his first voyage, and at his expense undertook in 1596 the second voyage to Guiana, identified the locality of the Dorado with this lake. "The Indians," says

[1] Discovery of Guiana, present edition, p. 13.

Keymis, "to show the worthiness of Dessekebe (Essequibo), for it is very large and full of islands in the mouth, do call it the brother of Orenoque; it lieth southerly in the land, and from the mouth of it unto the head they pass in twenty days; then taking their provisions, they carry it on their shoulders one day's journey; afterwards they return to their canoes, and bear them likewise to the side of a lake, which the Jaos call Raponowini, the Charibes Parime, which is of such bigness that they know no difference between it and the main sea. There be infinite numbers of canoes in this lake, and I suppose it is no other than that whereon Manoa standeth." And,

> "...... to give to airy nothings
> A local habitation and a name,"

from that period the isthmus which is formed by the rivers Rupununi and Parima became the classical soil of El Dorado de Parima.

Subsequent geographers, as Sanson (between 1656 and 1669), D'Anville (1760), La Crux Olmedilla (1775), and Surville (1778), retained the Laguna Parima, or Mar Blanco, but varied its locality in the most arbitrary manner. Sanson and D'Anville appear to have been doubtful whether to adopt it or not: for instance Sanson, in his chart of the river of the Amazons (1680), left out the Lake Parima, which appeared in his first map; while D'Anville omitted it in the first edition of 'L'Amérique Méridionale,' but inserted it in the second edition, published in 1760.

The researches of the most eminent traveller of our

age, to whom every branch of physical science is indebted—the celebrated Humboldt—was the first who, by reasoning, founded upon personal experience and an inspection of every document relating to the regions which had been made the locality of this inland lake, proved the non-existence of this White Sea, or Laguna de Parima.

Humboldt observes, that if a geographer intended to construct a map of South America on astronomical observations, he would find to the north of the Amazon a *terra incognita*, three times as long as Spain; or, that if a line be drawn west of Cayenne, through the falls of the Maroni and the Essequibo, Vieja Guayana, along the right bank of the Orinoco to Esmeralda, and thence through the confluence of the Rio Branco with the Rio Negro along the latter river as far as Vistoza, on the left bank of the Amazon, and to the sources of the Oyapok, there would be an area of 432,000 square miles on which not a single position has been astronomically determined. Thus wrote Humboldt twenty-five years ago. If we except the country to the east of the 55th meridian, these are the very regions which we have explored during our eight years' wanderings in Guiana between the years 1835 and 1844, and we can fully certify that the reasoning at which Humboldt arrived, by judiciously comparing and considering the documents relating to the origin of the White Sea or Lake Parima, are borne out by the geography of nature. There is no inland sea in existence. The inundations of those extensive savannahs during the tropical winter, which cover 14,000 square miles, and are encompassed by the Sierra Pacaraima to the north, the Canuku, Taripona, and Carawaimi mountains to the south, the thick forest of the Essequibo and isolated mountains to the east, and the mountains of the Mocajahi and Parima to the west,—gave rise, no doubt, to the fable of the White Sea, assisted by the ignorance of Europeans of the Indian language[1].

We shall not enumerate the various expeditions which were undertaken for the conquest of El Dorado,—a phantom which has by some been regarded as a device of Satan "to lure men to destruction," and viewed by others as the means of spreading Christianity and enlarging our geographical knowledge. The quaint remarks of John Hagthorpe, a well-known author of the early part of the seventeenth century, and a contemporary of Ralegh, are very amusing: he says, "Sir Walter Rawley knewe very well when

[1] Notwithstanding the proofs of the non-existence of this White Sea or Lake Parima, a work was published in New York in 1844 with the pompous title of 'El Dorado;' it is illustrated by a Map on which the Lake Parima figures in its whole extent. The author, Mr. Van Heuvel, visited the coast regions of Guiana without penetrating into the interior, and his conclusions respecting this lake rest only upon what he learned from some Indians, whose language he did not understand, and upon the maps of Sanson, D'Anville and others of the last century; and although fully acquainted with Humboldt's writings, "who," he says, "effaced without sufficient grounds that wondrous lake," Mr. Van Heuvel has fully restored it, and gives to it a length of from two hundred to two hundred and fifty miles, and a breadth of about fifty miles. Out of it flow the rivers Parima and Takutu into the Rio Negro and the Amazon; the Cuyuni, the Siparuni, and the Mazaruni, into the Essequibo; and the Paragua into the Orinoco. A single step backwards in our geographical knowledge is much to be regretted, and all who take interest in that science ought to aid in preventing the dissemination of such absurdities.

he attempted his Guyana businesse, who err'd in nothing so much (if a free man may speak freely) as in too much confidence in the relations of the countrie: For who knowes not the policy and cunning of the fat Fryers, which is to stirre up and animate the Souldiers and Laytie to the search and inquisition of new Countries, by devising tales and coments in their Cloysters where they live at ease, that when others have taken payne to bring in the harvest, they may feed upon the best and fattest of the croppe[1]?"

Though we cannot go all lengths with Hagthorpe, there seems to be much truth in his observation. It is remarkable that the copy which Antonio de Berreo[2] had received of the pretended journey of Juan Martinez came originally from his confessor. Ralegh expressly states, that when Martinez had given up all hope of life, and was receiving the sacrament at the hands of his confessor, "he delivered these things with the relation of his travels, and also called for his calabazas, or gourds of the gold beads, which he gave to the church and friars to be prayed for[3]."

[1] 'England's Exchequer, or a discourse of the sea and navigation, with some things thereunto coincident concerning plantations; by John Hagthorpe, Gent. London, 1625.'

[2] As the name of Berreo occurs here for the first time in this volume, we may observe that it should perhaps have been written more properly Berrio, as we find it in Father Simon's Noticias; but as Ralegh, with all contemporary English and some French authors, have written it as above, we have, for the sake of conformity with the original work of Ralegh, assumed the mode of spelling it Berreo throughout. According to some he married the daughter, according to others the adopted child, of Gonzalo Ximenes de Quesada. Fray Simon calls her the niece of the great Adelantado, but all agree that she inherited his riches.

[3] Discovery of Guiana, p. 20 of the present edition.

The account which Ralegh gives of the Amazons and the headless men has received severe censure. We shall leave our observations on the subject of the latter to a future opportunity, observing only that Hartsinck in his work on Guiana, published in 1770, gravely asserts the existence of a race of negroes in Surinam whose hands and feet were forked like the claw of a lobster, consisting merely of a thumb and a finger.

With regard to the account of the Amazons, it is not given as from personal observation, but as a report received from Indians, and current at the period when Ralegh wrote his Guiana voyage, and which even Condamine the French Academician considered probable, adducing many testimonies in its favour in a discourse delivered before the French Academy. The account of a tribe of Amazons is almost coeval with the discovery of America. Christopher Columbus was told that the small island of Madanino or Matinino (Montserrat) was inhabited by warlike women[1]. Orellana in his descent of the Marañon was cautioned at the mouth of the Napo by an old chieftain, to beware of the warlike women, and asserts that he afterwards met females fighting in the ranks of men. Hernando de Ribeira, the follower of Cabeza de Vega the Conquistador of Paraguay, asserts, in 1545, that he heard of a nation of Amazons, who lived on the western side of a large lake, which was poetically called the Mansion of the Sun, because that orb sank

[1] Peter Martyr, Dec. i. lib. 2. Select Letters of Christopher Columbus, translated and edited for the Hakluyt Society by R. H. Major, Esq., p. 15.

into it. D'Acuña expressed his firm belief in their existence, and fixed their abode on the river Cunuriz. It is a strange coincidence that, according to Ralegh, there is a province in Guiana called Canuri, governed by a woman, and we might almost question whether the close resemblance of these two words is accidental[1]. D'Acuña observes: "When their neighbours visit them (the Amazons) at a time appointed by them, they receive them with their bows and arrows in their hands, and exercise them as if to engage with enemies; but knowing their object, they lay them down, and receive them as their guests, who remain with them a few days[2]." Andrew Thevet, in his 'Antarctic,' has made the arrival of the Amazons' guests the subject of an illustration[3]. We observe from several quotations given by Ralegh that he was well acquainted with Thevet's publication, a translation of which by Bynneman appeared in 1568, and we may therefore suppose that he had preconceived an opinion in favour of their existence before he left England: in this however he was not singular; the belief was entertained by thousands at that period. Father Cyprian Baraza, a Jesuit missionary, at the close of the seventeenth century gave an account of the existence of Amazons to the west of the Paraguay in 12° south latitude. We have already alluded to the statement which M. de Condamine made before

[1] Discovery of Guiana, present edition, p. 108.

[2] We quote this passage from the English translation of D'Acuña's 'Discovery of the River Amazon.'

[3] 'Les Singularités de la France Antarctique, par F. André Thevet,' p. 124. Paris, 1558.

the Academy, and the existence of such reports was confirmed thirty years after by Ribeiro, a Portuguese astronomer, without however expressing his own faith in these traditions[1]. The missionary Gili heard from an Indian of the Quaqua tribe, that the Aikeambenanos, literally 'the women living alone,' inhabited the banks of the Cuchivero, which falls into the Orinoco opposite the island of Taran, between Caycara and Alta Gracia. Condamine further adduces the testimony of two Spanish Governors of the province of Venezuela, Don Diego (? Francisco) Portales and Don Francisco Torralva, which agreed in substance that a tribe of warlike women dwelt in the interior of Guiana. Count Pagan, in his history of the river Amazon, observes in his florid style, "que l'Asie ne se vante plus de ses comptes véritables ou fabuleuses des Amazones, l'Amérique ne lui cède point cet avantage . . . Et que le fleuve de Thermodoon, ne soit plus enflé de la gloire de ces conquérantes, la rivière de Coruris [Cunuriz] est aussi fameuse pour ses belles guerrières[2]." L'Abbé Guyon expresses a similar opinion in his 'Histoire des Amazones anciennes et modernes,' but it is evident that the faith in their existence rests upon D'Acuña's report.

In these accounts, which have been transmitted to us by the early historians, we observe a manifest desire to invest all that related to the new continent

[1] Ribeiro de Sampaio, 'Diario da viagem no anno de 1774 et 1775,' p. 27 *et seq*.

[2] 'Relation de la rivière des Amazones, par le Comte de Pagan,' chap. xlix. p. 157.

with an air of marvel. It is however extraordinary that, if the tradition originated with Europeans, it was not only still in existence at the time of Condamine's voyage, but is even now current among all the Indian tribes who have had intercourse with the Caribs. The Indians of the lower Corentyn, of the Essequibo and Rupununi, declared to us in the gravest manner during our travels in these regions, that the separate hordes of females still live on the upper part of the Corentyn, in a country called Marawonne. The accounts we received respecting the country they inhabited were accompanied by such details, that the tradition assumed some probability. We were told that when we should have passed high above the great cataracts in the Corentyn, at the point where two huge rocks, called Pioomoco and Surama, rise from each bank of the river and bound it like a portal, we might consider ourselves in the land of the Woruisamocos. We received similar accounts from the Macusis, who reside on those savannahs which form the supposed site of Keymis's El Dorado. When travelling over these plains we frequently came to sequestered spots where we observed a great quantity of broken pottery, which our Macusi Indians invariably adduced as a proof of the former residence of the Woruisamocos on these places. Of all Guianians however the Caribs are the most versed in wonderful tales, and all agree in the facts, that such a republic existed in the interior of Guiana, towards the head of the Corentyn, and in a district which no European ever visited; that these females are called Woruisamocos; that they shoot with bow and arrow, and use the *cura* or blow-pipe; that they cultivate their own grounds, and hold no intercourse with other Indians, except once a year, when they permit the men to visit them in parties of twenties; and that if their offspring prove a male infant they kill it, but rear up the female children.

Orellana, in his descent of the Marañon, met with hostile Indians at the river Cunuriz who opposed his advance, and among their number were females, who appeared quite as warlike as the men. This is the origin of the fable of the American Amazons, but the locality being once fixed, succeeding centuries have been unable to efface the tradition that Amazons exist in some part or other of Guiana. Several expeditions have been sent at different times to explore the Rio Trombetas, all of which were stopped by the large cataracts; in some instances the explorers were murdered by the savage Indians who inhabit the upper branches: hence those parts of that river remained perfectly unknown, and were considered the abode of the bellicose dames. M. Montravel, commanding the French man-of-war 'La Boulonnaise,' surveyed the Amazon as high up as the Rio Negro in the years 1842–1844, and heard a similar account when in the neighbourhood of the Rio Trombetas. We have therefore from the south as well as from the north the same tradition, that the Amazons of the New World inhabit a central district of Guiana. Our route in 1844, when traversing these very regions, and descending the chief branch of the Trombetas from its source to its junction with the Wanamu, has, unfortunately for the interest attached to this romance, driven the warlike dames from one of their last hiding-places. The result of this fatiguing and perilous journey has only strengthened our conviction that the existence of this republic of women was one of those inventions designed merely to enhance the wonders of which the New World was regarded as the seat. It would however be unjust to condemn Ralegh's proneness to a belief in their existence, when we find that even Southey, the learned historian of Brazil, makes this remark: "Had we never heard of the Amazons of antiquity, I should without hesitation believe in those of America; their existence is not the less likely for that reason, and yet it must be admitted that the probable truth is made to appear suspicious by its resemblance to a known fable[1]."

The next point to be considered is the censure which Ralegh has incurred from his enemies for his exaggerated representations of the mineral riches of Guiana. The ore which he presented to the Lord High Admiral Howard and Sir Robert Cecil was alleged to have been obtained from Africa; he refutes this charge in the preface to his 'Discoverie of Guiana'; and the strongest evidence of his belief in the mineral wealth of Guiana is afforded by the two expeditions undertaken at his expense in the following years with the object of discovering mines in Guiana. Oldys relates that he saw some of the ore brought by Sir Walter Ralegh from Guiana, which had been carefully preserved in his family, and which,

[1] Southey's History of Brazil, p. 609.

at the period when Oldys wrote Ralegh's life, was in the possession of Captain William Elwes. It cannot be doubted that Guiana possesses gold; there are various instances on record of this metal being found, but none where it has been met with in sufficient quantities to render its working profitable. Humboldt says that, from what he observed in that part of America, he is led to think "that gold, like tin, is sometimes disseminated in an almost imperceptible manner in the mass of granite rocks itself, without our being able to admit that there is a ramification and an interlacing of small veins. Not long ago the Indians of Emaramada found in the Quebrada del Tigre a piece of native gold two lines in diameter. It was rounded, and appeared to have been washed along by the waters." We saw a piece of native gold twice that size in the hands of Fray Josè at Fort San Joachim, which he assured us had been found in the river Takutu; and we ourselves observed minute particles of gold in the dry bed of that river. Strange to say, the gold which Fray Josè showed us was upon white quartz, the "harde white sparr" described by Ralegh.

In 1721 the Council of Ten in Holland granted a privilege, whereby it was enacted that all persons disposed to work mines in Guiana might do so upon certain conditions, and Mr. Hildebrand, a miner, was sent from Holland for that purpose. A shaft was sunk at a short distance from the first cataracts in the Cuyuni, but the small quantity of ore found did not repay the expenses of working it, and the attempt was abandoned. Hildebrand went afterwards up the river Siparuni, a tributary of the Essequibo, and is said to have met with ore there.

Several of the natives who came on board of Columbus's ship, when lying at anchor in the Gulf of Paria, wore pieces of gold on their breasts; he made inquiries as to where they found the gold, and they all directed him to an elevated tract of land lying westward, at no great distance on the confines of their own country[1].

The testimony of Mr. Robert Duddeley, who was afterwards knighted, is fully corroborative of the prevalent opinion of the abundance of gold in Guiana. Duddeley arrived in Trinidad on the 1st of February, 1595, consequently several days previous to Sir Walter Ralegh's leaving England. He states that a party whom he sent to examine the Orinoco informed him, on their return, that an Indian chief gave them some plates of gold, and told them of "another rich nation, that sprinkled their bodies with gold, and seemed to be gilt." Robert Harcourt also furnishes evidence of the general belief of the abundance of gold in Cayenne; and though the reports of Sparrey and Keymis may be considered partial, and written in the interest of Ralegh, the same cannot be said of Duddeley and Harcourt. The existence of auriferous regions in Guiana was attested by the latter, who observes, that Anthony Canabre an Indian brought him a piece of a "rocke of white sparre" which held both

[1] Select Letters of Columbus, translated and edited for the Hakluyt Society by R. H. Major, Esq., pp. 121, 124.

gold and silver[1]. Nor are Ralegh and his contemporaries the only persons who assert that there is gold in Guiana. Baron d'Ouily received information from a Spaniard, towards the latter part of the seventeenth century, of the existence of ore in Guiana, and entered into a contract with some people from Zealand, in consequence of which some of the ore was brought to Holland, 120 lbs. of which contained 2½ ounces of fine gold and one ounce of silver; a similar quantity of another kind contained more, others less, and some neither gold nor silver. Otto Kay, who mentions this in his 'Pertinente Beschryvinge van Guiana' (Amsterdam, 1676), says, that he conversed with Hendrick Harmensz, who commanded the soldiers near the mines, and who told him that they had been merely worked near the surface.

We have attempted to exculpate Ralegh from some of the gravest accusations of bad faith and gratuitous inventions that have been brought against him. Many remarks to a similar purpose will be found in the following pages, where passages in the body of the work have called forth the animadversions of the historians and biographers of this great man.

The pure and nervous style in which the 'Discoverie of Guiana' is written imparts to it a lasting charm. Camden characterizes it as an elegant production; and it attracted such attention when it first appeared, that it was translated into the principal European languages. It may not be uninteresting to

[1] Robert Harcourt: 'A Relation of a Voyage to Guiana.' Edition of 1626, p. 53.

enumerate here the different editions which have appeared of this work, the first of which bears the date of 1596. The general belief that during Ralegh's lifetime only one edition of his Voyage was separately published, is erroneous, as on a recent comparison of two copies bearing the date of 1596, we have observed some trifling typographical differences[1]. The 'Discovery of Guiana' was reprinted verbatim in 'Hakluyt's Voyages'[2], and since in Birch's 'Works of Ralegh'[3], Cayley's 'Life of Sir Walter Ralegh'[4], and in the 'Works of Sir Walter Raleigh,' published by the directors of the Clarendon press[5]. A few years after the publication of the original, an abridged Latin translation[6] appeared in 1599 in Nuremberg, at the cost of the celebrated geographer and collector Levinus Hulsius. This is embellished by five curious representations: the first, of the Tivitivas living on the tops of trees; a representation of "Manoa o el

[1] This refers to the ornamental letters; the initials of Sir Walter Ralegh (W. R.) at the end of his Preface and Address to the Reader, and the catchword at the end of the pages.

[2] Richard Hakluyt: 'The principal Navigations, Voyages, Traffiques and Discoveries of the English nation,' etc. folio. London, 1599, vol. iii. p. 627.

[3] Thomas Birch: 'The Works of Sir Walter Ralegh, Knight.' 8vo. London, 1751, vol. ii. p. 139.

[4] Arthur Cayley, jun.: 'The Life of Sir Walter Raley, Knight.' 4to. London, 1805, vol. i. p. 142.

[5] 'The Works of Sir Walter Raleigh, Knight, now first collected, to which are prefixed the Lives of the Author by Oldys and Birch.' 8vo. Oxford, 1829, vol. viii. p. 391.

[6] 'Brevis et admiranda descriptio regni Guianæ, auri abundantissimi, in America seu Novo Orbe sub linea equinoctiali siti. Quod nuper admodum, annis nimirum 1594, 1595 et 1596 per generosum D. D. Gualtherum Ralegh equitem Anglum, detectum est, etc. Impensis Levini Hulsii. 4to. Noribergæ, 1599.'

Dorado," with part of the Essequibo river, and the Indians occupied in carrying their boats and cargoes over land to the Lake Roponowini, as related by Keymis; the third plate represents the joyful reception of the men, and subsequent amusements of the Amazons with their friends; while the fourth shows how these warlike dames dealt with their enemies: their prisoners are hung up by the feet to trees, and serve as targets for their skill in archery; others are preparing fires for roasting the victims: the most interesting however is the fifth plate, which exhibits the Ewaipanoma or men without heads[1]. A translation in German seems to have been coeval with the Latin one[2]. A literal translation is likewise contained in the eighth part of De Bry's 'Collection of Ameri-

[1] Attached to this volume is a "Tabula Locorum quorum in libello hoc mentio fit," which as a document of the geographical knowledge of the western hemisphere at that period is highly curious. As Hulsius' edition is now very scarce, that geographical table may prove of interest. The degrees of longitude are reckoned eastwards from the extreme north-western point of the island of Ferro (long. 18° 7′ 30″ west of Greenwich), and the latitude is, with two exceptions, north of the equator.

	Grad. long.	Grad. lat.		Grad. long.	Grad. lat.
Amapaia	313	2 Sept.	Jaos	325	3 Sept.
Amazones Fluv.	338	0	Iwaiponoma	315	1 ...
Capuri Fluv.	322	7 Sept.	Macureguarai	316	3 ...
Cassipa	315	3 ...	Manoa	320	1 ...
Cassipagotes	316	1½ ...	Morequito	317	4 ...
Dorado	320	1 ...	Orenoque Fluv.	116*	5 ...
Demorary Fluv.	325	5 ...	Parima Lacus	320	0 ...
Essebeke Fluv.	322	3 ...	Trinidado	321	9 ...
Guiana	310	1 ...			

[2] 'Kurtze wunderbare Beschreibung des Goldreichen Königreichs Guiana in America, von Herrn Waltherio Raleigh.' Frankfurt am Main, 4to. F. Hulsius, Wittibe, 1599.

* So in the MS., but evidently an error, and intended for 316.

can Navigations and Voyages,' which was published in Latin, German and French, and is now of great rarity[1]; it is accompanied by a curious map of that part of South America. Oldys observes, "There are accounts of two editions of Sir Walter Ralegh's Voyage to Guiana in Dutch, one in 4to, which must be this of his Discovery, and the other in 1619." Edmund Howes, in his addition to Stow's Annals, says, "it has been translated into all languages." A French translation appeared in 1722, in the second volume of F. Coreal's Voyages[2].

An interesting manuscript in the British Museum contains a list of the captains and gentlemen who accompanied Sir Walter on his first Guiana voyage; it is entitled, 'An abstract of diuerse memorable thinges worthy the noting, selected out of Sir Walter Raleighes first booke of his discoverie of Guyana and by hym performed in Anno Domini 1595[3].' The following extract contains the list:—

"Thursday the vi of February, I departed England,

[1] De Bry: 'Collectiones Peregrinationum in Indias Orientales et Occidentales. Folio. Francofurti, 1590–1599. Americæ Pars viii.' It is entitled, 'Verissima Descriptio auriferi et præstantissimi Regn. Guiana, quod hisce temporibus, a veteribus regni Peru incolis habitatur, et a posteris Guiana-Capa potentissimi quondam in Peru Regis, possidetur, una cum descriptione ditissimarum Regionum et provinciarum Emeria, Aromaia, et Amapaia, anno 1595 per nobilissimum et fortissimum Gualtherum Ralegh equitem Anglum inventarum.'

[2] 'Relation de la Guiane, du Lac de Parima et des provinces d'Emeria, d'Arromaia et d'Amapaia, découvertes par le Chevalier Walter Raleigh.'

[3] Brit. Mus. Ayscough's Cat. No. 3272. It appears to be a contemporary copy, perhaps transcribed from Sir Walter's own manuscript; however this list has not been published in any of the editions of his Voyage known to us.

being accompanied with diuerse Captaines and Gentlemen whose names were these:

Captain George Gifford, Vice Admirall,
Captain Calfeild,
Captain Amiotts Preston,
Captain Thynne,
Captain Laurence Keymis,
Captain Eynos,
Captain Whiddon,
Captain Clarke,
Captain Crosse,
Captain Facy,
My cousin Butsheade George,
My nephew John Gilbert,
John Dowglass Master of myne owne shipp,
Mr. Edward Porter,
Lieutenant Hewes,
My cousin Greeneueile,
— Connock,
Anthoney Wells,
— King, M[r] of the Lions whelpe,
Jerom Farrar,
Thomas Upton,
Nicholas Mellechapp, Surgeon (he is now, 1618, dwelling in Ludlow)."

The Voyage described in the following pages was directed to a river of which very little was known, at the time when Ralegh undertook to reach the main stream from Trinidad by one of the numerous channels which intersect the delta; the better to elucidate the account of his slow progress and hair-breadth escapes, we prefix a few general remarks on the Orinoco.

During his third voyage Columbus discovered the island of Trinidad, and entered the Gulf of Paria, which he called Golfo de las Perlas. The low land which forms the delta of the Orinoco he named Terra de Gracia; the strong currents prevented his examining that part of the coast, and he considered the four great outlets of the Orinoco to be arms of the sea, and called the coast of Paria which partly surrounds the gulf Isla Santa[1]. Vincente-Yanez Pinçon gave the first information of this great river, which he called Rio Dulce[2], and that name was preserved for some time on the maps of the sixteenth century. In a highly interesting manuscript map in the British Museum[3], supposed to have been executed towards the end of the first third of the sixteenth century, the eastern branch (Boca de Navios) is called Rio Doulce; and the oceanic delta, Costa Bassa, el Palmar, and Anegada; the latter name no doubt refers to its being so frequently under water. The most western branch (Manamo) is called Comari. Diego de Ordaz, who in 1531 ascended the river as high up as the cataract of Atures, heard for the first time the name of Orinoco, and affirms that from its mouth to the

[1] Herrera (Historia general de los Hechos de los Castellanos en las islas y tierra firma del mar Oceano. Madrid, 1601—1615.), Dec. iii. lib. 3. pp. 79, 81.

[2] Grynæus, De Navigatione Pinzoni, pp. 119, 120.

[3] Add. MSS. No. 5413.

confluence with the Meta it is called Uriaparia, and from that point it goes by the name of the Orinucu[1]. Baron Humboldt enumerates the following names which the Orinoco bears in one or other part of its course; Baraguan, Yuyapari, Yjupari, Huriaparia, Uriapari, Viapari, Paragua, Bazagua, Parava[2]. To these may be added Rio de Paria, Urinucu, Raleana[3], Worinoque[4]; and we have ourselves heard it called Riunucku by the Maiongkong and Guinau Indians, who inhabit the upper branches of this great river. The Gran Boca or Boca de Navios is called East Capuri, Vinikebery, Winikeberi, and Varima, in some of the early maps[5].

The uncertainty of the situation of its sources has in a great measure been removed by our journey in 1839–40. We approached within thirty miles of the head of the chief branch, when we were obliged to retreat in consequence of an expected attack of the Kirishanas, a tribe of savage Indians alike hostile to the whites and their Indian neighbours[6]. According to the Indians who accompanied us, we were then a

[1] Herrera, Dec. iv. p. 219; Dec. v. p. 22.

[2] Humboldt's Personal Narrative, English translation, vol. v. p. 806.

[3] Keymis bestowed this name upon it in honour of his General, Sir Walter Ralegh.

[4] Wori signifies a woman in the Macusi language; Worinakui is a female name by no means uncommon among that tribe.

[5] See 'La Guaiane ou Coste Sauvage autrement El Dorado, par Père Du Val d'Abbeville,' Paris, 1654; and 'Terreferme, par Sanson d'Abbeville.' Paris, 1656.

[6] Journal of the Royal Geographical Society of London, vol. x. pp. 231, 232.

journey of a day and a half from the sources of the Orinoco; and from the information which we procured in that vicinity, we assume their geographical position to be in latitude 2° 30′ north, and longitude 64° 50′ west. At a distance of one hundred and fifteen miles (sixty to a degree) from its sources, the Orinoco sends off the remarkable branch which connects that river with the Rio Negro, a tributary of the great Amazon. It is called Casiquiare, and receives several rivers in its course, until it falls above San Carlos into the Rio Negro[1]. From this remarkable bifurcation the course of the Orinoco to Angostura is seven hundred and fifty miles; and from that place to the Boca de Navios, where its main branch flows into the Atlantic Ocean, two hundred and fifty-five miles; its whole course would therefore be about one thousand one hundred and twenty geographical miles. The hydrographical system of the Orinoco, including its tributaries, extends over a surface of two hundred and seventy thousand square miles, and receives four hundred and thirty-six rivers, and more than two thousand rivulets and streams. The superficial area of its basin covers an extent half as large again as the kingdom of Spain.

The Caroni, one of the tributaries of the Orinoco, to the mouth of which Ralegh extended his journey, joins the latter river on its left bank, in latitude 8° 8′

[1] During our expedition in February 1839, we passed through that remarkable natural canal from the Orinoco into the Rio Negro. See Journal of the Royal Geographical Society, vol. x. p. 248.

north according to Humboldt, but in 8° 15′ north according to Codazzi[1]. This river, which drains a surface of twenty-six thousand square miles, has the source of its main branch in the remarkable sandstone mountains of Roraima, and receives upwards of fifty large tributaries. About sixty-three miles below the mouth of the Caroni, or one hundred and seventeen miles from the Boca de Navios or Punta Barima, the Orinoco sends off its first branch, called Brazo[2] Macareo, to the north, and forms that remarkable oceanic delta which is intersected by seventeen large branches and a number of smaller ones. The nearest branches communicate with each other, and form a network and labyrinth of islands, which extend between Punta Barima, the most eastern point[3], and Caño Vagre, the most western outlet, over a distance of one hundred and fifty miles in a direct line.

These numerous branches are divided into two chief portions, of which the one between the Bocas Vagre and Macareo is called the upper or western

[1] Humboldt's Personal Narrative, Engl. translation, vol. v. p. 795. In the map which accompanies this edition we have however adopted Colonel Codazzi's position (8° 15′ north), since Humboldt himself did not extend his journey to the Caroni.

[2] The Macareo is called Brazo only from its efflux to where it divides into two chief arms, the western of which is the Caño Manamo, which Ralegh ascended, and the eastern the Caño Macareo, which he selected on his return.

[3] According to our observations, made whilst the Boundary Expedition was encamped at this point, the geographical position of this point is found to be in latitude 8° 35′ 48″, and longitude 60° 18′ 30″; much confusion hitherto prevailed, Punta Sabaneta being frequently mistaken for Punta Barima.

delta (Hororotomaka of Ralegh), and the other the lower or eastern (Pallamos of Ralegh); the former are likewise called the Bocas Chicas, or "little mouths." The bocas of the upper delta disembogue into the Gulf of Paria, Golfo Triste, or Golfo de las Perlas of Columbus, a basin which is formed by the coast of Paria and the island of Trinidad. It is from east to west nearly ninety miles in length, and from north to south thirty-six miles in breadth. Columbus gave to the celebrated passage, between the projecting point or promontory of Paria (Punta de la Pena) and the north-western point of Trinidad (Punta Monos), the name of the Dragon's Mouth, and it is supposed that it once formed an isthmus by which the present island of Trinidad was connected with the mainland. A similar supposition prevails respecting the Serpent's Mouth, the entrance to the gulf between the south-western point of Trinidad (Punta de Icacos) and Punta Foleto on the coast of the Orinoco, somewhat east of the Boca de Paternales. If this supposition be correct, the Gulf of Paria once formed an inland basin, which by some convulsions of nature burst its barrier and flowed into the powerful currents of the Atlantic and the Orinoco.

The impetuosity with which the waters issue from the different mouths of these outlets is so great, that during the periodical swelling, or the rainy season, the water of the ocean is pressed backwards, and causes currents and counter-currents, which it requires much local knowledge to overcome in navigating the coast; but the assertion of Depons, that the water of the Orinoco remains fresh at more than thirty leagues from its mouth, can only be considered fabulous[1]. In the months of July, August and September, when the Orinoco is highest, the water is fresh at a distance of six miles from Punta Barima[2]. The waters in the Gulf of Paria are during that period along the shore fresh, but the middle of the basin is salt, though in a less degree than the adjacent sea. Along the whole coast, from the river Corentyn to the Gulf of Paria, certain localities are subjected to "rollers" or ground-swells,—a peculiar phænomenon, which is ascribed to the meeting and combination of contrary currents, shallow water, and the effect of winds. The sea approaches on such occasions in undulating masses, which suddenly rise to large ridges crested with foam, and form billows that break with the greatest impetuosity against any object they meet in their course. The roaring of the waves resembles thunder, and when an unfortunate vessel is exposed to their fury, the spray is dashed high up the rigging to the mast-head: we speak from experience, as the schooner on board of which we sailed got unfortunately among the rollers when bound for the Orinoco. Columbus has described the phænomenon very graphically, and upon his description Sir Wal-

[1] Travels in South America by F. Depons. English translation, vol. ii. p. 342.

[2] During our encampment at Punta Barima we procured fresh water only after the ebb had continued for three or four hours, but from June to September the water is said to be always fresh.

ter Scott seems to have based the following forcible verses[1] :—

> . . . . "The battle's rage
> Was like the strife which currents wage
> Where Orinoco, in his pride,
> Rolls to the main no tribute tide,
> But 'gainst broad Ocean urges far
> A rival sea of roaring war;
> While in ten thousand eddies driven
> The billows fling their foam to heaven,
> And the pale pilot seeks in vain,
> Where rolls the river, where the main."

We shall here conclude this sketch of the life and exploits of Ralegh, which has already extended to a greater length than we at first proposed; but, as this work forms in a manner the climax of Ralegh's fame and adventures, we hope to be excused for enlarging on those circumstances of his life and character which serve to elucidate its narrative.

[1] Rokeby, Canto I. xiii.

THE DISCOVERIE OF THE LARGE, RICH AND BEWTIFVL EMPIRE OF GVIANA, WITH

a relation of the Great and Golden City *of* Manoa *(which the ſpaniards call* El *Dorado)* And the prouinces of *Emeria, Arromaia, Amapaia* and other Countries, with their riuers, adioyning.

Performed in the yeare 1595. by Sir *W. Ralegh*, Knight, Captaine of her *Maieſties Guard, Lo. Warden* of the Stanneries, and her Highneſſe Lieutenant generall of the Countie of Cornewall.

Jmprinted at London by Robert Robinson

1596.

TO THE RIGHT HONORABLE MY

ſingular good Lord and kinſman,

Charles Howard, knight of the Garter, *Barron, and Counceller, and of the Admiralls of England the moſt renowned*: And to the Right Honorable Sr *Robert Cecyll* Knight, Counceller in her Highnes priuie Councels.

FOR your Honors many Honorable and friendlie partes, I haue hitherto only returned promises; and nowe for answere of both your aduentures, I haue sent you a bundle of papers which I haue deuided betwene your Lo. and Sr Robert Cecyl *in these two respectes chiefly: First for that it is reason, that wastful factors, when they haue consumed such stockes, as they had in trust, doe yeeld some cullor for the same in their account, secondly for that I am assured that whatsoeuer shalbe done, or written by me, shall neede a double protection and defence. The trial that I had of both your loues, when I was left of all, but of malice and reuenge, makes me still presume that you wil be pleased (knowing what little power I had to performe ought, and the great aduantage of forwarned enimies) to answere that out of knowledge, which others shall but obiect out of malice. In my more happie times as I did especially honour you both, so I found that your loues sought me out in the darkest shadow of aduersitie, and the same affection which accom-*

panied my better fortune, sored not away from me in my manie miseries: all which though I cannot requite, yet I shal euer acknowledge: and the great debt which I haue no power to pay, I can doe no more for a time but confesse to be due. It is true that as my errors were great, so they haue yeelded verie grievous effects, and if ought might haue been deserued in former times to haue counterpoysed any part of offences, the frute thereof (as it seemeth) was long before fallen from the tree, and the dead stocke onely remained. I did therefore euen in the winter of my life, Vndertake these trauels, fitter for boies lesse blasted with mis-fortunes, for men of greater abilitie, and for mindes of better incouragement, that thereby if it were possible I might recouer but the moderation of excesse, and the least tast of the greatest plentie formerly possessed. If I had knowen other way to win, if I had imagined how greater aduentures might haue regained, if I coulde conceiue what farther meanes I might yet vse, but euen to appease so powerefull displeasure, I would not doubt but for one yeare more to holde fast my soule in my teeth, til it were performed. Of that little remaine I had, I haue wasted in effect al herein, I haue vndergone many constructions, I haue been accompanyed with many sorrows, with labour, hunger, heat, sicknes, and peril: It appeareth notwithstand that I made no other brauado of going to sea, then was ment, and that I was neither hidden in Cornwell[1] *or else where, as was supposed. They haue grosly belied me, that foreiudged that I wolde rather become a seruant to the Spanish king, the return, and the rest were much mistaken, who woulde haue perswaded, that I was too easeful and sen-*

[1] Amongst the various reports which were spread after the return of Sir Walter Ralegh from his first voyage to Guiana, for the purpose of injuring him, or to derogate from the merit connected with it, it was also asserted that he himself had never left England, and had been lying secreted in Cornwall until the return of his vessels, when he made his re-appearance, and from the accounts rendered to him by his lieutenants of their exploits, concocted the relation of his voyage. The accusation is too absurd to be entitled to the slightest consideration.

suall to vndertake a iorney of so great trauel. But, if what I haue done receiue the gratious construction of a painful pilgrimage, and purchase the least remission, I shall thinke all too little, and that there were wanting to the rest, many miseries: But if both the times past, the present, and what may be in the future, doe all by one graine of gall continue in an eternall distast, I doe not then knowe whether I should bewaile my selfe either for my too much trauel and expence, or condemne my selfe for doing lesse then that, which can de serue nothing. From my selfe I haue deserued no thankes, for I am returned a begger, and withered, but that I might haue bettred my poore estate, it shall appeare by the following discourse, if I had not onely respected her Maiesties future Honor, and riches. It became not the former fortune in which I once liued, to goe iourneys of picorie[1]*, and it had sorted ill with the offices of Honor, which by her maiesties grace, I hold this day in England, to run from Cape to Cape, and from place to place, for the pillage of ordinarie prizes. Many yeares since, I had knowledge by relation, of that mighty, rich, and beawtifull Empire of* Guiana, *and of that great and Golden Citie, which the spanyards call* El Dorado, *and the naturals* Manoa[2]*, which Citie was conquered, reedified, and inlarged by a yonger sonne of* Guainacapa *Emperor of* Peru, *at such time as* Francisco Pazaro *and others conquered the saide Empire, from his two elder brethren* Guascar, *and* Atabalipa, *both then contending for the same, the one being fauoured by the* Oreiones *of* Cuzco, *the other by the people of* Caximalca. *I sent my seruant* Iacob Whiddon *the yeer before, to get knowledge of the passages, and I had some light from Captaine* Parker *sometime my seruant, and nowe attending on your Lo. that such a place there*

1 Derived probably from the Spanish *picaro*, 'a rogue,' *pickeer*, 'to rob or pillage.' (See Halliwell, Dict. of Arch. and Prov. Words.)

2 As the names and circumstances here alluded to occur again in the Voyage itself, the reader is referred to the notes there attached in explanation of Sir W. Ralegh's allusions.

was to the southward of the great bay of Charuas, *or* Guanipa: *but I found that it was* 600 *miles farther off, then they supposed, and manie other impediments to them vnknowne and vnheard. After I had displanted* Don Anthonio de Berreo, *who was vpon the same enterprize, leauing my ships at* Trinedado, *at the port called* Curiapan, *I wandred* 400 *miles, into the said countrey by land and riuer: the particulars I will leaue to the following discourse. The countrey hath more quantity of Gold by manifolde, then the best partes of the* Indies, *or* Peru: *All the most of the kings of the borders are already become her Maiesties vassals: and seeme to desire nothing more then her Maiesties protection and the returne of the English nation. It hath another grounde and assurance of riches and glory, then the voiages of the west* Indies, *and an easier way to inuade the best parts therof, then by the common course. The king of* Spaine *is not so impouerished by taking* 3 *or* 4 *port townes in* America *as we suppose, neither are the riches of* Peru, or Nueua Espania *so left by the sea side, as it can be easily washt away, with a great flood, or springtide, or left drie vpon the sandes on a lowe ebbe. The port townes are few and poore in respect of the rest within the land, and are of little defence, and are onely rich when the fleets are to receiue the treasure for spaine: And we might thinke the spaniards verie simple hauing so manie horses and slaues, that if they coulde not vpon two daies warning, carrie all the Golde they haue into the land, and farre enough from the reach of our footmen especiallie the* Indies *being (as it is for the most part) so mountainous, so full of woods, riuers, and marishes. In the port townes of the prouince of* Vensuello[1], *as* Cumana,

[1] The enumeration of ports, cities, and places which follow in this page and the succeeding, attest the extensive geographical knowledge which Sir W. Ralegh had acquired of the regions, which during the sixteenth century were the scenes of Spanish adventure in search of El Dorado. It is observed of him by Oldys, "There was not an expert soldier or seaman but he consulted, nor a printed or manuscript discourse but he perused;" and al-

Coro, *and* S. Iago (*whereof* Coro *and* S. Iago *were taken by Captaine* Preston[1] *and* Cumana *and* S. Iosephus *by vs*) *we found not the value of one riall of plate in either: but the Cities of* Barquasimeta[2], Valentia, S. Sebastian, Cororo, S. Lucia, Alleguna, Marecabo, *and* Truxillo, *are not so easely inuaded: neither doth the burning of those on the coast impouerish the king of spayne anie one ducket, and if we sacke the riuer of* Hache[3], S. Marta, *and* Cartagena, *which are the portes of* Nueuo reyno *and* Popayan. *There are besides within the land which are indeed rich and populous, the townes and Cities of* Merida, Lagrita, S. Christofero, *the great Cities of*

though this relates more expressly to his preparations for the Guiana voyage, his epistle dedicatory affords sufficient proof of his general knowledge of the geography of the northern half of South America.

1 Santiago de Léon de Caracas (*Caracasia, Leopolis,* in Latin documents), the present capital of the republic of Venezuela, was founded in 1567 by Diego de Losada in the valley of San Francisco. The fleet of Captain Amias Preston and George Somers, consisting of four vessels, appeared before Cumana on the 21st of May, 1595; but the inhabitants paid a large sum of money to save the town from being plundered and burnt down, and it was consequently spared. A part of the crew landed, and reached by a most difficult and dangerous path Santiago Léon de Caracas, which they took on the 29th of May, and remained there until the 3rd of June; but as they could not come to an understanding with the inhabitants respecting their contribution, they set the town and some of the neighbouring places on fire, and regained their vessels without having lost a single man. (Hakluyt, iii. 578.)

2 Barquisimeta, Valencia, San Sebastian, Corora, Santa Lucia, Alleguna, Maracaybo and Truxillo, are cities and towns situated in the repnblic of Venezuela; so also are Merida, La Grita, San Cristóbal (S. Christofero of Ralegh); the last is called in Latin documents of that time *S. Christophori Fanum.*

3 Nuestra Señora de los Remedios del Rio de la Hacha, situated on the mouth of a river bearing the same name, was founded by Nicolas Federman, who called it N. S. de las Nievas. Its name was changed as above in 1594. Sir Francis Drake appeared before it with his fleet in 1595, and although its inhabitants wished to save the pillage of their city and the houses from being burnt down by paying thirty-four thousand ducats, it was nevertheless set on fire on the 1st of December. Santa Marta and Nombre-de-Dios shared a similar fate in the following month of January.

Pampelone[1], S. Fede Bogota, Tunia *and* Mozo *where the* Esmeralds *are founde, the townes and Cities of* Morequito[2], velis, la villa de Leua, Palma, vnda, Angustura, *the greate Citie of* Timana, Tocaima, S. Aguila, Pasto, Iuago, *the great city of* Popaian *it selfe*[3], Los Remedios, *and the rest. If we take the ports and villages within the bay of* Vraba[4] *in the kingdome or riuers of* Dariena, *and* Caribana, *the cities and townes of S.* Iuan de Roydas[5], *of* Cassaris, *of* Anteocha, Carramanta,

[1] Pamplona (Pampejopolis Nova), Santa Fé de Bogota, Tunja, and Muzo (Mozo of Ralegh) are situated in the republic of New Granada, of which Bogota forms the capital. Muzo, or, as it was pompously called, "La Santissima Trinidad de los Muzos," founded in 1560, was at that period much famed for its rich mines of emeralds. (Herrera, Dec. viii. lib. i. cap. 15—17. Piedrahita, lib. xii. cap. 6.)

[2] Mariquita (Mariolum or Marichisia), Velez (Velis of Ralegh), Leyba or Leiva (Leua of Ralegh), la Palma, Honda (Vnda of Ralegh), Angostura, Tymana, Tocayma, Remedios, settlements and towns on the river Magdalena or Rio Grande and its tributaries, were mostly all founded between 1536 and 1570. They are situated within the "Departamento de Cundinamarca," so famed in the fable of El Dorado.

[3] The foundation of San Juan de Pasto (Pastum or Fanum S. Juan ad Pastos) was laid on the 17th of July 1539, in the valley of Guacanquer, by Captain Lorenzo de Aldaña, by the command of Gonzalo Diaz de Pinedo. The town was afterwards removed into the valley of Tris, and was called Villa Viçosa de Pasto. (Herrera, Dec. vi. lib. vii. cap. 1.) Santiago or San Yago (Juago of Ralegh) is situate at the eastern foot of the Andes, on the river Casiana, a tributary of the Rio Meta. The city of Popayan (Popajanum) was founded by Sebastian de Belalcazar, in 1536, on an extensive plain, watered by the Rio del Molino. (Genealogias del Nuevo reyno de Granada, liii. p. 121.) The latitude of Popayan is 2° 26′ north, the longitude 76° 40′ west.

[4] The Golf of Uraba, or of Darien, by which name it is much better known, was one of the first places on the shores of the Caribbean Sea where the Spaniards erected settlements. Ojeda received from the king a grant of that part of the coast which extended from Cap de la Vela to the middle of the Gulf of Uraba; and the country which extended from the other half of the gulf to Cap Gracias-à-Dios was granted to Diego de Nicuesa. The latter was named Castilla-del-Oro, the former Nueva Andalucia (Herrera, Nov. Orbis, cap. 8). The north-eastern point of the Gulf of Uraba is called Point Caribana.

[5] San Juan de Rodas, Caceres (Cassaris of Ralegh), Antioquia, Cara-

Cali, *and* Anserma *haue golde enough to pay the Kinge part, and are not easily inuaded by the way of the* Ocean *or if* Nombre de Dios *and* Panama[1] *be taken in the prouince of* Castillo de oro, *and the villages vpon the riuers of* Cenu *and* Chagre[2]. Peru *hath besides those and besides the magnificent cities of* Quito *and* Lima *so many Ilands, portes, Cities, and mines, as if I should name them with the rest, it would seeme incredible to the reader: of all which because I haue written a particuler treatise of the west* Indies[3], *I will omit their repetition at this time, seing that in the saide treatise I haue anatomized the rest of the sea townes as well of* Nicaragua, Iucata, Nueua Espanna[4], *and the Ilands, as those of the Inland, and by what meanes they may be best inuaded, as farre as any meane Iudgement can comprehend. But I hope it shall appeare that there is a*

manta, Cali, Ançerma (Anserma of Ralegh), are cities and towns situate on the banks of the river Cauca and its tributaries. The Cauca falls into the river Magdalena.

[1] Diego de Nicuesa erected a fort in a bay about eighteen miles to the east of Portobello, which he considered so convenient, that he called out, "Paremos à qui en el nombre de Dios,"—Let us remain here in the name of God; from which circumstance it was called Nombre de Dios. The foundation of a town was likewise laid, which was increased by Diego de Albites in 1517; the situation was however so unhealthy that Philip the Second ordered the town to be removed to Portobello. Herrera observes that during the first twenty-eight years of the occupation of Peru by the Spaniards more than forty thousand Spaniards died of its unhealthy climate, and a similar number in Nombre de Dios alone. Pedrarias Davila, governor of Darien, founded Panama (Panæmium) in 1518. The whole province of Nueva Andalucia obtained at a later period the name of Castilla-del-Oro.

[2] The river Zinu falls into the Gulf of Morrosquillo opposite the island of Fuerte. Chagres lies on the isthmus of Panama. Quito, the capital of the republic of Ecuador, and Lima of Peru, are too well known to require further designation.

[3] As previously observed, this composition was never printed, and the manuscript appears to have been lost.

[4] Nicaragua, formerly a province of Mexico, forms now part of Guatemala. Yucatan, a province of Mexico. Mexico itself was formerly called Nueva España.

way found to answere euerie mans longing, a better Indies for her maiestie then the King of Spain hath any, which if it shall please her highnes to vndertake, I shall most willingly end the rest of my daies in following the same: If it be left to the spoyle and sackage of common persons, if the loue and seruice of so many nations be despised, so great riches, and so mightie an Empyre refused, I hope her Maiestie will yet take my humble desire and my labour therein in gracious part, which if it had not beene in respect of her highnes future honor and riches, I could haue laid hands and ransomed many of the kings and Cassiqui *of the Country, and haue had a reasonable proportion of gold for their redemption: But I haue chosen rather to beare the burthen of pouerty, then reproch, and rather to endure a second trauel and the chaunces therof, then to haue defaced an enterprise of so great assurance, vntill I knew whether it pleased God to put a disposition in her princely and royall heart either to follow or foreslow the same: I wil therefore leaue it to his ordinance that hath onely power in al things, and do humblie pray that your honors wil excuse such errors, as without the defence of art, ouerrun in euery part, the following discourse, in which I haue neither studied phrase, forme, nor fashion, and that you will be pleased to esteeme me as your owne (though ouer dearly bought) and I shall euer remaine ready to doe you all honour and seruice.*

W: R.

To the Reader.

BEcause there haue been diuers opinions conceiued of the golde oare brought from *Guiana,* and for that an Alderman of London and an officer of her maiesties minte, hath giuen out that the same is of no price, I haue thought good by the addition of these lines to giue aunswere as well to the said malicious slaunder, as to other obiections. It is true that while we abode at the Iland of *Trinedado,* I was informed by an Indian, that not farre from the Port, where we ancored, there were founde certaine minerall stones which they esteemed to be gold, and were thereunto perswaded the rather for that they had seen both English and French men gather, and imbarque some quantities thereof: vppon this liklyhoode I sent 40 men and gaue order that each òne should bring a stone of that myne, to make triall of the goodnesse, which being performed, I assured them at their returne that the same was *Marcasite,* and of no riches or value: Notwithstanding diuers trusting more to their owne sence, then to my opinion, kept of the saide *Marcasite,* and haue tried thereof, since my returne, in diuers places. In *Guiana* it selfe I neuer sawe *Marcasite,* but all the rocks, mountaines, all stones in the plaines, in woodes, and by the riuers sides are in effect thòrow shining, and appeare marueylous rich, which being tried to be no *Marcasite,* are the trew signes of rich mineralles, but are no other then *El madre del oro* (as the Spanyards terme them) which is the mother of golde, or as it is saide by others the scum of gold: of diuers sortes of these manie of my companie brought also into England, euerie one taking the fayrest for the best, which is not generall. For mine owne partte, I did not countermand any mans desire, or opinion, and I could haue aforded them little if I shoulde haue denied them the pleasing of their owne fancies therein: But I was resolued that golde must be found either in graines separate from the stone (as it is in most of al the riuers in *Guiana*) or else in a kinde of hard stone, which we call the white Sparre, of which I saw diuers hils, and in sundrie places, but had neither tyme, nor men, nor instruments fitte to labour. Neere vnto one of the riuers I founde of the saide white Sparre or flint a very great ledge, or banke, which I endeuored to breake by al the meanes I coulde, because there appeared on the out side some small graines of gold, but finding no meane to worke the same vppon the vpper part, seeking the sides and circuite of the sayd rock, I founde a clift in the same, from whence with daggers, and with the heade of an ax, we gotte out some small quantitie thereof, of which kinde of white stone (wherein golde is engendred) we sawe diuers hils and rocks in euerie part of *Guiana*, wherein we trauelled. Of this there hath beene made manie trialls, and in London, it was first assaide by Master *Westwood* a refiner dwelling in wood-street, and it helde after the rate of 12000 or 13000 pounds a tunne. Another sort was afterward tried by Master *Bulmar* and Master *Dimoke* assay master, and it held after the rate of 23000 pounds a tunne. There was some of it againe tried by Master *Palmer* comptroller of the minte, and Master *Dimoke* in golde smiths hall, and it helde after 26900 pounds a tunne. There was also at the same time, and by the same persons a triall made of the dust of the said myne which held 8 pound 6 ounces weight of gold, in the hundred: there was likewise at the same time a triall made of an Image of Copper made in *Guiana*, which helde a third part gold, besides diuers trialls made in the countrey, and by others in London. But because there came of ill with the good, and belike the said Alderman was not presented with the best, it hath pleased him therefore to scandall all the rest, and to deface the enterprize as much as in him lyeth. It hath also been concluded by diuers, that if there had been anie such oare in *Guiana*, and the same discouered, that I woulde haue brought home a greater quantitie thereof: first I was not bounde to satisfie anie man of the quantitie, but such onely as aduentured, if any store had been returned thereof: but it is verie true that had all their mountaynes beene of massie gold, it was impossible for vs to haue made anie longer staye to haue wrought the same: and whosoeuer hath seene with what strength of stone, the best golde oare is inuironned, hee will not thinke it easie to be had out in heaps, and especiallie by vs who had neither men, instrumentes, nor time (as it is saide before) to performe the same: There were on this discouerie, no lesse than 100 personnes, who can all witnesse, that when we past any braunch of the riuer to vewe the land within, and staid from our boats but six houres, wee were driuen to wade to the eyes, at our returne: and if we attempted the same the day following, it was impossible either to forde it, or to swim it, both by reason of the swiftnesse, and also for that the borders were so pestred with fast woods, as neither bote nor man could finde place, either to land, or to imbarque: for in Iune, Iuly, August, and September, it is impossible to nauigate any of those riuers, for such is the furie of the *Current,* and there are so many trees and woods ouerflowne, as if anie boate but touch vppon anie tree or stake, it is impossible to saue any one person therein: and ere we departed the land, it ran with that swiftnesse, as we draue downe most commonly against the winde, little lesse than one hundred miles a day: Besides our vessels were no other than wherries, one little barge, a small cockboate, and a bad Galiota, which wee framed in hast for that purpose at *Trinedado,* and those little boates had nyne or ten men apeece, with all their victuals, and armes. It is further true, that we were about 400 miles from our shippes, and had bene a moneth from them, which also we left weakely mande in an open roade, and had promised our return in 15 dayes. Others haue deuised that the same oare was had from Barbery, and that we caried it with vs into *Guiana*: surely the singularitie of that deuice, I do not well comprehend, for mine owne parte, I am not so much in loue with these long voiages, as to deuise, thereby to cozen my selfe, to lie hard, to fare worse, to be subiected to perils, to diseases, to ill sauours, to be parched and withered, and withall to sustaine the care and labour of such an enterprize, excepte the same had more comfort, then the fetching of *Marcasite* in *Guiana,* or bying of gold oare in Barbery. But I hope the better sort will iudge me by themselues, and that the way of deceipt, is not the way of honor or good opinion: I haue herein consumed much time, and many crowns, and I had no other respecte or desire then to serue her maiesty and my Country thereby. If the spanishe nation had beene of like beleefe to these detractors, we should litle haue feared or doubted their attempts, wherewith we now are daily threatned. But if we now consider of the actions both of *Charles* the fifte, who had the Maydenhead of *Peru*, and the aboundant treasures of *Atabalipa*, together with the affaires of the Spanish king now liuing, what territories he hath purchased, what he hath added to the actes of his predecessors, how many kingdoms he hath indangered, how many armies, garrisons, and nauies, he hath and doth maintaine, the greate losses which he hath repayred, as in 88 aboue 100 sayle of greate shippes with their artillery, and that no yere is lesse vnfortunate but that many vessels, treasures, and people are deuoured, and yet notwithstanding he beginneth againe like a storme to threaten shipwracke to vs all, we shall finde that these abilities rise not from the trades of sackes, and Ciuil Orenges, nor from ought else that either Spaine, Portugal, or any of his other prouinces produce: It is his Indian Golde that indaungereth and disturbeth all the nations of Europe, it purchaseth intelligence, creepeth into Councels, and setteth bound loyalty at libertie, in the greatest Monarchies of Europe. If the Spanish king can keepe vs from forraine enterprizes, and from the impeachment of his trades, eyther by offer of inuasion, or by besieging vs in Britayne, Ireland, or else where, he hath then brought the worke of our perill in greate forwardnes. Those princes which abound in treasure haue greate aduantages ouer the rest, if they once constraine them to a defensiue warre, where they are driuen once a yeare or oftner to cast lots for their own garments, and from such shal al trades, and entercourse, be taken away, to the general losse and impouerishment of the kingdom, and common weale so reduced: besides when men are constrained to fight, it hath not the same hope as when they are prest and incouraged by the desire of spoyle and riches. Farther it is to be doubted how those that in time of victorie seeme to affect their neighbour nations, will remaine after the first view of misfortunes, or ill successe; to trust also to the doubtfulnes of a battel, is but a fearefull and vncertaine aduenture, seeing therein fortune is as likely to preuaile, as vertue. It shall not be necessary to alleage all that might be said, and therefore I will thus conclude, that whatsoeuer kingdome shalbe inforced to defend it selfe, may be compared to a body daungerouslie diseased, which for a season may be preserued with vulgar medicines, but in a short time, and by little and little, the same must needs fall to the ground, and be dissolued. I haue therefore laboured all my life, both according to my small power, and perswasion, to aduance al those attempts, that might eyther promise return of profit to our selues, or at last be a lett and impeachment to the quiet course, and plentiful trades of the Spanish nation, who in my weake iudgement by such a warre were as easily indaungered and brought from his powerfulnes, as any prince in Europe, if it be considered from how many kingdomes and nations his reuenewes are gathered, and those so weake in their owne beings, and so farre seuered from mutuall succor. But because such a preparation and resolution is not to be hoped for in hast, and that the time which our enemies embrace, can not be had againe to aduantage, I will hope that these prouinces, and that Empyre now by me discouered shall suffice to inable her Maiesty, and the whole kingdome, with no lesse quantities of treasure, then the king of Spayne hath in all the Indies, east and west, which he possesseth, which if the same be considered and followed, ere the Spanyards enforce the same, and if her Maiesty will vndertake it, I wilbe contented to lose her highnes fauour and good opinion for euer, and my life withall, if the same be not found rather to exceed, then to equall whatsoeuer is in this discourse promised or declared. I will nowe referre the reader to the following discourse with the hope that the perilous and chargeable labors and indeuours of such as thereby seeke the profit and honor of her Maiesty, and the English nation, shall by men of qualitie and vertue receiue such construction, and good acceptance, as them selues would looke to be rewarded withall in the like.

W: R.

THE DISCOVERIE

OF

GVIANA.

ON Thursday the 6 of Februarie in the yeare 1595, we departed *England*, and the sunday following had sight of the North cape of *Spayne*, the winde for the most part continuing prosperous; wee passed in sight of the *Burlings* and the rocke[1], and so onwardes for the *Canaries*, and fell with *Fuerte ventura* the 17 of the same moneth, where we spent two or three daies, and relieued our companies with some fresh meate. From thence wee coasted by the *Gran Canaria*, and so to *Tenerife*, and staied there for the Lyons whelp your Lordships ship, and for Captaine *Amys Preston* and the rest; but when after 7 or 8 daies we found them not, wee departed and directed our course for *Trinedado* with mine owne shippe, and a small barke of Captaine *Crosses* onely (for we had before lost sight of a small Gallego on the coast of *Spayne*, which came with vs from *Plymmouth*): wee arriued at *Trinedado* the 22 of March, casting ancour at Point *Curiapan*, which the Spanyards call *Punto de Gallo*[2], which is

[1] The isles of Berlengas, Burlings or Biorlings, and Cape Roca or the rock of Lisbon, on the coast of Portugal.

[2] Curiapan is the south-western point of Trinidad, now called Hicacos or Icacos; it forms with Punta Foletto, or Foleto, the Serpent's Mouth. Christopher Columbus cast anchor here on the 3rd of August, 1498, and

situate in 8 degrees or there abouts: we abode there 4 or 5 daies, and in all that time we came not to the speach of anie Indian or Spaniard: on the coast we saw a fire, as we sailed from the point *Carao*[1] towards *Curiapan*, but for feare of the Spaniards, none durst come to speake with vs. I my selfe coasted it in my barge close abord the shore and landed in euery Coue, the better to know the iland, while the ships kept the chanell. From *Curiapan* after a fewe daies we turned vp Northeast to recouer that place which the Spaniards cal *Puerto de los Hispanioles*, and the inhabitants *Conquerabia*[2], and as before (reuictualing my barge) I left the shippes and kept by the shore, the better to come to speach with some of the inhabitantes, and also to vnderstand the riuers, watring places and portes of the iland which (as it is rudely done) my purpose is to send your lordship after a few daies. From *Curiapan* I came to a port and seat of Indians called *Parico*, where we found a fresh-water riuer[3], but sawe no people. From thence I rowed to another port, called by the naturals *Piche*, and by the Spaniardes *Tierra de Brea*[4]. In the way betweene both were diuers little brooks

called it Punta del Arenal. A sand-bank, situated round the point to the north-west, bears to this day the name of "los Gallos." Sir Robert Duddley, who anchored at Point Curiapan on the 1st of February 1595, called the bay under the point Pelican's Bay, from the abundance of these birds there. (Hakluyt, vol. iii. p. 574.) The geographical position of Point Icacos is 10° 2′ 30″ north latitude, and 61° 57′ west longitude from Greenwich. It will be observed that Ralegh considers himself two degrees further south than he was in reality, and this refers to his whole Orinoco journey.

[1] The point Carao is now called Negra Point: in some of the Spanish charts this point and the small river to the windward of it are named Punta y rio Curao.

[2] Puerto d'España, or Port of Spain, the capital of Trinidad.

[3] Punta del Cedro, or Cedar Point, forms the northern point of this bay. It is no longer known by the name of Parico.

[4] The celebrated pitch-lake of Trinidad near Punta la Brea is situated on the leeward side of the island, on a small peninsula: it is nearly circular, and about a mile and a half in diameter. The usual appearance of the pitch or asphaltum is that of pit-coal, but in hot weather it is liquid. When mixed with grease, oil, or common pitch, to acquire fluidity, it is well-

of fresh water, and one salt riuer that had store of oisters vpon the branches of the trees[1], and were very salt and wel tasted. Al their oisters grow vpon those boughs and spraies, and not on the ground: the like is commonlie seene in the West Indies and else where. This tree is described by *Andrewe Theuet* in his French *Antartique*, and the forme figured in his booke as a plante verye straunge, and by *Plinie* in his XII. booke of his naturall historie. But in this ilande, as also in *Guiana*, there are verie manie of them.

At this point called *Tierra de Brea* or *Piche* there is that abundance of stone pitch, that all the ships of the world may be therewith loden from thence, and wee made triall of it in

adapted for preserving the bottoms of ships against the destructive worm, the *Terēdo navalis*. Admiral Cochrane made several experiments to use it for nautical purposes, which failed, as it was requisite to mix such a large quantity of oil with it to render it pliable, that it far surpassed the price of common pitch.

[1] The first accounts brought to Europe of oysters growing on trees raised as great astonishment as the relation of El Dorado itself; and to those who were unacquainted with the fact that these molluscous animals select the branches of the tree, on which they fix themselves during high water, when they are immersed, it may certainly sound strange and wonderful that shells, which as we know live in Europe on banks in the depths of the sea, should be found in the West Indies on the branches of trees. They attach themselves chiefly to the mangrove tree (*Rhizophora Mangle*, Linn.), which grows along the shore of the sea and rivers with brackish water, and covers immense tracts of coast, rooting and vegetating in a manner very peculiar to that tree, even as far as low-water mark. Sir Walter Ralegh, in his History of the World (book i. chap. iv. section 2), compares it erroneously with the Indian fig-tree (*Ficus indica*), which Becanus considered to be the tree of knowledge, or of life. Ralegh observes in his description that he had seen five hundred oysters hanging on one of the branches (which he calls cords) of a mangrove tree. The water flowing off during ebb leaves the branches with the oysters attached to them high and dry. Three species of mollusca are chiefly found on the mangrove trees, namely *Ostrea Rhizophoræ* (Auct.?), *O. folium*, and a species of *Mytilus*. The *O. Rhizophoræ* is eaten, and in Porto Rico the price of a barrel of these mangrove oysters is a piaster. We differ with Ralegh respecting their superior taste; they are at the best mere substitutes for an European oyster, very small, and not so delicate.

trimming our ships to be most excellent good, and melteth not with the sunne as the pitch of *Norway*, and therefore for ships trading the south partes very profitable. From thence we went to the mountaine foote called *Annaperima*[1], and so passing the riuer *Carone*, on which the Spanish Citie was seated, we met with our ships at *Puerto de los Hispanioles* or *Conquerabia*.

This iland of *Trinedado* hath the forme of a sheep-hook, and is but narrow; the north part is very mounteynous, the soile is very excellent and wil beare sugar, ginger, or any other commodity that the Indies yeeld. It hath store of deare, wyld porks, fruits, fish and fowle. It hath also for bread sufficient *Mais*, *Cassaui*[2], and of those roots and fruits which are common euery where in the West *Indies*. It hath diuers beasts, which the *Indies* haue not: the Spaniards confessed that they found grains of gold in some of the riuers, but they hauing a purpose to enter *Guiana* (the *Magazin* of all rich mettels) cared not to spend time in the search therof any farther. This iland is called by the people therof *Cairi*, and in it are diuers nations: those about *Parico* are called *Iaio*; those at *Punto Carao* are of the *Arwacas*, and betweene *Carao* and *Curiapan* they are called *Saluaios*; betweene *Carao* and *Punto Galera*[3] are the *Nepoios*, and those about the Spanish Citie tearme themselues *Carinepagotos*[4]. Of the rest of the nations, and of other portes and

[1] This hill, in the neighbourhood of San Fernando, is now called Naparima, and has given its name to the whole district.

[2] These two plants supply the most useful food of the Indian tribes; they form their staff of life. The grains of the first (*Zea Mays*, Linn.) furnish the Indian corn or maize, and from the roots of the second (*Manihot utilissima*, Pohl), although itself a strong poison in its natural state, the Indians prepare a nutritious substitute for bread.

[3] The north-eastern point of Trinidad is called at present Punta de la Galera; but Columbus designated the south-eastern point of the island under that name, on account of a rock which has the appearance of a vessel under sail. It is now known as Punta Galeota.

[4] The number of Indians, the remnant of those numerous tribes who inhabited Trinidad at the period when Ralegh visited it, amounted in 1831 to seven hundred and sixty-two.

riuers I leaue to speake heere, beeing impertinent to my purpose, and meane to describe them as they are situate in the particular plot and description of the iland, three partes whereof I coasted with my barge, that I might the better discribe it.

Meeting with the ships at *Puerto de los Hispanioles*, we found at the landing place a company of Spanyardes who kept a guard at the descent, and they offering a signe of peace I sent Captaine *Whiddon* to speake with them, whome afterward to my great griefe I left buried in the said iland after my returne from *Guiana*, beeing a man most honest and valiant. The Spanyards semed to be desirous to trade with vs, and to enter into tearms of peace, more for doubt of their own strength then for ought else, and in the end vpon pledge, some of them came abord: the same euening there stale also abord vs in a small *Canoa* two Indians, the one of them being a *Casique* or Lord of people called *Cantyman*, who had the yeare before beene with Captaine *Whiddon*, and was of his acquaintance. By this *Cantyman* wee vnderstood what strength the Spaniardes had, how farre it was to their Citie, and of *Don Anthonio de Berreo*[1] the gouernour, who was said to be slaine in his second attempt of *Guiana*, but was not.

While we remained at *Puerto de los Hispanioles* some Spaniardes came abord vs to buy lynnen of the company, and such other thinges as they wanted, and also to view our shippes and company, all which I entertained kindly and feasted after our manner: by meanes whereof I learned of one and another as much of the estate of *Guiana* as I could, or as they knew, for those poore souldiers hauing beene many yeares without wine, a fewe draughtes made them merry, in which moode they vaunted of *Guiana* and of the riches therof, and all what they knew of

[1] Don Antonio de Berreo y Oruña, who figures so conspicuously in Ralegh's voyage, was governor of Trinidad, and married to a daughter of the great Adelantado Gonzalo Ximenes de Quesada, the founder of "Nuevo reyno de Granada," from whom he had inherited his treasures, and the desire to discover the boundless riches of Guiana.

the waies and passages, my selfe seeming to purpose nothing lesse then the enterance or discouerie thereof, but bred in them an opinion that I was bound onely for the reliefe of those english, which I had planted in *Virginia*[1], whereof the brute was come among them, which I had performed in my returne if extremity of weather had not forst me from the said coast.

I found occasions of staying in this place for two causes: the one was to be reuenged of *Berreo*, who the yeare before betraied 8 of Captaine *Whiddons* men, and toke them while he departed from them to seeke the *E. Bonauenture*, which arriued at *Trinedado* the day before from the East *Indies*: in whose absence *Berreo* sent a *Canoa* abord the pinnace onely with *Indians* and dogs inuiting the company to goe with them into the wods to kil a deare, who like wise men in the absence of their Captaine followed the *Indians*, but were no sooner one harquebush shot from the shore, but *Berreos* souldiers lying in ambush had them all, notwithstanding that he had giuen his worde to Captaine *Whiddon* that they should take water and wood safelie: the other cause of my stay was, for that by discourse with the *Spaniards* I daily learned more and more of *Guiana*, of the riuers and passages, and of the enterprize of *Berreo*, by what meanes or fault he failed, and how he meant to prosecute the same.

While we thus spent the time I was assured by another *Casique* of the north side of the iland, that *Berreo* had sent to *Marguerita* and to *Cumana* for souldiers, meaning to have giuen me a *Cassado* at parting, if it had bin possible. For although he had giuen order through all the iland that no *Indian* should come aborde to trade with me vpon paine of hanging and quartering, (hauing executed two of them for the same which I afterwardes founde) yet euery night there came some with most

[1] The conduct of Ralegh, who was charged with a callous abandonment of the poor settlers in Virginia, has been much censured. This passage is one proof among many which we possess, that although he had given up his patent to a company of merchants, he continued to take a strong interest in the fate of the first adventurers in Virginia.

lamentable complaints of his cruelty, how he had deuided the iland and giuen to euery soldier a part, that he made the ancient *Casiqui* which were Lordes of the country to be their slaues, that he kept them in chains, and dropped their naked bodies with burning bacon, and such other torments, which I found afterwards to be true: for in the city after I entred the same, there were 5 of the Lords or litle kings (which they cal *Casiqui* in the west Indies) in one chaine almost dead of famine, and wasted with torments: these are called in their own language *Acarewana*[1], and now of late since English, French, and Spanish are come among them, they cal themselues *Capitaynes,* because they perceiue that the chiefest of euery ship is called by that name. Those fiue *Capitaynes* in the chaine were called *Wannawanare, Carroaori, Maquarima, Tarroopanama,* and

[1] Humboldt considers that Acarewana signifies, in one of the different Carib or Caribisi dialects, a chief or any person in command. This supposition is correct; more accurately it refers to the commander or head of the tribe to which he who speaks and makes use of the word belongs. The name of a chief or commander in the general sense of the word is Tepotori * in the Macusi language, but if the speaker alludes to the chief of his own tribe or horde, he would say Epotoriwana; that is, our headman or chieftain. As Ralegh observes, these petty chieftains call themselves now capitan or captain. Esakamapung in the Caribisi, or Tepotorokung in the Macusi dialect, signifies a great captain or chief who has command over a number of inferior chiefs; it is perhaps analogous to 'king' in the English language.

The metaphorical application of the word tepotori in the Macusi language deserves a passing observation as it affords an instance of the similarity of the metaphors employed in the infancy of languages in general. The largest of a number of apples, oranges or any other objects would be called by a Macusi tepotori, the chieftain or captain. This application reminds us of our own expression in childhood for the largest apple or orange among a number, which playfully would be called "the captain;" and if we follow the idea suggested by this application, it will lead us to the most striking qualifications required for a leader.

* The editor begs here to observe, that in the orthography which he has adopted for Indian words he has used the sound of the vowels which they possess in the Italian, and for the consonants that which they have in the English language.

Aterima. So as both to be reuenged of the former wrong, as also considering that to enter *Guiana* by small boats, to depart 400 or 500 miles from my ships, and to leaue a garison in my backe interessed in the same enterprize, who also daily expected supplies out of Spaine, I should haue sauoured very much of the Asse: and therfore taking a time of most aduantage, I set vpon the *Corp du guard* in the euening, and hauing put them to the sword, sente Captaine *Calfeild* onwards with 60 soldiers, and my self followed with 40 more and so toke their new city which they called *S. Ioseph*[1], by breake of day: they abode not any fight after a few shot, and al being dismissed but onely *Berreo* and his companion, I brought them with me abord, and at the instance of the Indians I set their new city of *S. Iosephs* on fire.

The same day arriued Captaine *George Gifford* with your Lordships ship, and Captaine *Keymis* whom I lost on the coast of Spaine, with the *Gallego*, and in them diuers Gent. and others, which to our little army was a great comfort and supply.

We then hastened away towards our purposed discouery, and first I called all the Captaines of the iland together that were enemies to the Spaniards, for there were some which *Berreo* had brought out of other countries, and planted there to eat out and wast those that were natural of the place, and by my Indian interpreter, which I caried out of England, I made them vnderstand that I was the seruant of a Queene, who was the great *Casique* of the north, and a virgin, and had more *Casiqui* vnder her then there were trees in their iland: that she was an enemy to the *Castellani*[2] in respect of their tyrannie and oppression,

[1] St. Joseph is now almost abandoned since Port of Spain became the capital. The number of inhabitants amounted in 1831 to six hundred and four.

[2] Among the Indian tribes of the Upper Orinoco and its northern tributaries, the Ventuari, Padamo, &c., the descendants of the Spaniards are still called Castilanos. When the Macusis speak of the Spanish inhabitants of the Lower Orinoco about Angostura, they call them sometimes Carrakinio (perhaps from Caracas?), but more frequently Españolos. The descendants of the Portuguese or Brazilians are called in the Carib dialects

and that she deliuered all such nations about her, as were by them oppressed, and hauing freed all the coast of the northern world from their seruitude had sent me to free them also, and withal to defend the countrey of *Guiana* from their inuasion and conquest. I shewed them her maiesties picture which they so admired and honored, as it had beene easie to haue brought them idolatrous thereof[1].

The like and a more large discourse I made to the rest of the nations both in my passing to *Guiana*, and to those of the borders, so as in that part of the world her maiesty is very famous and admirable, whom they now call *Ezrabeta Cassipuna Aquerewana*, which is as much as *Elizabeth*, the great princesse or greatest commaunder. This done wee left *Puerto de los Hispanioles*, and returned to *Curiapan*, and hauing *Berreo* my prisonour I gathered from him as much of *Guiana* as he knewe.

This *Berreo* is a gent. well descended, and had long serued the Spanish king in *Millain*, *Naples*, the lowe Countries and else where, very valiant and liberall, and a Gent. of great assurednes, and of a great heart: I vsed him according to his estate and worth in all things I could, according to the small meanes I had.

and by the Guianians in general Caraiwa; those of the Teutonic races, as the English, German and Dutch, Parana-ghiri, signifying Sea-people. Caraiwa is a foreign word, and has been introduced from the Tapuyas; it signifies 'white man.'

[1] Ralegh possessed the indispensable accomplishment of a courtier of Queen Elizabeth's reign, namely the art of flattery, in a high degree. We refer to his poetry and his letters of adulation written to the Queen during the period he was for the first time confined in the Tower; nay, even the romantic incident of the cloak, which, as Fuller tells us, led to his favour with the Queen, proves him the accomplished courtier. The adulation which pervades the account of his discovery, from the commencement to the end, does not astonish us therefore; but we venture to say, from the knowledge we possess of the character and taste of the Indian, that a representation of Zuccaro's portrait of her Majesty, now at Hampton Court, in which she is presented in a fantastic dress, and which, we must confess, does not convey to our imagination the idea of beauty, would have had many more attractions for the assembled multitude of admiring Indians than the portrait which Ralegh showed to them.

I sent Captaine *Whiddon* the yeare before to get what knowledge he could of *Guiana*, and the end of my iorney at this time was to discouer and enter the same, but my intelligence was farre from trueth, for the country is situate aboue 600 English miles further from the sea, then I was made beleeue it had beene, which afterward vnderstanding to be true by *Berreo*, I kept it from the knowledge of my companie, who else woulde neuer haue beene brought to attempt the same: of which 600 miles I passed 400[1] leauing my shippes so farre from me at ancor in the sea, which was more of desire to performe that discouery, then of reason, especially hauing such poore and weake vessels to transport our selues in; for in the bottom of an old *Gallego* which I caused to be fashioned like a Galley, and in one barge, two wherries, and a ship bote of the Lyons whelpe, we caried 100 persons and their victuals for a moneth in the same, being al driuen to lie in the raine and wether, in the open aire, in the burning sunne, and vpon the hard bords, and to dresse our meat, and to carry al manner of furniture in them, wherewith they were so pestred and vnsauery, that what with victuals being most fish, with the weete clothes of so many men thrust together and the heate of the sunne, I will vndertake there was neuer any prison in England, that coulde be founde more vnsauory and lothsome, especially to my selfe, who had for many yeares before beene dieted and cared for in a sort farre differing.

If Captaine *Preston* had not beene perswaded that he should haue come too late to *Trinedado* to haue found vs there (for the moneth was expired which I promised to tarry for him there ere he could recouer the coast of Spaine) but that it had pleased God he might haue ioyned with vs, and that wee had entred the countrey but some ten daies sooner ere the riuers were ouer-

[1] The farthest point which Ralegh reached on his Orinoco journey was the mouth of the river Caroni, one hundred and twenty-five miles distant in a direct line from Punta Curiapan or Punta de Gallo, or at the utmost about two hundred and fifty miles, according to the windings of the Caños and Brazos.

flowen, we had aduentured either to haue gone to the great City of *Manoa*, or at least taken so many of the other Cities and townes neerer at hand, as would haue made a royall returne: But it pleased not God so much to fauour me at this time: if it shalbe my lot to prosecute the same, I shall willingly spend my life therein, and if any else shalbe enabled thereunto, and conquere the same, I assure him thus much, he shall performe more then euer was done in *Mexico* by *Cortez*, or in *Peru* by *Pacaro*, whereof the one conquered the Empire of *Mutezuma*, the other of *Guascar*, and *Atabalipa*[1], and whatsoeuer Prince shall possesse it, that Prince shalbe Lorde of more gold, and of a more beautifull Empire, and of more Cities and people, then eyther the king of Spayne, or the great Turke.

But because there may arise many doubtes, and how this Empire of *Guiana* is become so populous, and adorned with so manie greate Cities, Townes, Temples, and threasures, I thought good to make it knowen, that the Emperour now raigning is discended from those magnificent Princes of *Peru* of whose large territories, of whose pollicies, conquests, edifices, and riches *Pedro de Cieza*, *Francisco Lopez*[2], and others haue written large discourses: for when *Francisco Pacaro*, *Diego Almagro* and others conquered the said Empire of *Peru*[3], and had put to death

[1] Ralegh alludes by the name of Pacaro to Francisco Pizarro, by Mutezuma to Montezuma, by Guascar to Huascar, by Atabalipa to Atahualpa. The Inca Guaynacapa Upangi, or Huayna Capac, divided his empire of Peru amongst his two sons, Huascar-Inca and Atahualpa.

[2] Pedro de Cieça de Leon, author of the 'Cronica del Peru,' the first part of which was published in 1553, in Sevilla. Francisco Lopez de Gomara published his History of the Indies and the Conquest of Mexico in 1552–53.

[3] The empire of the Incas was divided after the conquest in two governments, namely la Nueva Castilla, extending from Quito to Cuzco, and to sixty leagues above Chincha; and that of la Nueva Toledo, which extended for two hundred leagues from Chincha towards the Tierras del Estrecho or Straits of Magalhaens. The Marquis Francisco Pizarro was appointed governor of the first, and Diego de Almagro, his companion in the conquest, of the second.

Atabalipa sonne to *Guaynacapa*, which *Atabalipa* had formerly caused his eldest brother *Guascar* to be slaine, one of the younger sonnes of *Guaynacapa* fled out of *Peru*, and tooke with him many thousandes of those souldiers of the Empyre called *Oreiones*, and with those and many others which followed him, he vanquished al that tract and valley of *America* which is situate betweene the great riuers of *Amazones* and *Baraquona*, otherwise called *Orenoke* and *Maranion*[1].

[1] The remarks of Humboldt on this subject are to the following effect:—"The flight of Manco-Inca, brother of Atahualpa, to the east of the Cordilleras, no doubt gave rise to the tradition of a new empire of the Incas in Dorado. It was forgotten that Caxamarca and Cuzco, two towns where the princes of that unfortunate family were at the time of their emigration, are situated to the south of the Amazon, in the latitude of 7° 8′ and 13° 21′ south, and consequently four hundred leagues south-west of the pretended town of Manoa on the lake Parima (3° 30′ north latitude). It is probable, that from the extreme difficulty of penetrating into the plains east of the Andes, covered with forests, the fugitive princes never went beyond the banks of the Beni. The following is what I learnt with certainty respecting this emigration of the family of the Inca, some sad vestiges of which I saw on passing Caxamarca. Manco-Inca, acknowledged as the legitimate successor of Atahualpa, made war without success against the Spaniards. He retired at length into the mountains and thick forests of Vilcabamba, which are accessible either by Huamanga and Antahuaylla, or by the valley of Yucay north of Cuzco. Of the two sons of Manco-Inca, the eldest, Sayri-Tupac, surrendered himself to the Spaniards upon the invitation of the viceroy of Peru, Hurtado de Mendoza. He was received with great pomp at Lima, was baptized there, and died peaceably in the fine valley of Yucay. The youngest son of Manco-Inca, Tupac-Amaru, was carried off by stratagem from the forests of Vilcabamba and beheaded on pretext of a conspiracy formed against the Spanish usurpers. At the same period thirty-five distant relatives of the Inca Atahualpa were seized, and conveyed to Lima, in order to remain under the inspection of the Audiencia. It is interesting to inquire whether any other princes of the family of Manco-Capac have remained in the forests of Vilcabamba, and if there still exist any descendants of the Incas of Peru between the Apurimac and the Beni. This supposition gave rise in 1741 to the famous rebellion of the Chuncos, and to that of the Amajes and Campos, led on by their chief, Juan Santos, called the false Atahualpa. The late political events of Spain have liberated from prison the remains of the family of Jose Gabriel Condorcanqui, an artful and intrepid man, who, under the name of the

The Empyre of *Guiana* is directly east from *Peru* towards the sea, and lieth vnder the Equinoctial line, and it hath more abundance of Golde then any part of *Peru,* and as many or more great Cities then euer *Peru* had when it florished most: it is gouerned by the same lawes, and the Emperour and people obserue the same religion, and the same forme and pollicies in gouernment as was vsed in *Peru,* not differing in any part: and as I haue beene assured by such of the *Spanyardes* as haue seene *Manoa* the emperiall Citie of *Guiana,* which the *Spanyardes* cal *el Dorado,* that for the greatnes, for the riches, and for the excellent seate, it farre exceedeth any of the world, at least of so much of the world as is knowen to the Spanish nation: it is founded vpon a lake of salt water of 200 leagues long like vnto *mare caspiū*[1]. And if we compare it to that of *Peru,* and but reade the report of *Francisco Lopez* and others, it wil seeme more then credible, and because we may iudge of the one by the other, I thought good to insert part of the 120 chapter of *Lopez* in his generall historie of the *Indies,* wherein he discribeth the court and magnificence of *Guaynacapa,* auncestor to the Emperour of *Guiana,* whose very words are these. *Todo el seruicio de su casa, mesa, y cozina era de oro, y de plata, y quando menos de plata, y cobre por mas rezio. Tenia en su recamara estatuas huecas de oro que parecian gigantes, y las figuras al propio, y tamanon de quantos animales, aues, arboles, y yeruas produze la tierra, y de quantos peces cria la mar y aguas de sus reynos. Tenia assi mesmo sogas, costales, cestas, y troxes de oro y plata, rimeros de palos de oro, que pareciessen lenna raiada para quemar. En fin no auia cosa en su tierra, que no la tuuiesse de oro contrahecha: y aun*

Inca Tupac-Amaru, attempted in 1781 that restoration of the ancient dynasty, which Ralegh had projected in the times of Queen Elizabeth." (Humboldt's Personal Narrative, English translation, vol. v. note at p. 854.)

[1] We have here the first allusion to that great lake in the interior of Guiana, which for two centuries remained a geographical problem. This is perhaps the proper place to draw the particular attention of the reader to the observations which the editor has made on the non-existence of such a lake in his Introduction to this edition.

dizen, que tenian los Ingas vn vergel en vna isla cerca de la Puna, donde se yuan a holgar, quando querian mar, que tenia la ortaliza, las flores, yarboles de oro y plata, inuencion y grandeza hasta entonces nunca vista. Allende de todo esto tenia infinitissima cantidad de plata, y oro por labrar en el Cuzco, que se perdio por la muerte de Guascar, ca los Indios lo escondieron, viendo que los Españoles se lo tomauan, y embriauan a España. That is, All the vessels of his home, table, and kitchin were of gold and siluer, and the meanest of siluer and copper for strength and hardnes of the mettal. He had in his wardroppe hollow statues of golde which seemed giants, and the figures in proportion and bignes of all the beastes, birdes, trees and hearbes, that the earth bringeth forth: and of all the fishes that the sea or waters of his kingdome breedeth. Hee had also ropes, budgets, chestes and troughs of golde and siluer, heapes of billets of golde that seemed woode, marked out to burne. Finally there was nothing in his countrey, whereof hee had not the counterfeat in gold: Yea and they say, The *Ingas* had a garden of pleasure in an iland neere *Puna,* where they went to recreate themselues, when they would take the ayre of the sea, which had all kind of garden hearbes, flowers and trees of Gold and Siluer, an inuention, and magnificence til then neuer seene: Besides all this, he had an infinite quantitie of siluer and gold vnwrought in *Cuzco* which was lost by the death of *Guascar,* for the Indians hid it, seeing that the Spaniards tooke it, and sent it into Spayne.

And in the 117 chapter *Francisco Picarro* caused the Golde and Siluer of *Atabalipa* to bee weyed, after hee had taken it, which *Lopez* setteth downe in these wordes following.

Hallaron cinquenta y dos mil marcos de buena plata, y vn millon y trezientos y veinte y seys mil, y quinientos pesos de oro, which is: They founde fiftie and two thousand markes of good siluer, and one million, and three hundred twentie and sixe thousand and fiue hundred pesoes of golde.

Nowe although these reportes may seeme straunge, yet if wee consider the many millions which are daily brought out of *Peru* into Spaine, wee may easely beleeue the same, for wee finde that by the abundant treasure of that countrey, the Spanish King vexeth all the Princes of Europe, and is become in a fewe yeares from a poore king of *Castile* the greatest monarke of this part of the worlde, and likelie euery day to increase, if other Princes forsloe the good occasions offered, and suffer him to adde this Empire to the rest, which by farre exceedeth all the rest: if his golde now indaunger vs, hee will then be vnresistable. Such of the Spaniards as afterwarde endeuoured the conquest thereof (whereof there haue beene many as shall bee declared heereafter) thought that this *Inga* (of whome this Emperor now liuing is descended) tooke his way by the riuer of *Amazones*, by that braunch which is called *Papamene*, for by that way followed *Oreliano*[1] (by the commaundement of the Marquis *Pacarro* in

[1] Ralegh commits in his Guiana Voyage frequent mistakes in the orthography of names and the chronological succession of events. His 'History of the World' proves how careful he became in aftertimes. The celebrated journey, the result of which was the discovery of the Upper Amazon, was undertaken in 1540–1541. Gonzalo Pizarro, the brother of the Marquis of Pizarro, and Francisco Orellana started in 1540 from Zumaque, where they had met by accident, and descended the river Coca in search of El Dorado, which they had been told was situated on the banks of a mighty river into which the Coca flowed. They encountered great difficulties, and many of their followers having fallen sick, Pizarro resolved to construct a vessel or brigantine, upon which he embarked his invalids and one hundred thousand livres in gold. The expedition was at that time suffering the greatest want; he therefore desired Orellana to take charge of the brigantine and to go in search of provisions, and if successful to return with supplies. The strong current of the river Coca, which further below takes the name of Napo, carried him rapidly along, and having entered a river of great size, he doubted not that this was the one on which Dorado was said to be situated. Orellana determined on the last day of December 1540 not to return, which he felt persuaded to be impossible against the current, and to leave Pizarro and his companions to their fate. He followed the current of the great stream, and in his descent he met with a host of Indians who opposed his landing. He saw among their ranks females fighting as valiantly as the men, and this circumstance tended to confirm the report which he had previously heard of the existence of American Amazons, from which the river received its name. Others called it, in honour after its discoverer, Orellana. The mouth and

the yeare 1542) whose name the riuer also beareth this day, which is also by others called *Maragnon,* althogh *Andrew Theuet* doth affirm that between *Maragnon* and *Amazones* there are 120 leagues: but sure it is that those riuers haue one head and beginning, and that *Maragnon* which *Theuet* describeth is but a braunch of *Amazones* or *Oreliano,* of which I wil speake more in an other place. It was also attempted by *Diego Ordace*[1], but whether before *Oreliano* or after I knowe not: but it is now

the lower part of the river were known at a much earlier period than Orellana's voyage, under the name of Marañon. Peter Martyr, Oviedo, Pedro Cieça, and Zarate called it in 1513 Marañon. Garcilasso de la Vega, Herrera, and, as Ralegh observes, likewise Andrew Thevet, made two separate rivers of the Amazon and Marañon, flowing widely apart. Father Rodriguez gives a long disquisition "Si las Amazonas, el Marañon, y el rio Orellano son diversos, ò uno mismo." (El Marañon y Amazonas, lib. i. cap. 5.) It is now usual to call the river, from its source near Cajatambo in Peru to the junction with the Huallaga, Marañon; from thence to the confluence of the Rio Negro, Solimoes; and from the Rio Negro to its embouchure into the Atlantic, the Amazon (Rio das Amazonas). The Indians call it Paranna-vacu, or Great River. Its course is computed at four thousand English miles. (See Herrera, decad. iv. lib. vi. cap. 3; decad. vi. lib. viii. cap. 6 et 7; lib. ix. cap. 2 to 6; decad. vii. lib. iv. cap. 8 et 9. Pedro de Cieça, cap. 40. Acuña, in "el Marañon y Amazones," lib. ii. cap. 10.)

[1] Diego de Ordaz, one of the officers who followed Cortez to Mexico and New Spain, and whom Charles the Fifth permitted to bear a burning volcano in his arms to commemorate his feat of having taken sulphur out of the crater of the Peak of Popocatepetl, is considered to have been the first who ascended the Orinoco to any distance. In 1531 he reached the Cataract of Atures, where the difficulty of overcoming this impediment, and the hostility of the Indians, obliged him to return. Alonso de Herrera was commanded by Geronimo de Ortal, who had been authorized by the king to continue the discoveries of Diego de Ordaz, to ascend in 1533 the Orinoco, and he entered the Meta, where in a battle with the Indians he met his death from a poisoned arrow. Alvaro de Ordaz, his lieutenant, conducted the remains of the expedition to the Casua fuerte de Paria, a fortified post erected by Antonio Sedeño in the territory of the Cacique Yuripari, of which Ortal had taken forcible possession. (Fr. Simon: "Segunda Noticia historial de las Conquistas de Tierra-firme," cap. 17 to 26; Tercera Noticia, cap. 20 to 30. Caulin, "Historia de la Nueva-Andalucia," lib. ii. cap. 5, 6 et 7. Herrera, decad. v. lib. v. cap. 6; lib. vi. cap. 15, etc.)

little lesse then 70 yeares since that *Ordace* a knight of the order of *Saint Iago* attempted the same: and it was in the yeare 1542 that *Oreliano* discouered the riuer of *Amazones*; but the first that euer sawe *Manoa* was *Iohannes Martines* master of the munition to *Ordace*. At a porte called *Morequito* in *Guiana*[1] there lyeth at this daie a great ancor of *Ordaces* shippe, and this port is some 300 miles within the lande, vpon the greate riuer of *Orenoque*.

I rested at this port fowre daies: twentie daies after I left the shippes at *Curiapan*. The relation of this *Martynes* (who was the first that discouered *Manoa*) his successe and end is to be seene in the Chauncery of *Saint Iuan de puerto rico*, whereof *Berreo* had a coppie[2], which appeared to be the greatest incou-

[1] The port of the Cazique Morequito, or, as we are informed by Francis Sparrey, the country of Aromaia (Purchas, vol. iv. chap. 11. 1248), was probably where San Miguel is now situated, about twelve miles to the east of the mouth of the river Caroni, or about one hundred and seventy miles from the sea. Sanson, in his chart of Guiana, published in 1679, places Morequito on the left bank of the Orinoco, which is evidently an error.

[2] The copy which Berreo had received of the pretended journey of Juan Martinez, induced him to send his camp-master, Domingo de Vera, to Spain, to prepare an expedition for the conquest of Dorado, or as it began then to be called, the Laguna de la Gran Manoa. Domingo de Vera acquitted himself so well in his mission, that he induced king Philip the Second to embark seventy thousand ducats in the expedition: the city of Sevilla advanced five thousand ducats, and placed five vessels at De Vera's disposition. Several officers who had distinguished themselves during the wars in Flanders and Italy, the younger sons of nobles, and numerous veteran soldiers, joined the expedition, which was ultimately composed of two thousand individuals. To prevent such a number of persons being without spiritual assistance, ten ecclesiastics and a rich canon of the cathedral, upon whom the title of administrator-general was conferred, accompanied De Vera. Besides these secular priests there were twelve monks, for the conversion of souls among the heathens. The expedition set out on the 23rd of February 1595 from the port of San Lucar, consequently only seventeen days later than Ralegh from Plymouth, and arrived on the 16th of April 1595. There prevails, however, great confusion respecting the dates of this expedition, and in the great work of Roubaud, 'L'Histoire de l'Asie, de l'Afrique, et de l'Amérique, Paris, 1775,' it is stated that it occurred in 1594. It is our opinion that De Vera arrived in

ragement as well to *Berreo* as to others that formerly attempted the discouery and conquest. *Oreliano* after he failed of the discouerie of *Guiana* by the said riuer of *Amazones*, passed into Spaine, and there obtained a patent of the king for the inuasion and conquest, but died by sea about the Ilands, and his fleet beeing seuered by tempest, the action for that time proceeded not. *Diego Ordace* followed the enterprize, and departed Spaine

Trinidad in 1596, in which we are confirmed by a passage in Keymis's Journal, who expressly informs us, Domingo de Vera had only been sent into Spain five months before Ralegh's arrival at Trinidad: and the Indian whom he took at the Caroni confessed that Berreo "daily looked for his son from Nuevo Reyno, for his camp-master from Trinidad, and for horses from the Caracas." The arrival of De Vera's expedition could not have taken place in March or April 1595, as in that instance they would have met Ralegh's ships, who did not leave the island of Trinidad before the end of June. Suffice it to say, that this great expedition met with such disasters, sufferings and wretchedness, that only a few are said to have returned to Spain to relate the misfortunes of the two thousand adventurers who started from San Lucar. Epidemics, famine, shipwreck, and the war-clubs of the Indians, swept away all but that small number.

Humboldt supposes that the narrative of Juan Martinez, which gave rise to this unfortunate enterprise, was founded on the adventures of Juan Martin de Albujar, who in the expedition of Pedro de Silva in 1570 was taken prisoner by the Caribs or Caribisi of the Lower Orinoco, and who settled ultimately at Carora, after having long wandered with Indian tribes, and made several excursions to Santa Fé de Bogota. As already observed in the introduction to this edition, John Hagthorpe considers the whole relation "an invention of the fat fryers;" but if Juan Martin de Albujar was the author of the story in the hands of Berreo, it is more than probable that he composed it from what he had learned from the Spaniards about the adventures of Felipe de Urre, or more properly Philip von Huten, and combined it with the accounts he heard from the Caribs, who among all Indian tribes to this day are considered the most superstitious and the greatest story-tellers. According to a manuscript which we had in our hands while in Demerara, a tribe of Mahanaos is said to have inhabited the tributaries of the Rio Branco, Takutu, and Rupununi, of whom he must have learned through the Caribs, who possessed settlements on the skirts of the savannahs; and as those regions are annually inundated to a great extent, the great expanse of the inundation, which may have reached the villages of the Mahanaos, gave rise to the fable of the Laguna de Manoa, or del Dorado, or de Parima.

with 600 soldiers and 30 horse, who arriuing on the coast of *Guiana* was slaine in a muteny with the most part of such as fauoured him, as also of the rebellious part, in so much as his ships perished, and few or none returned, neither was it certainely knowen what became of the said *Ordace*, vntill *Berreo* found the ancor of his ship in the riuer of *Orenoque*; but it was supposed, and so it is written by *Lopez*, that he perished on the seas, and of other writers diuersly conceiued and reported. And heereof it came that *Martynes* entred so farre within the lande and arriued at that Citie of *Inga* the Emperor, for it chaunced that while *Ordace* with his armie rested at the port of *Morequito* (who was either the first or second that attempted *Guiana*), by some negligence, the whol store of powder prouided for the seruice was set on fire, and *Martines* hauing the chief charge was condemned by the generall *Ordace* to be executed forthwith: *Martines* being much fauored by the soldiers had al the meane possible procured for his life, but it could not be obtained in other sort then this: That he shuld be set into a *Canoa* alone without any victual, onely with his armes, and so turnd loosse into the great riuer: but it pleased God that the *Canoa* was carried downe the streame, and that certain of the *Guianians* met it the same euening, and hauing not at any time sene any Christian, nor any man of that colour, they caried *Martynes* into the land to be wondred at, and so from towne to towne, vntill he came to the great Citie of *Manoa*, the seate and residence of *Inga* the Emperor. The Emperor after he had beheld him, knew him to be a Christian (for it was not long before that his brethren *Guascar* and *Atabalipa* were vanquished by the Spaniards in *Peru*) and caused him to be lodged in his pallace, and well entertained: hee liued 7 moneths in *Manoa*, but not suffered to wander into the countrey any where: hee was also brought thither all the waie blindfield, led by the Indians, vntill he came to the entrance of *Manoa* it selfe, and was 14 or 15 daies in the passage: he auowed at his death that he entred the City at *Noon,* and then they vncouered his face, and that he trauelled al that daie til night thorow the Citie, and the next day from sun rising to sun setting, ere he came to the pallace of *Inga.* After that *Martynes* had liued 7 moneths in *Manoa,* and began to vnderstand the language of the country, *Inga* asked him whether he desired to returne into his own countrey, or would willingly abide with him: but *Martynes* not desirous to stay, obtained the fauour of *Inga* to depart, with whom he sent diuers *Guianians* to conduct him to the riuer of *Orenoque* all loden with as much gold as they could carrie, which he gaue to *Martines* at his departure: but when he was arriued neere the riuers side, the borderers which are called *Orenoqueponi* robbed him and his *Guianians* of all the treasure (the borderers beeing at that time at warres with *Inga,* and not conquered) saue onely of two great bottels of gords, which were filled with beads of gold curiously wrought, which those *Orenoqueponi* thought had ben no other thing then his drink or meate or grain for foode with which *Martynes* had libertie to passe, and so in *Canoas* he fell down by the riuer of *Orenoque* to *Trinedado,* and from thence to *Marguerita,* and so to *Saint Iuan de puerto rico,* where remaining a long tyme for passage into *Spayne* he died. In the time of his extreme sicknesse, and when he was without hope of life, receauing the *Sacrament* at the handes of his Confessor, he deliuered these thinges, with the relation of his trauels, and also called for his *Calabaza* or gords of the gold beades which he gaue to the Church and friers to be praied for. This *Martynes* was he that christned the citie of *Manoa,* by the name of *El Dorado,* and as *Berreo* informed me vpon this occasion. Those *Guianians* and also the borderers, and all others in that tract which I haue seen are marueylous great drunkardes, in which vice I think no nation can compare with them: and at the times of their solemne feasts when the Emperor carowseth with his Captayns, tributories, and gouernours, the manner is thus. All those that pledge him are first stripped naked, and their bodies annoynted al ouer with a kinde of white *Balsamum* (by them called *Curcai*)[1] of which there is great plenty and yet very deare amongst them, and it is of all other the most pretious, wherof we haue had good experience : when they are annointed all ouer, certaine seruants of the Emperor hauing prepared gold made into fine powder blow it thorow hollow canes vpon their naked bodies, vntill they be al shining from the foote to the head, and in this sort they sit drinking by twenties and hundreds and continue in drunkennes somtimes sixe or seuen daies togither: the same is also confirmed by a letter written into *Spaine* which was intercepted, which master *Robert Dudley* told me he had seen. Vpon this sight, and for the abundance of gold which he saw in the citie, the Images of gold in their Temples, the plates, armors, and shields of gold which they vse in the wars, he called it *El Dorado*. After *Oreliano* who was emploied by *Pacaro* afterwards *Marques Pacaro* conqueror and gouernor of *Peru*, and the death of *Ordace* and *Martynes*, one *Pedro de Osua*[2], a knight of

[1] The Indians possess different kinds of gum with which they anoint themselves, and which exude from different species of trees of the genera *Amyris* and *Calophyllum*. The most precious is however a gum coming from a tree the true botanical character of which is still unknown to us, but which we consider to belong to the natural order of *Amyridaceæ*. It possesses a grateful balsamic odour, and is called Acuyari or Acayarlou by the Guianians, who consider an inhalation of its fragrant odour when burning beneficial for the lungs of consumptive persons.

[2] Pedro de Ursua descended, towards the end of 1560, the river Papamene (called at present Rio Caqueta or Yupura) in search of El Dorado. It was during this expedition that Lopez de Aguirre rose against him in revolt, and Ursua was slain, as related by Sir Walter Ralegh. When Aguirre was in the height of his bloody career, and had received the epithet of the Tyrant, he wrote a most remarkable letter of defiance to Philip the Second of Spain. Don Gonzales Ximenes de Quesada arrested his course of murder and rapine, and attacked him and his band in the valley of Cerinca, twelve leagues from Tienja. Surrounded on all sides, he first killed his daughter, whom he had destined for his successor, and allowed himself cowardly to be taken prisoner. He was conducted to the island of Trinidad, where he was executed and his body quartered; his house was demolished, and the place where it stood strewn with salt. There are some doubts among historians whether Aguirre, with Ursua's expedition,

Nauarre attempted *Guiana,* taking his way from *Peru,* and built his brigandines vpon a riuer called *Oia,* which riseth to the southward of *Quito,* and is very great: this riuer falleth into *Amazones,* by which *Osua* with his companies descended, and came out of that Prouince which is called *Mutylones*: and it seemeth to me that this Empire is reserued for her Maiestie and the *English* nation, by reason of the hard successe which all these and other *Spaniards* found in attempting the same, wherof I will speake brieflie, though impertinent in some sort to my purpose. This *Pedro de Osua* had among his troupes a *Biscayn* called *Agiri,* a man meanlie borne, and bare no other office than a Surgeant or *Alferez*: but after certaine months, when the soldiers were grieued with trauels and consumed with famine, and that no entrance could be found by the branches or body of *Amazones,* this *Agiri* raised a muteny, of which hee made himselfe the head, and so preuailed as he put *Osua* to the sword, and all his followers, taking on him the whole charge and commandement with a purpose not onely to make himselfe Emperor of *Guiana,* but also of *Peru,* and of al that side of the *West Indies*: he had of his partie seuen hundred soldiers, and of those many promised to draw in other captains and companies to deliuer vp towns and forts in *Peru,* but neither finding by the saide riuer any passage into *Guiana,* nor any possibilitie to returne towards *Peru* by the same *Amazones,* by reason that the descent of the riuer made so great a currant, he was inforced to desemboque at the mouth of the said *Amazones,* which cannot be lesse than a thousand leagues from the place where they imbarqued: from thence he coasted the land till he arriued at *Marguerita* to the North of *Mompatar,* which is at this daie

descended the Amazon to its embouchure, or whether he ascended the Rio Negro, its tributary the Rio Branco, and by the short "portage" crossed to the Rupununi, a tributary of the Essequibo, which river he followed to the Atlantic. (See Fr. Pedro Simon, not. vi. cap. 30–39. Piedrahita, Historia general de la conquistas del nuevo reyno de Granada, lib. vii. cap. 8. Purchas, vol. iv. lib. vii. cap. 11. Pagan, Relation de la rivière des Amazones, cap. 39, &c.)

called *Puerto de Tyranno,* for that he there slue *Don Iuan de villa Andreda,* gouernor of *Marguerita,* who was father to *Don Iuan Sermiento* gouernor of *Marguerita* when Sir *Iohn Burgh* landed there, and attempted the *Iland. Agiri* put to the sword all others in the Iland that refused to be of his partie, and tooke with him certaine *Cemerones,* and other desperate companions: From thence he went to *Cumana,* and there slew the *Gouernor,* and dealt in all as at *Marguerita*: he spoiled all the coast of *Caracas,* and the prouince of *Vensuello,* and of *Rio de hache,* and as I remember it was the same yeer that Sir *Iohn Hawkins* sailed to Saint *Iuan de Lua* in the *Iesus* of *Lubeck,* for himselfe told me that he met with such a one vpon the coast that rebelled, and had sailed downe all the riuer of *Amazones. Agiri* from hence landed about *Sancta Marta,* and sacked it also, putting to death so many as refused to be his followers, purposing to inuade *Nueuo reyno de Granada,* and to sack *Pampelone, Merida, Lagrita, Tunia,* and the rest of the cities of *Nueuo reygno,* and from thence againe to enter *Peru*: but in a fight in the said *Nueuo reygno* he was ouerthrowne, and finding no way to escape, he first put to the sword his own children, foretelling them that they should not liue to be defamed or opbraid by the *Spaniards* after his death, who would haue tearmed them the children of a *Traytor* or *Tyrant,* and that sithence he could not make them Princes, he woulde yet deliuer them from shame and reproch : These were the ends and tragedies of *Oreliano, Ordace, Osua, Martynes,* and *Agiri.*

After these followed *Ieronimo Ortal de Saragosa*[1] with 130

[1] Geronimo de Ortal was attached to the expedition of Don Diego de Ordas as treasurer, and received king Philip's commands after the death of Ordas to continue the conquest of New Andalusia. He was nominated governor of Paria, and despatched Alonso de Herrera (see *ante,* note at p. 16) to ascend the Orinoco. He commanded likewise Augustin Delgado to proceed to the coast of Neveri and to establish himself in the neighbourhood of Maracapana, where he constructed a fort which he called Asiento de San Miguel de Neveri. This was afterwards taken possession of by Antonio Sedeño. (Pedro Simon, Tercera Noticia, cap. 20–30. Cau-

soldiers, who failing his entrance by sea was cast with the currant on the coast of *Paria,* and peopled about *S. Miguell de Neueri.* It was then attempted by *Don Pedro de sylua* a *Portugues*[1] of the familie of *Rigomes de sylua,* and by the fauour which *Rigomes* had with the king, he was set out, but he also shot wide of the mark, for being departed from *Spaine* with his fleete, he entred by *Maragnon* or *Amazones,* where by the nations of the riuer, and by the *Amazones* he was vtterly ouerthrowen, and himselfe and all his armie defeated, onely seuen escaped, and of those but two returned.

After him came *Pedro Hernandez de Serpa,* and landed at *Cumana* in the *West Indies,* taking his iourney by land towards *Orenoque,* which may bee some 120 leagues; but ere he came to the borders of the said riuer, he was set vpon by a nation of Indians called *Wikiri,* and ouerthrowen in sort, that of 300 soldiers, horsemen, many Indians, and *Negros,* there returned but 18: others affirm that he was defeated in the very entrance of *Guiana,* at the first ciuill towne of the Empire called *Macureguarai.* Captaine *Preston* in taking *S. Iago de Leon* (which was by him and his companies very resolutely performed, being a great towne, and far within the land) held a gentleman prisoner who died in his ship, that was one of the companie of *Hernandez de Serpa,* and saued among those that escaped, who witnessed what opinion is held among the *Spaniards* thereabouts of the

lin, Historia de la Nueva-Andalucia, lib. ii. cap. 7. Herrera, dec. v. lib. v. vi. vii. ix.)

[1] Don Pedro de Silvia, having received permission to attempt the conquest of El Dorado, departed from the port of Burburuta and traversed the Llanos. Abandoned by his soldiers, he returned in March 1570 to Barcquizemeto, from whence he went to Peru and embarked ultimately for Spain. He was killed on his return by the Caribs. (Oviedo, lib. vi. cap. 1 et 5.) Ralegh confounds evidently the expedition of Don Malavez de Silvia with the above, who departed in 1568 from Pernambuco and entered the Amazon. On his return to Portugal, he equipped three ships and two caravels to continue the discoveries of Orellana; but all his vessels, with the exception of the caravel, on board of which was De Silvia himself, were lost in the Amazon.

great riches of *Guiana,* and *El Dorado* the citie of *Inga.* Another *Spaniard* was brought aboord me by captaine *Preston,* who told me in the hearing of himselfe and diuers other gentlemen, that he met with *Berreos* Campmaster at *Caracas,* when he came from the borders of *Guiana,* and that he saw with him fortie of most pure plates of golde curiously wrought, and swords of *Guiana* decked and inlaid with golde, feathers garnished with golde, and diuers rarities which he carried to the *Spanish* king.

After *Hernandez de Serpa* it was vndertaken by the *Adelantado, Don Gonzales Cemenes de Casada*[1], who was one of the chiefest in the conquest of *Nueuo reyno,* whose daughter and heire *Don Anthonio de Berreo* maried: *Gonzales* sought the passage also by the riuer called *Papamene,* which riseth by *Quito* in *Peru,* and runneth southeast 100 leagues, and then falleth into *Amazones,* but he also failing the entrance, returned with the losse of much labour and cost: I tooke one captaine *George* a *Spaniard* that followed *Gonzales* in this enterprise. *Gonzales* gaue his daughter to *Berreo* taking his oth and honor to follow the enterprise to the last of his substance and life, who since as he hath sworne to me hath spent 300000 ducates in the same, and yet neuer could enter so far into the land as my selfe with that poore troupe or rather a handfull of men, being in all about 100 gentlemen, soldiers, rowers, bote-keepers, boies, and of all

[1] Don Gonzales Ximenes de Quesada, the founder of Nuevo reyno de Granada, returned in 1538 to Spain to give an account of his conquests and exploits. Ralegh confounds the brother of Don Gonzales, captain Hernan Perez de Quesada, with the great adelantado. Having understood that beyond the mountains west of New Granada existed great store of gold and emeralds, he departed on the 1st of September 1541, accompanied by an expedition of two hundred and seventy Spaniards, nearly two hundred horses, and five thousand Indians of the Moxcas tribe. He reached the river Papamene, and after great hardships and loss of men and horses, returned with the remainder of the expedition to New Granada. (Herrera, decad. vii. lib. iv. cap. 12. Piedrahita, part i. lib. ix. cap. 3.) As already observed, Ralegh commits great mistakes, and frequently confounds the heroes of the numerous expeditions in search of El Dorado, nor does he bind himself to a chronological order in the relation of his predecessors in search of the phantom of Gran Manoa.

sorts : neither could any of the forepassed vndertakers, nor *Berreo* himselfe discouer the country, till now lately by conference with an ancient king called *Carapana* he got the true light thereof: for *Berreo* came aboue 1500 miles, ere he vnderstood ought, or could finde any passage or entrance into any part thereof, yet he had experience of all these forenamed, and diuers others, and was perswaded of their errors and mistakings. *Berreo* sought it by the riuer *Cassanar,* which falleth into a great riuer called *Pato, Pato* falleth into *Meta,* and *Meta* into *Baraquan,* which is also called *Orenoque.*

He tooke his iourney from *Nueuo reyno de Granada* where he dwelt, hauing the inheritance of *Gonzales Cemenes* in those parts : he was followed with 700 horse, he draue with him 1000 head of cattell, he had also many women, Indians, and slaues[1]. How all these riuers crosse and encounter, how the countrie lieth and is bordred, the passage of *Cemenes,* and of *Berreo,* mine owne discouerie, and the way that I entred, with all the rest of the nations and riuers, your Lordship shall receiue in a large Chart or Map, which I haue not yet finished, and which I shall most humbly pray your Lordship to secret, and not to suffer it to passe your own hands; for by a draught thereof all may bee preuented by other nations[2]. For I know it is this very yeere sought by the French, although by the way that they now take, I feare it not much. It was also told me ere I departed England, that *Villiers* the Admirall was in preparation for the planting of *Amazones,* to which riuer the French haue made diuers voiages, and returned much gold and other rarities. I spake with a captaine of a French ship that came from thence, his ship riding in *Falmouth,* the same yeere that my ships came first from *Virginia.*

[1] We are only acquainted with the details of Berreo's expedition through Sir Walter Ralegh's account.

[2] It appears he never executed this map, or if he did so, it has been lost. Jodocus Hondius constructed from the account of Ralegh's and Keymis's voyages the map entitled "Nieuwe Caerte van het goudrycke landt Guiana, 1599." Levinus Hulsius availed himself of it for the construction of his map "Nova et exacta delineatio Americæ partis australis, etc., 1599."

There was another this yeere in *Helford* that also came from thence, and had been 14 moneths at an ancor in *Amazones*, which were both very rich. Although as I am perswaded, *Guiana* cannot be entred that way, yet no doubt the trade of gold from thence passeth by branches of riuers into the riuer of *Amazones*, and so it doth on euery hand farre from the countrey it selfe, for those Indians of *Trenedado* haue plates of gold from *Guiana*, and those *Canibals* of *Dominica* which dwell in the Ilands by which our ships passe yeerly to the *West Indies*, also the Indians of *Paria*, those Indians called *Tucaris, Chochi, Apotomios, Cumanagotos*, and all those other nations inhabiting nere about the mountaines that run from *Paria* thorow the Prouince of *Vensuello*[1], and in *Maracapana*, and the Canibals of *Guanipa*, the Indians called *Assawai, Coaca, Aiai*, and the rest (all which shall be described in my description as they are situate) haue plates of gold of *Guiana*. And vpon the riuer of *Amazones Theuet* writeth that the people weare *Croissants* of gold, for of that form the *Guianians* most commonly make them: So as from *Dominica* to *Amazones* which is aboue 250 leagues, all the chiefe Indians in al parts weare of those plates of *Guiana*. Vndoubtedly those that trade [with the] *Amazones* returne much gold, which (as is aforesaid) commeth by trade from *Guiana*, by some branch of a riuer that falleth from the countrey into *Amazones*, and either it is by the riuer which passeth by the nations called *Tisnados*, or by *Carepuna*. I made inquirie amongst the most ancient and best traueled of the *Orenoqueponi*, and I had knowledge of all the riuers between *Orenoque* and *Amazones*, and was very desirous to vnderstand the truth of those warlike women, bicause of some it is beleeued, of others not: And though I digresse from my

[1] Alonso de Ojeda gave the name to the province of Venezuela. During his voyage with Amerigo Vespucci in 1498 he coasted along Terra firma, and landed at a village which consisted of twenty-six huts built upon piles, and connected with each other by drawbridges, which he compared with Venice, from which circumstance he called the place Venezuela, or Little Venice.

purpose, yet I will set downe what hath been deliuered me for truth of those women, and I spake with a *Casique* or Lord of people that told me he had been in the riuer, and beyond it also. The nations of these women are on the south side of the riuer in the Prouinces of *Topago,* and their chiefest strengths and retraicts are in the Ilands scituate on the south side of the entrance, some 60 leagues within the mouth of the said riuer. The memories of the like women are very ancient as well in *Africa* as in *Asia*: In *Africa* those that had *Medusa* for *Queene*: others in *Scithia* neere the riuers of *Tanais* and *Thermadon*: we find also that *Lampedo* and *Marthesia* were *Queens* of the *Amazones*: in many histories they are verified to haue been, and in diuers ages and Provinces: But they which are not far from *Guiana* do accompanie with men but once in a yeere, and for the time of one moneth, which I gather by their relation to be in Aprill. At that time all the Kings of the borders assemble, and the Queenes of the *Amazones,* and after the Queens haue chosen, the rest cast lots for their *Valentines.* This one moneth, they feast, daunce, and drinke of their wines in abundance, and the Moone being done, they all depart to their owne Prouinces. If they conceiue, and be deliuered of a sonne, they returne him to the father, if of a daughter they nourish it, and reteine it, and as many as haue daughters send vnto the begetters a Present, all being desirous to increase their owne sex and kinde, but that the cut of the right dug of the brest I do not finde to be true. It was farther told me, that if in the wars they tooke any prisoners that they vsed to accompany with those also at what time soeuer, but in the end for certaine they put them to death: for they are said to be very cruell and bloodthirsty, especially to such as offer to inuade their territories[1]. These *Amazones* haue likewise great store of these plates of golde, which they recouer by exchange chiefly for a kinde of greene stones, which the

[1] The subject of the Amazons of America has been fully treated in the Introduction to this edition, to which the reader is referred.

Spaniards call *Piedras Hijadas,* and we vse for spleene stones, and for the disease of the stone we also esteeme them : of these I saw diuers in *Guiana,* and commonly euery king or *Casique* hath one, which their wiues for the most part weare, and they esteeme them as great iewels[1].

But to returne to the enterprise of *Berreo,* who (as I haue said) departed from *Nueuo reyno* with 700 horse, besides the prouisions aboue rehearsed; he descended by the riuer called *Cassanar,* which riseth in *Nueuo reyno* out of the mountaines by

[1] Ralegh alludes here to the Amazon stones, which were formerly considered to cure diseases of the liver; hence they received the name of "piedras del higado." These stones it was pretended came from the country of the women without husbands. They are of a green colour and of a cylindrical form, about two inches long, and perforated. The price of a cylinder of that size was, as Humboldt relates, from twelve to fifteen piasters. They were considered as amulets, and preserved the wearer against nervous diseases and liver complaints, fevers, and the bite of snakes. The Caribs and Waccawais, who among the Indian tribes replace our Jew pedlars, in former times brought them frequently to Demerara, where they are known by the name of Macuaba, or Calicot stones. They are now seldom seen; one of the last which the editor recollects was worn by a child of the Warrau nation on the river Corentyne. The Indians on the river Uaupes wear similar stones, but of different colour and substance, as a token of chieftainship and noble descent, and according to the length of the cylinder and the depth of the perforation may be recognized their grade and nobility. The author of these remarks possesses one of these cylinders which is $3\frac{6}{10}$ inches long and $3\frac{1}{2}$ inches in circumference. Humboldt observes that the spot which produces the Amazon stones is rather unknown than concealed by the Indians. He learned in San Carlos and in the neighbouring villages, that the sources of the Orinoco, and in the missions of the Caroni and at Angostura, that the sources of the Rio Branco, were the site of these stones. (Humboldt's Personal Narrative, English translation, vol. v. pp. 383–387.) During our travels in Guiana we ascertained that these two rivers have their sources at no great distance from each other; hence there is some probability in the assertion. This does not prevent us from mentioning here, that there is, near the source of one of the chief branches of the river Caroni, at Mount Roraima, a mineral substance (jasper) resembling in colour verde-antique; it is translucent, and sometimes found in thin plates, which give a sonorous sound similar to the one described by Humboldt, and it is of so hard a substance that it is used in lieu of flint by the natives (the Arecunas), who besides carry on with it a trade of barter with other tribes.

the citie of *Tunia,* from which mountaine also springeth *Pato,* both which fall into the great riuer of *Meta,* and *Meta* riseth from a mountaine ioining to *Pampelone* in the same *Nueuo reyno de Granada*: these as also *Guaiare,* which issueth out of the mountains by *Timana,* fall all into *Baraquan,* and are but of his heads, for at their comming togither they lose their names, and *Baraquan* farther down is also rebaptized by the name of *Orenoque*[1]. On the other side of the citie and hils of *Timana* riseth *rio grande,* which falleth into the sea by *Sancta Marta.* By *Cassonar* first, and so into *Meta, Berreo* passed, keeping his horsemen on the banks, where the countrie serued them for to march, and where otherwise he was driuen to embarque them in botes which he builded for the purpose, and so came with the currant down the riuer of *Meta,* and so into *Baraquan*[2]. After he entred that great and mightie riuer, he began dailie to loose of his companies both men and horse, for it is in many places

[1] We have already referred in the Introduction to the different names of the Orinoco. The mountains of Baraguan narrow the bed of the river considerably, and form almost a strait, from which the river, not only in its immediate neighbourhood, but as high up as the Guaviare, received the name of Baraguan.

[2] The general correct geographical knowledge which Sir Walter Ralegh had acquired of these regions is really wonderful. Near the port of Marayal the two rivers, the Rio Negro and the Rio de Aguas Blancas or Umadea, unite, and from hence it receives the name of Meta. Ralegh is however mistaken in considering that the river rises near Pamplona, which is situated nearly two hundred miles to the north of it. On ascending the Meta and the Rio Negro to reach Santa Fé de Bogota, travellers disembark near the Passo de la Cabulla, from whence the capital of New Granada is only eight to ten leagues distant. The river which passes Patuto, formerly a mission, is no doubt the one to which Ralegh alludes when speaking of the Pato. After its confluence with the Tocaragua and the Tama, it is called Cassanare, and flows ultimately into the Meta. As we have had already an opportunity to observe, we know only Berreo's expedition from Ralegh's account; according to contemporary historians, this personage made his appearance in Trinidad about 1584, where he was installed as Governor; and he is acknowledged to have been the founder of San Joseph de Oruña in Trinidad and of Santo Thomé de la Guayana, on the right bank of the Orinoco, in the year 1591. (Caulin, Historia Corografica de la Nueva-Andalucia, p. 175.)

violentlie swift, and hath forcible eddies, many sands, and diuers Ilands sharpe pointed with rocks: But after one whole yeere, iourneying for the most part by riuer, and the rest by land, he grew dailie to fewer numbers, for both by sicknes, and by encountring with the people of those regions, through which he trauelled, his companies were much wasted, especially by diuers incounters with the *Amapaiens*: And in all this time he neuer could learne of any passage into *Guiana*, nor any newes or fame thereof, vntill he came to the farther border of the said *Amapaia*, eight daies iourney from the riuer *Caroli*, which was the farthest riuer that we entred. Among those of *Amapaia*, *Guiana* was famous, but few of these people accosted *Berreo*, or woulde trade with him the first three months of the six which he soiourned there. This *Amapaia* is also maruellous rich in gold (as both *Berreo* confessed, and those of *Guiana* with whom I had most conference) and is situate vpon *Orenoke* also. In this countrey *Berreo* lost 60 of his best soldiers, and most of all his horse that remained of his former yeeres trauell: but in the end after diuers encounters with those nations they grew to peace, and they presented *Berreo* with 10 Images of fine gold among diuers other plates and *Croissants*, which as he sware to me and diuers other gentlemen were so curiouslie wrought, as he had not seene the like either in *Italy*, *Spaine*, or the *Lowe Cuntries*: and he was resolued that when they came to the hands of the *Spanish* king, to whom he had sent them by his Campmaster, they would appeer very admirable, especially being wrought by such a nation as had no Iron instrument at all, nor anie of those helps which our goldsmiths haue to worke withall. The particular name of the people in *Amapaia* which gaue him these peeces are called *Anebas*, and the riuer of *Orenoque* at that place is aboue 12 *English* miles brode, which may be from his out fall into the sea 700 or 800 miles[1].

[1] The statement of the breadth of the Orinoco is here greatly exaggerated. Its breadth from the mouth of the Arauca to the junction of the river Meta varies between a mile and a half to two miles and a half.

This Prouince of *Amapaia* is a verie low and a marish ground neere the riuer, and by reason of the red water which issueth out in small branches thorow the fenny and boggie ground, there breed diuers poysonfull wormes and serpents, and the Spaniards not suspecting, nor in anie sort foreknowing the danger were infected with a greeuous kind of flux by drinking therof, and euen the very horses poisoned therewith : In so much as at the end of the six months that they abode there, of all there troups, there were not left aboue 120 soldiers, and neither horse nor cattle[1]. For *Berreo* hoped to haue found *Guiana* by 1000 miles neerer than it fell out to be in the end, by means wherof they susteined much want and much hunger, oppressed with greeuous diseases, and all the miseries that could be imagined. I demanded of those in *Guiana* that had trauelled *Amapaia* how they liued with that tawnie or red water when they trauelled thither, and they told me that after the *Sun* was neere the middle of the skie, they vsed to fill their pots and pitchers with that water, but either before that time, or towards the setting of the *Sun* it was dangerous to drinke of, and in the night strong poison. I learned also of diuers other riuers of that nature among them which were

Humboldt found the river near the mission of Uruana, which is sixty miles below the Meta, seventeen thousand four hundred feet, or three English statute miles broad, while at the Baraguan it is only five thousand six hundred and eighty-five feet, or about one mile broad. The mouth of the Meta is about six hundred nautical miles from the sea. (Humboldt, Personal Narrative, vol. iv. p. 504; vol. v. p. 639.)

[1] During our wanderings over the Savannahs we experienced frequently the pernicious influence of the waters, chiefly during the dry season, when nearly every river is scorched up, and the water, turbid in appearance, is only found collected in small pools. In 1835, while traversing with Lieutenant Haining the Savannahs of the Mahu or Ireng, the author of these notes quenched his thirst from one of the pools, and suffered to such a degree from flux that he almost despaired of recovering. Similar instances befell our people repeatedly, whom we could not restrain from drinking this water in spite of our warning. We cannot explain to ourselves why according to Ralegh's account the water proved less pernicious if filled in pots at noon, except that being allowed to stand quiet, the foreign particles with which it was impregnated evaporated or fell to the bottom.

also (while the *Sun* was in the *Meridian*) verie safe to drink, and in the morning, euening, and night, woonderfull dangerous and infectiue. From this Prouince *Berreo* hasted away assoone as the *Spring* and beginning of *Summer* appeered, and sought his entrance on the borders of *Orenoque* on the south side, but there ran a ledge of so high and impassable mountaines as he was not able by any means to march ouer them, continuing from the east sea into which *Orenoque* falleth, euen to *Quito* in *Peru*: neither had he means to carrie victuall or munition ouer those craggie, high, and fast hils, being all wooddy, and those so thicke and spiny, and so full of prickles, thorns, and briers, as it is impossible to creepe thorow them: he had also neither friendship among the people, nor any interpreter to perswade or treate with them, and more, to his disaduantage, the *Casiqui* and kings of *Amapaia* had giuen knowledge of his purpose to the *Guianians*, and that he sought to sacke and conquer the Empire, for the hope of their so great abundance and quantities of gold: he passed by the mouths of many great riuers, which fell into *Orenoque* both from the north and south, which I forbeare to name for tediousnes, and bicause they are more pleasing in describing than reading.

Berreo affirmed that there fell an hundred riuers into *Orenoque* from the north and south, whereof the lest was as big as *Rio grande*, that passeth between *Popayan* and *Nueuo reyno de granada* (*Rio grande* being esteemed one of the renowmed riuers in al the west Indies, and numbred among the great riuers of the world[1]:) But he knew not the names of any of these, but *Caroli*

[1] The Rio Grande or Rio de la Magdalena has its source in 1° 58′ north latitude, about forty miles south of Popayan, and falls into the Atlantic in 11° 2′ north latitude: its course is therefore about nine degrees of latitude. None of the tributaries of the Orinoco has the size of the Rio Magdalena. The Meta, the largest tributary of the Orinoco, has a course of about five hundred miles. The country through which the Rio de la Magdalena flows was explored in 1536–38 by Gonzalo Ximenes de Quesada, the father-in-law (or, according to Fray Simon, the uncle) of Antonio de Berreo. He conquered the indigenous tribes, and founded on the 6th of

only, neither from what nations they descended, neither to what Prouinces they led, for he had no meanes to discourse with the inhabitants at any time: neither was he curious in these things, being vtterlie vnlearned, and not knowing the east from the west. But of al these I got som knowledge, and of manie more, partly by mine own trauel, and the rest by conference: of som one I lerned one, of others the rest, hauing with me an Indian that spake many languages, and that of *Guiana* naturally. I sought out al the aged men, and such as were greatest trauelers, and by the one and the other I came to vnderstand the situations, the riuers, the kingdoms from the east sea to the borders of *Peru*, and from *Orenoque* southward as far as *Amazones* or *Maragnon*, and the regions of *Maria Tamball*[1], and of all the kings of Prouinces and captains of townes and villages, how they stood in tearms of peace or war, and which were friends or enimies the one with the other, without which there can be neither entrance nor conquest in those parts, nor els where: For by the dissention betweene *Guascar* and *Atabalipa*, *Paçaro* conquered *Peru*, and by the hatred that the *Traxcallians* bare to *Mutezuma*, *Cortez* was victorious ouer *Mexico*[2], without which both the one

August, 1538 (the day of Transfiguration), the city of Santa Fé de Bogota, which became the capital of the Nuevo Reyno de Granada. (Piedrahita, part i. lib. vi. cap. 1, 2 and 4; Florez de Ocariz, preludio 35, p. 61.) Sébastian de Belalcazer founded in 1536 the city of Popayan (Popajanum).

[1] Peter Martyr speaks of a number of "fortunate and fruitful isles," situated somewhere in the sea near the coast of Paria, inhabited by men of meek nature and easy of access, but possessing neither gold nor precious stones. The inhabitants, he says, call these regions Mariatamball. (Peter Martyr, decad. i. chap. 9.) If the isles and islets Blanca, Orchilla and Los Roques are not meant by it, they are imaginary.

[2] After Cortez had defeated the Tlascalans, Xicotencatl, their chief, offered peace, and signed a treaty of alliance. The republic of Tlascala had always been hostile to Montezuma, and six thousand Tlascalans accompanied Cortez on his first expedition to Mexico. They remained his faithful allies, and afterwards assisted materially in the conquest of the great city. (Historia verdadera de la Conquista de la Nueva España por Bernal Diaz del Castillo. Madrid, 1632, cap. 73, 149, &c. Prescott's History of the Conquest of Mexico, vol. ii. pp. 10, 415.

and the other had failed of their enterprize, and of the great honor and riches, which they attained vnto.

Now *Berreo* began to grow into despaire, and looked for no other successe than his predecessors in this enterprize, vntill such time as he arriued at the Province of *Emeria* towards the east sea and mouth of the riuer, where he found a nation of people very fauorable, and the countrey full of all maner of victuall. The king of this land is called *Carapana*, a man very wise, subtill, and of great experience, being little lesse than 100 yeeres old: In his youth he was sent by his father into the Iland of *Trinedado*, by reason of ciuill warre among themselues, and was bred at a village, in that Iland, called *Parico*: at that place in his youth he had seene many Christians both French and Spanish, and went diuers times with the Indians of *Trinedado* to *Marguerita* and *Cumana* in the west Indies[1], (for both those places haue euer been releeued with victuall from *Trinedado*) by reason whereof he grew of more vnderstanding, and noted the difference of the nations, comparing the strength and armes of his country with those of the Christians, and euer after tempo-rized so, as whosoeuer els did amisse, or was wasted by con-tention, *Carapana* kept himselfe and his country in quiet and plentie: he also held peace with *Caribas* or *Canibals*[2] his neighbors, and had free trade with all nations whosoeuer els had war.

Berreo soiourned and rested his weake troupe in the towne of *Carapana* six weeks, and from him learnd the way and passage to *Guiana*, and the riches and magnificence thereof: but being then vtterly disable to proceed, he determined to trie his fortune

[1] Not only the archipelago, but likewise the coast of terra firma from the Gulf of Darien to Paria, were called at that period the West Indies.

[2] Carib and Cannibal were synonymous at that period. "Edaces hu-manarum carnium novi helluones anthropophagi, Caribes alias Canibales appellati," reports Peter Martyr of Angleria. The royal decree of Queen Isabella in 1504 declared the Caribs undeserving of Christian commisera-tion, and all Indians who bore that name were condemned to slavery and might be sold or exterminated.

another yeere, when he had renewed his prouisions, and regathered more force, which he hoped for as wel out of Spain, as from *Nueuo reyno*, where he had left his son *Don Anthonio Xemenes* to second him vpon the first notice giuen of his entrance, and so for the present embarqued himselfe in *Canoas*, and by the branches of *Orenoque* arriued at *Trinedado*, hauing from *Carapana* sufficient Pilots to conduct him. From *Trinedado* he coasted *Paria*, and so recouered *Marguerita* : and hauing made relation to *Don Iuan Sermiento* the gouernour of his proceeding, and perswaded him of the riches of *Guiana*, he obtained from thence 50 soldiers, promising presentlie to returne to *Carapana*, and so intò *Guiana*. But *Berreo* meant nothing lesse at that time, for he wanted manie prouisions necessarie for such an enterprize, and therfore departing from *Marguerita* seated himselfe in *Trinedado*, and from thence sent his Campmaster, and his Sargeant maior back to the borders to discouer the neerest passage, into the Empire, as also to treat with the borderers, and to drawe them to his partie and loue, without which, he knew he could neither passe safelie, nor in anie sort be releeued with victuall or ought els. *Carapana* directed this companie to a king called *Morequito*, assuring them that no man could deliuer so much of *Guiana* as *Morequito* could, and that his dwelling was but fiue daies iourney from *Macureguarai*, the first ciuill towne of *Guiana*.

Now your Lordship shall vnderstand that this *Morequito*, one of the greatest Lords or Kings of the borders of *Guiana*, had two or three yeeres before beene at *Cumana*, and at *Marguerita* in the west Indies, with great store of plates of gold, which he carried to exchange for such other things as he wanted in his owne countrey, and was dailie feasted, and presented by the gouernors of those places, and held amongst them some two moneths, in which time one *Vides*[1] gouernor of *Cumana* wan him to be his conductor into *Guiana*, being allured by those *Croissants* and Images of gold which he brought with him to

[1] Don Francisco de Vides.

trade, as also by the ancient fame and magnificence of *El Dorado*: whereupon *Vides* sent into Spaine for a Patent to discouer and conquer *Guiana*, not knowing of the precedence of *Berreos* patent, which as *Berreo* affirmeth was signed before that of *Vides*: so as when *Vides* vnderstood of *Berreo*, and that he had made entrance into that territorie, and foregone his desire and hope, it was verilie thought that *Vides* practised with *Morequito* to hinder and disturbe *Berreo* in all he could, and not to suffer him to enter through his *Seignory*, nor anie of his companies, neither to victuall, nor guide them in anie sort; for *Vides* gouernor of *Cumana*, and *Berreo* were become mortall enimies, as well for that *Berreo* had gotten *Trinedado* into his Patent with *Guiana*, as also in that he was by *Berreo* preuented in the iourney of *Guiana* it selfe: howsoeuer it was I know not, but *Morequito* for a time dissembled his disposition, suffered Spaniards, and a Frier (which *Berreo* had sent to discouer *Manoa*) to trauell through his countrey, gaue them a guide for *Macureguarai* the first towne of ciuill and apparelled people, from whence they had other guides to bring them to *Manoa* the great citie of *Inga*: and being furnished with those things, which they had learned of *Carapana*, were of most price in *Guiana*, went onward, and in eleuen daies arrived at *Manoa*, as *Berreo* affirmeth for certain: although I could not be assured therof by the Lord which now gouerneth the Prouince of *Morequito*, for he told me that they got all the gold they had, in other townes on this side *Manoa*, there being many very great and rich, and (as he said) built like the townes of Christians, with many roomes.

When these ten Spaniards were returned, and readie to put out of the border of *Arromaia*, the people of *Morequito* set vpon them, and slew them all but one that swam the riuer, and tooke from them to the value of 40000. pesoes of golde, and as it is written in the storie of *Iob*, one onelie liued to bring the newes to *Berreo*, that both his nine soldiers and holie father were benighted in the saide Prouince. I my selfe spake with the Captaines of *Morequito* that slew them, and was at the place where it was executed. *Berreo* inraged heerewithall sent all the strength he could make into *Arromaia,* to be reuenged of him, his people, and countrey: but *Morequito* suspecting the same fled ouer *Orenoque,* and thorow the territories of the *Saima,* and *Wikiri,* recouered *Cumana,* where he thought himselfe very safe with *Vides* the gouernor: But *Berreo* sending for him in the kings name, and his messengers finding him in the house of one *Fashardo* on the sudden ere it was suspected, so as he could not then be conueied away, *Vides* durst not deny him, as well to auoide the suspition of the practise, as also for that an holy father was slaine by him and his people. *Morequito* offred *Fashardo* the weight of three quintals in gold, to let him escape, but the poore *Guianian* betraid of all sides was deliuered to the Campmaster of *Berreo,* and was presently executed[1].

After the death of this *Morequito,* the soldiers of *Berreo* spoiled his territorie, and tooke diuers prisoners, among others they tooke the vnckle of *Morequito* called *Topiawari,* who is now king of *Arromaia,* (whose sonne I brought with me into *England*) and is a man of great vnderstanding and pollicie: he is aboue 100 yeeres old, and yet of a very able bodie: the *Spanyards* led him in a chain 17 daies, and made him their guide from place to place betweene his countrey and *Emeria* the prouince of *Carapana* aforesaid, and was at last redeemed for 100 plates of gold, and diuers stones called *Piedras Hijadas,* or

[1] This account of Berreo receives some confirmation from the author of 'Relation of the Habitations, and other Observations of the River Mariwin,' which follows Harcourt's Voyage in Purchas's Collections (Book vi. chap. xvii.). Purchas states in the margin, "I found this fairly written among M. Hakluyt's papers, but know not who was the author." It is however conjectured that the MS. originated with Fisher, the cousin of Robert Harcourt. He observes that he conversed with a Yaio who came down the river Selinama (Surinam), and who told him that he had been present with Morequito and Putimay when the nine Spaniards and the friar were killed by Morequito's people, that Morequito had been put to death and a great many Indians hanged. He himself was taken prisoner, tormented with pincers, and his ears nailed to wood; but he ultimately succeeded in making his escape.

Spleen stones. Now *Berreo* for executing of *Morequito* and other cruelties, spoiles, and slaughters done in *Arromaia* hath lost the loue of the *Orenoqueponi,* and of all the borderers, and dare not send any of his soldiers any farther into the land than to *Carapana,* which he calleth the port of *Guiana*: but from thence by the helpe of *Carapana* he had trade farther into the countrey, and alwaies appointed 10 *Spaniards* to reside in *Carapanas* towne[1]; by whose fauor and by being conducted by his people, those ten searched the countrey thereabouts as well for mines, as for other trades and commodities.

They haue also gotten a nephew of *Morequito,* whom they haue Christened and named *Don Iuan,* of whom they haue great hope, endeuoring by all means to establish him in the said prouince. Among manie other trades those *Spaniards* vsed in *Canoas* to passe to the riuers of *Barema, Pawroma,* and *Dissequebe,* which are on the south side of the mouth of *Orenoque,* and there buie women and children from the *Canibals,* which are of that barbarous nature, as they will for 3 or 4 hatchets sell the sonnes and daughters of their owne brethren and sisters, and for somewhat more euen their own daughters: heerof the Spaniards make great profit, for buying a maid of 12 or 13 yeeres for three or fower hatchets, they sell them againe at *Marguerita* in the west Indies for 50 and 100 pesoes, which is so many crownes[2].

The master of my ship *Io. Douglas* tooke one of the *Canoas* which came loden from thence with people to be sold, and the

1 We have little doubt that the place which Ralegh calls the port of Guiana is Santo Thomè. He does not mention in direct terms the settlement which Berreo had made as early as 1591; perhaps policy directed him to keep the existence of a Spanish settlement in Guiana a secret.

2 By means of the interlacing of rivers between the Barima, Guainia or Waini, the Morocco and Pomoroon, an active contraband trade was formerly carried on between the Dutch and the Spaniards, which is not yet quite extinct, though a more enlightened commercial policy has removed those enormous duties which encouraged its prosecution. At the early period to which Ralegh alludes the Caribs availed themselves of these communications to trade in Indian slaves. Francis Sparrey relates that he purchased for a common knife eight young females.

most of them escaped, yet of those hee brought, there was one as well fauored, and as well shaped as euer I saw anie in England, and afterward I sawe many of them, which but for their tawnie colour may bee compared to anie of *Europe*[1]. They also trade in those riuers for bread of *Cassaui*, of which they buy an hundred pound weight for a knife, and sell it at *Marguerita* for ten pesoes. They also recouer great store of cotten, brasill wood, and those beds which they call *Hamacas* or brasill beds[2], wherein in hot countries all the Spaniards vse to lie commonlie, and in no other, neither did we our selues while we were there: By means of which trades, for ransom of diuers of the *Guianians*,

[1] During our eight years' wandering among the tribes of Guiana who inhabit the vast regions from the coasts of the Atlantic to the interior, between the Cassiquiare and the upper Rio Trombetas, we have met with many an Indian female who in figure and comeliness might have vied with some of our European beauties. Although they are rather small in size, their hands and feet are generally exquisite, their ankles well-turned, and their waists, left to nature and not forced into an artificial shape by modern inventions, resemble the *beau ideal* of classical sculpture. Ralegh is not the only one profuse in praise of these tawny beauties: we have Ligon, who gives us a description of Yarico (*Yaricu* signifies a flower in the Macusi language), whose love and cruel fate kindled the poetic fire of Addison and gave rise to his pathetic tale of Inkle and Yarico. The early Spanish historians laud in unmeasured terms the beauty of the young Indian slave Doña Marina, who became the property of Alonso Hernandez de Puerto Carréro, and having learned the Spanish language rendered herself of great use to Cortez as interpreter during the conquest. (Ligon's History of Barbados, p. 54. Bernal Diaz, Historia de la Conquista, cap. 36. Prescott's Discovery of Mexico, vol. i. p. 268.)

[2] During the voyage of Alonzo de Ojéda and Americo Vespucci in 1498 we find already hammocks mentioned. They are woven upon handlooms, or in many instances they form merely a kind of network made of the fibres of the Ita palm (*Mauritia flexuosa*), silkgrass (*Bromelia*, spec.?) or cotton. They are used by all the Indian tribes, and upon the return of the first navigators of America they were introduced in lieu of the bulky cots on board of vessels. The Indian females are very expert in the manufacture of hammocks and cotton-cloth. We have met among the Pianoghottos and Drios, tribes who inhabit the regions between the sources of the Rio Trombetas, the Marowini and Corentyne, and who had never been in contact with Europeans, cotton-cloth woven for waist-laps merely in a primitive way on a hand-loom, of so fine a texture that they might have done honour to a European manufactory.

and for exchange of hatchets and kniues, *Berreo* recouered some store of gold plates, eagles of gold, and Images of men and diuers birds, and dispatched his Campmaster for Spaine with all that he had gathered, therewith to leuy soldiers, and by the shew therof to draw others to the loue of the enterprize: and hauing sent diuers Images as well of men as beasts, birds and fishes so curiouslie wrought in gold, doubted not but to perswade the king to yeeld to him some further helpe, especiallie for that this land hath neuer been sacked, the mines neuer wrought, and in the Indies their works were well spent, and the gold drawn out with great labor and charge: he also dispatched messengers to his son in *Nueuo reyno* to leuy all the forces he could, and to come down the riuer of *Orenoque* to *Emeria,* the prouince of *Carapana,* to meet him: he had also sent to *Sant Iago de Leon* on the coast of the *Caracas* to buy horses and mules.

After I had thus learned of his proceedings past and purposed: I told him that I had resolued to see *Guiana,* and that it was the end of my iourney, and the cause of my comming to *Trinedado,* as it was indeed, (and for that purpose I sent *Ia. Whiddon* the yeere before to get intelligence, with whom *Berreo* himselfe had speech at that time, and remembred how inquisitiue *Ia. Whiddon* was of his proceedings, and of the countrey of *Guiana*[1],) *Berreo* was striken into a great melancholie and

[1] It will be recollected by the readers of Southey's Life of Sir Walter Ralegh (Lives of the British Admirals, vol. iv.), that he doubts whether Berreo ever was a prisoner of Sir Walter Ralegh. Such an assertion is contradicted by this passage. Captain James Whiddon was then with Ralegh, and if it were possible that Ralegh could have been deceived in the man, Whiddon would have removed that mistake. Dr. Southey bases his assertion on the circumstance that neither Pedro Simon nor Oviedo y Baños make the slightest allusion to Ralegh. His voyage to Guiana was translated into Latin, German and Dutch; and Hondius, a well-known geographer of that period, constructed from Ralegh's and Keymis's relations a map of their journey. The intercourse then existing between the Austrian states, Holland, and Spain no doubt brought one of these translations, if not the original, to the knowledge of the Spaniards; and Ralegh's assertion of having made a man of Berreo's renown a prisoner would surely have found contradiction, had it not been an incontrovertible fact. We cannot conceive upon what grounds Dr. Southey

sadnes, and vsed all the arguments he could to disswade me, and also assured the gentlemen of my company that it would be labor lost: and that they should suffer many miseries if they proceeded: And first he deliuered that I could not enter anie of the riuers with any barke or pinace, nor hardly with anie ships bote, it was so low, sandie, and full of flats, and that his companies were daily grounded in their *Canoas* which drew but twelue inches water: he further saide that none of the countrey would come to speake with vs, but would all flie, and if we followed them to their dwellings, they would burne their owne townes, and besides that the way was long, the winter at hand, and that the riuers beginning once to swel, it was impossible to stem the currant, and that we could not in those smal botes by any means carry victuall for halfe the time, and that (which indeed most discouraged my company) the Kings and Lords of all the borders and of *Guiana* had decreed, that none of them should trade with any Christians for gold, bicause the same would be their owne ouerthrow, and that for the loue of gold the Christians meant to conquer and dispossesse them of all together.

Many and the most of these I found to be true, but yet I resoluing to make trial of all whatsoeuer hapned, directed Captaine *George Gifford* my Vice-admirall to take the *Lions whelp*, and Captaine *Calfield* his barke to turne to the eastward, against

considered himself justified in questioning the identity of Berreo. We must confess however that there is a great deal of confusion between the periods of Sir Walter Ralegh's arrival at Trinidad and that of the famed expedition of Domingo de Vera, which may have given rise to it. Fray Pedro Simon is, by his own showing, in error when he states that the expedition under De Vera left San Lucar on the 23rd of February, 1595. It is evident, from what he observes in the commencement of the tenth chapter (Noticia, vii.), that Berreo dispatched his campmaster only the very year in which further on he says the expedition left as early as February. (Noticia, vii. cap. 10, p. 596 *et seq.*) It is more than probable that De Vera sailed from San Lucar in 1596; and this agrees with Keymis's account, who observes, that during his expedition up the Orinoco in 1596, Berreo, who was then at Santo Thomè, expected daily his campmaster from Spain. The expedition under De Vera could not have arrived in 1595, as in that case they would have met Ralegh's ships at Trinidad. Caulin has merely copied his account of De Vera's expedition from Fray Simon.

the brize what they could possible, to recouer the mouth of a riuer called *Capuri*[1], whose entrance I had before sent Captaine *Whiddon* and *Io. Douglas* the master, to discouer, who founde some nine foote water or better vpon the flood, and fiue at lowe water, to whom I had giuen instructions that they shoulde ancor at the edge of the shold, and vpon the best of the flood to thrust ouer, which shold *Iohn Douglas* boyed and bekonned for them before: but they laboured in vain, for neither could they turne it vp altogither so farre to the east, neither did the flood continue so long, but the water fell ere they coulde haue passed the sands, as we after founde by a second experience: so as now we must either giue ouer our enterprize, or leauing our ships at aduenture 400 mile behind vs, to run vp in our ships botes, one barge, and two wherries, but being doubtfull how to carrie victuals for so long a time in such bables, or anie strength of men, especiallie for that *Berreo* assured vs that his sonne must be by that time come downe with manie soldiers, I sent away one *King* maister of the *Lions whelp* with his ships bote to trie another branch of a riuer in the bottome of the bay of *Guanipa*[2], which was called *Amana*, to prooue if there were water to be found for either of the small ships to enter: But when he came to the mouth of *Amana*[3], he found it as the rest, but staied not to dis-

[1] The river Capure has its origin in one of the numerous *lagunas* which exist between the branches or *bocas chicas*; it is however evident from what Ralegh observes hereafter, that he alludes here to the Caño Macareo. There is a communication by lateral branches between the Caños Vagre, Pedernales, Capure, Cucuina, and Macareo.

[2] The river Guanipa, which has its source in the small elevations or tableland (*Mesa*) of the same name, about twenty miles north-east of Pao, falls at the most southern point of the Golfo de Paria, or Triste (Golfo de la Balena or Golfo de las Perlas of Columbus and Ojedo) into a large bay which is protected by the island Cotoina. The river Guanipa has no communication with the Orinoco, nor with any of its numerous branches. The Caño Vagre, the most western branch of the delta, the Manamo (Amana of Ralegh) and the Pedernales disembogue into the same bay.

[3] The Boca Manamo, which, as already observed, falls into the great bay of Guanipa, is, next to the Macareo, the largest of the branches, and is considered to be one hundred and forty-five miles in length. A general description of the great river Orinoco and its delta has been given in the

couer it throughlie, bicause he was assured by an Indian his guide that the *Canibals* of *Guanipa* would assaile them with many *Canoas*, and that they shot poisonned arrowes, so as if he hasted not backe they should all be lost.

In the mean time fearing the worst I caused all the Carpenters we had to cut down a *Gallego* bote, which we meant to cast off, and to fit her with banks to row on, and in all things to prepare her the best they could, so as she might be brought to drawe but fiue foote, for so much we had on the bar of *Capuri* at lowe water: And doubting of *Kings* return I sent *Io. Douglas* againe in my long barge, as well to releeue him as also to make a perfect search in the bottom of that baie: For it hath beene held for infallible that whatsoeuer ship or bote shall fall therein, can neuer dessemboque againe, by reason of the violent currant which setteth into the said bay, as also for that the brize and easterlie wind bloweth directlie into the same, of which opinion I haue heard *Iohn Hampton* of *Plimmouth* one of the greatest experience of *England*, and diuers others besides that haue traded *Trinedado*[1].

I sent with *Iohn Douglas* an old *Cassique* of *Trinedado* for a Pilot, who tolde vs that we could not returne again by the bay or gulfe, but that he knew a by branch which ran within the land to the Eastward, and that he thought by it we might fall into *Capuri*, and so returne in fower daies: *Iohn Dowglas* searched those riuers, and found fower goodly entrances, whereof the least was as bigge as the *Thames* at *Wolwich*[2], but in the

Introduction; it remains however to be observed, that Ralegh gives to the Caño Manamo the name of a river, which enters the great laguna of Guanipa. The river Amana has its source in latitude 10° north, about fifteen miles to the north of Urica, and has no communication with the Orinoco or its branches.

[1] The currents of the ocean which set along the coast of Guiana in a west-north-west direction are powerfully increased by the fresh waters of the Bocas chicas, which with impetuosity sweep Punto Foleto, and render it almost impossible to reach the south-western point of Trinidad, where Ralegh's vessels were lying, from the Bay of Guanipa.

[2] The Bocas, of which John Douglas gives his report, are the Vagre, the small Caño Manamitos, the Manamo, and the Pedernales.

baie thitherward it was shole and but six foote water, so as we were now without hope of any ship or barke to passe ouer, and therefore resolued to go on with the botes, and the bottome of the *Gallego,* in which we thrust 60 men: In the *Lions whelps* bote and wherrie we carried 20. Captaine *Calfeild* in his wherrie carried ten more, and in my barge other ten, which made vp a hundred: we had no other meanes but to carrie victuall for a moneth in the same, and also to lodge therein as we could, and to boile and dresse our meat. Captaine *Gifford* had with him Master *Edw. Porter,* captaine *Eynos,* and eight more in his wherrie with all their victuall, weapons, and prouisions: Captaine *Calfield* had with him my cosen *Butshead Gorges* and eight more. In the galley, of gent. and officers my selfe had captaine *Thyn,* my cosen *Iohn Greenuile,* my nephew *Iohn Gilbert,* captaine *Whiddon,* captaine *Keymis, Edw. Hancocke,* captaine *Clarke,* lieutenant *Hewes, Tho. Vpton,* captaine *Facy, Ierome Ferrar, Antho. Wells, Will. Connock,* and about 50 more. We could not learne of *Berreo* any other waie to enter but in branches, so farre to the windeward as it was impossible for vs to recouer: for we had as much sea to crosse ouer in our wherries as betweene *Douer* and *Callys,* and in a great billow, the winde and currant being both very strong, so as we were driuen to go in those small botes directly before the winde into the bottome of the baie of *Guanipa,* and from thence to enter the mouth of some one of those riuers, which *Io. Dowglas* had last discouered[1], and had with vs for Pilote an *Indian* of *Barema,* a

[1] At the bottom of the bay disembogues the Caño Vagre, a branch of the Manamo, which flows off from the Manamo about fifteen miles higher up. The pilots, who are well acquainted with this labyrinth of islands and channels, select generally, during the summer or dry season, the Caños Pedernales or Manamo, for going from Trinidad to Angostura, if their vessels are of no greater burthen than twenty-five or thirty tons. During the rainy season, when the currents run with a swiftness of four or five miles an hour, it takes often twenty days to reach San Rafael de Barrancas, while the same distance may be accomplished with the current in four days; in returning, however, they give the preference to the Brazo Ma-

riuer to the south of *Orenoque,* betweene that and *Amazones,* whose *Canoas* we had formerlie taken as he was going from the said *Barema,* laden with *Cassaui* bread to sell at *Marguerita*: this *Arwacan* promised to bring me into the great riuer of *Orenoque,* but indeed of that which we entred he was vtterly ignorant, for he had not seene it in twelue yeeres before, at which time he was very yoong, and of no iudgement, and if God had not sent vs another helpe, we might haue wandred a whole yeere in that laborinth of riuers, ere we had found any way, either out or in, especiallie after we were past the ebbing and flowing, which was in fower daies: for I know all the earth doth not yeeld the like confluence of streames and branches, the one crossing the other so many times, and all so faire and large, and so like one to another, as no man can tell which to take: and if we went by the Sun or compasse hoping thereby to go directly one way or other, yet that waie we were also caried in a circle amongst multitudes of Ilands, and euery Iland so bordered with high trees, as no man could see any further than the bredth of the riuer, or length of the breach[1]: But this it chanced that entring into a

careo, the mouth of which lies south-east from the Soldiers' Passage, or Punto Icacos, which with the trade-wind enables the vessel to fetch the island of Trinidad. This is the branch which Ralegh calls erroneously the Capuri; there is likewise a Boca Capure, but as it lies south-west by west from Punto Icacos, it would be impossible to fetch it with the prevailing trade-wind; it is therefore evident that Ralegh means the Boca Macarco. The great entrance to the Orinoco (Boca de Navios) is sometimes called East Capure in old maps of Ralegh's period. The Macareo is considered to be one hundred and fifty miles in length, the Manamo one hundred and forty-five miles; they possess respectively a depth of from twelve to fifteen feet.

[1] The navigation of these branches is not without danger, and it frequently occurs that even the Indian pilots get bewildered. In such a case they follow the current, and having reached the gulf, enter one of the branches well known to them. In consequence of the difficulties connected with the navigation, and the danger of the climate, the sailors are in the habit of repeating the following lines:—

> "Quien se va à Orinoco
> Si no se muere, se volver à loco."

riuer, (which bicause it had no name we called the riuer of the *Red crosse*[1], our selues being the first *Christians* that euer came therein:) the 22 of *May* as we were rowing vp the same, we espied a smal *Canoa* with three *Indians*, which (by the swiftnes of my barge, rowing with eight oares) I ouertooke ere they could crosse the riuer, the rest of the people on the banks shadowed vnder the thicke wood gazed on with a doubtfull conceit what might befall those three which we had taken: But when they perceiued that we offred them no violence, neither entred their *Canoa* with any of ours, nor tooke out of the *Canoa* any of theirs, they then began to shew themselues on the banks side, and offred to traffique with vs for such things as they had, and as we drewe neere they all staide, and we came with our barge to the mouth of a little creeke which came from their towne into the great riuer.

As we abode there a while, our Indian Pilot called *Ferdinando* would needs go ashore to their village to fetch some fruites, and to drinke of their artificiall wines, and also to see the place, and to know the Lord of it against another time, and tooke with him a brother of his which he had with him in the iourney: when they came to the village of these people, the Lord of the Iland offred to lay hands on them, purposing to haue slaine them both, yeelding for reason that this Indian of ours had brought a strange nation into their territorie to spoyle and destroy them: But the Pilot being quicke and of a disposed body slipt their fingers, and ran into the woods, and his brother being the better footman of the two, recouered the creekes mouth, where we staied in our barge, crying out that his brother was slaine, with that we set hands on one of them that was next vs, a very old man, and brought him into the barge, assuring him that if we had not our Pilot againe, we would presently cut off his head. This old man being resolued that he should paie the losse of the

[1] It becomes more evident from Francis Sparrey's account (Purchas, iv. chap. 11) that it was the Caño Manamo, before it sends off the Caño Vagre, which Ralegh called the river of "the Red Crosse."

other, cried out to those in the woods to saue *Ferdinando* our Pilot, but they followed him notwithstanding, and hunted after him vpon the foote with their Deere dogs[1], and with so maine a crie that all the woods eckoed with the shoute they made, but at last this poore chased Indian recouered the riuer side, and got vpon a tree, and as we were coasting, leaped down and swam to the barge halfe dead with feare; but our good hap was, that we kept the other old Indian, which we handfasted to redeeme our Pilot withall, for being naturall of those riuers, we assured our selues he knew the way better than any stranger could, and indeed, but for this chance I thinke we had neuer founde the way either to *Guiana*, or backe to our ships: for *Ferdinando* after a few daies knew nothing at all, nor which way to turne, yea and many times the old man himselfe was in great doubt which riuer to take. Those people which dwell in these broken Ilands and drowned lands are generally called *Tiuitiuas*, there are of them two sorts, the one called *Ciawani*, and the other *Waraweete*.

The great riuer of *Orenoque* or *Baraquan* hath nine branches which fall out on the north side of his owne maine mouth: on the south side it hath seuen other fallings into the sea, so it desemboketh by 16 armes in al, betweene Ilands and broken ground, but the Ilands are verie great, manie of them as bigge as the Isle of *Wight* and bigger, and many lesse: from the first branch on the north to the last of the south it is at lest

[1] The Indian dogs hunt usually in full cry; they are trained to seize the game, and to stay its flight until the huntsman comes up to kill it. The Indian sets a great value on a good hunting-dog, and some of the tribes in the interior are famed for breeding them. We have known as much as fifteen to sixteen pounds sterling to have been paid by colonists for a good Indian hunting-dog. They are frequently trained to hunt only one peculiar kind of game, as deer, Peccaries (*Dicotyles torquatus*, F. Cuv.), Labas (*Cœlagenus subniger*, Desm.), &c.; others pursue several kinds indiscriminately: in the latter instance the Indian knows, by the peculiar barking of the dog when in chase, what he is hunting. The best dogs for hunting the Jaguar or tiger of America come from the Orinoco.

100 leagues, so as the riuers mouth is no lesse than 300 miles wide at his entrance into the sea, which I take to be farre bigger than that of *Amazones*: al those that inhabite in the mouth of this riuer vpon the seuerall north branches are these *Tiuitiuas*, of which there are two chiefe Lords which haue continuall warres one with the other: the Ilands which lie on the right hand are called *Pallamos*, and the land on the left *Hororotomaka*, and the riuer by which *Iohn Dowglas* returned within the land from *Amana* to *Capuri*, they call *Macuri*.

These *Tiuitiuas*[1] are a verie goodlie people and verie valiant, and haue the most manlie speech and most deliberate that euer

[1] Ralegh alludes here to the Uaraus or Waraus, of whom he tells us in the preceding page, that there are two sorts, the one called Ciawani and the other Waraweete. They are the Guaraunos or Guaraunu of the Spanish historians, an Indian tribe who principally inhabit the delta of the Orinoco, and the swampy coast between the rivers Pomeroon and Barima. The low land extends from the coast twenty to thirty miles into the interior, and is inundated during eight months out of twelve. Parallel to the coast rise small elevations or sand-reefs, some ten, some fifteen or even thirty feet high, consisting of a clayey soil, strongly mixed with sand, vegetable matter and iron ore (chiefly bog iron). Those hills are selected by the Waraus and Arawaaks as dwelling-places, the more so since the soil possesses great fertility. The inundated lands are thickly covered with Ita-trees (*Mauritia flexuosa*, Linn.), one of the most graceful palms, which furnishes to the Indian "*victum et amictum*," or rather bread and wine. The fibres of the young leaves are woven into hammocks, rŏpes and baskets; the trunk encloses a pith, which, like that of the *Sagus farinifera*, is converted into flour, or Aru, of which the Waraus bake a kind of bread, called Yaruma, and at a certain period of the year the trunk is tapped and yields a fluid possessing much saccharine matter, and which they ferment and use as a beverage. There are numerous other uses to which the Indians apply it, from which circumstance Father Gumilla called it "arbol de la vida," the tree of life.

The Waraus are to this day the most famous boat-builders, and furnish nearly the whole colony of Demerara with canoes. These are made of cedar (*Cedrela odorata*, Linn.) or of a tree called Bisci or Bisi, and are sometimes fifty feet in length and five to six feet broad. The Bisci grows generally on some of the higher land, surrounded with swamps and Ita palms: if the Warau Indian has singled out a tree from which he promises himself a good canoe, he constructs in the neighbourhood his temporary dwelling. For this purpose a spot where the Ita palm grows in thick clusters is

I heard of what nation soeuer. In the summer they haue houses on the ground as in other places: In the winter they dwell vpon the trees, where they build very artificiall townes and villages, as it is written in the Spanish storie of the *West Indies*, that those people do in the low lands neere the gulfe of *Vraba*: for betweene *May* and *September* the riuer of *Orenoke* riseth thirtie foote vpright, and then are those Ilands ouerflowen twentie foote high aboue the leuell of the ground, sauing some few raised grounds in the middle of them: and for this cause they are en-

selected, and the palm-trees are felled about four or five feet above the ground. In the neighbourhood of the Ita grows usually another graceful palm, the Manicole or Manica (*Euterpe*, species?), the slender trunk of which is split into laths, which serve to construct his floor. The Trouli (*Manicaria saccharifera*, Gaertn.), another tree of that family, which grows in groups, furnishes excellent thatch; and thus his hut is finished in a comparatively short time, and lasts the Indian for a longer period than he requires to form his canoe or gather the Ita starch. Fires are indispensable to the Indian by day and night; every one has under his hammock a fire burning during night, which he keeps up with great attention. To prevent therefore the floor being burnt through, it is covered with lumps of clay, on which the fire is made. During the period that the expedition, under the command of the author of these remarks, sojourned on the delta of the Orinoco, and which comprised some months of the rainy season, we have frequently seen houses constructed in the mode just described, but not a single instance wherein, as observed by Ralegh, they dwelt on trees. We can well suppose that the numerous fires which were made in each hut, and the reflexion of which was the stronger in consequence of the stream of vapour around the summit of trees in those moist regions, illuminated at night the adjacent trees; but the fire itself was scarcely ever made on the top of a tree. The inundation rises at the delta seldom higher than three or four feet above the banks of the rivers; and if the immediate neighbourhood of the sea and the level nature of the land be considered, this is an enormous rise. It is different in the interior, where local circumstances combine to raise the river from twenty-five to thirty-five, and as is asserted even to fifty feet above its general level. We do not deny that, in order to escape the attacks of the mosquitos, the Indian sometimes suspends his hammock from the tops of trees, and we have imitated their example and found ourselves less annoyed; but on such occasions no fires are made, nor could be made, under the hammock.

The Waraus are of somewhat darker complexion than the Caribs or Carabisi and Arawaaks. They are industrious, but most negligent in their

forced to liue in this maner. They neuer eate of anie thing that is set or sowen, and as at home they vse neither planting nor other manurance, so when they com abroad they refuse to feede of ought, but of that which nature without labor bringeth foorth. They vse the tops of *Palmitos* for bread[1], and kil Deere, fish and porks for the rest of their sustenance, they haue also manie sorts of fruits that grow in the woods, and great varietie of birds and foule.

And if to speake of them were not tedious and vulgare, surely

persons and villages: indeed the dirtiness of a Warau is proverbial among the other Indians. It appears almost as if their feet were peculiarly formed, or rather their toes spread out in such a manner as to enable them to walk on the muddy shores where another person would sink. Their language differs radically from that of the surrounding tribes, and is perfectly intelligible to the Arawaaks and Carib tribes. The Warau is despised by the other Indian tribes in consequence of his negligent habits. He smears his body with oil, and as he seldom takes the trouble to clean it, and his colour is besides of a darker hue, it is sometimes difficult, if it were not for his straight hair, to distinguish him from a negro. Their children are so much neglected that their fingers and toes are frequently destroyed by chigoes and their bodies crippled. (Journal of the Royal Geogr. Society, vol. xii. p. 175.)

[1] The foliage of the palm-trees, "the princes of the vegetable world," ends above in a green pyramidal spire, which contains numerous young leaves closely wrapped one over the other. The outer coating of this spire, which is coarse, splits, and adopting a nearly horizontal position, becomes the young leaf. The next in turn is still of a firm consistency and of a more beautiful green than the succeeding coating, while the thickness and vivid colour decrease until it reaches the third or fourth folding, when it becomes of a bright lemon colour, white within, but still of a tough consistence. On removing several of these exfoliations, the delicate Mountain-cabbage or Palmetto lies in many thin snow-white flakes in the middle. These flakes are the germs of succeeding leaves, and consequently the palm being deprived of them dies, reproduction being stayed. In taste it resembles an almond, and contains an oily substance in cell-like reservoirs. It is boiled and considered a great delicacy; it is likewise prepared as a salad, or eaten in a raw state. Necessity has forced us, during our exploring expeditions in Guiana, to make the Mountain-cabbage for weeks our chief sustenance; and at a period when, deprived of salt, we were obliged to eat it raw, we found it in that state highly injurious to our digestive organs.

we sawe in those passages of very rare colours and forms, not else where to be found, for as much as I haue either seen or read. Of these people those that dwell vpon the branches of *Orenoque* called *Capuri* and *Macureo*, are for the most part Carpenters of *Canoas*, for they make the most and fairest houses, and sell them into *Guiana* for gold, and into *Trinedado* for *Tobacco*, in the excessiue taking whereof, they exceede all nations, and notwithstanding the moistnes of the aire in which they liue, the hardnes of their diet, and the great labors they suffer to hunt, fish, and foule for their liuing, in all my life either in the Indies or in Europe did I neuer behold a more goodlie or better fauoured people, or a more manlie. They were woont to make warre vpon all nations, and especiallie on the *Canibals*, so as none durst without a good strength trade by those riuers, but of late they are at peace with their neighbors, all holding the *Spaniards* for a common enimie. When their commanders die, they vse great lamentation[1], and when they thinke the flesh of their bodies is putrified, and fallen from the bones, then they take vp the carcase againe, and hang it in the *Casiquies* house that died, and decke his skull with feathers of all colours, and hang all his gold plates about the bones of his armes, thighes, and legges. Those nations which are called *Arwacas*[2] which dwell on the south of

[1] The custom of bewailing the dead with great lamentations is more followed among the Waraus than other tribes. Their dead are usually buried in the ground under the hut which they inhabited; and if the deceased be a great man, the hut is burnt down over the grave; otherwise the nearest relations kindle a fire over the spot, which they keep burning day and night: the chief mourner slings his or her hammock over the grave, and does not leave it for days.

[2] The Arawaaks live frequently intermixed with the Waraus, otherwise they inhabit to this day the rivers on the southern bank of the Orinoco. They call themselves Arua or Aruwa, the name of the American tiger or jaguar (*Felis onza*, Linn.) in their language. The early Dutch colonists cultivated their goodwill, and they have always been attached to them since the settlement of Essequibo. The Arawaak is fairer than either the Carib or Warau, and the females, taken as a tribe, are the handsomest of all the Guianians we have met with.

Orenoque, (of which place and nation our Indian Pilot was) are dispersed in manie other places, and do vse to beate the bones of their Lords into powder, and their wiues and friends drinke it all in their seuerall sorts of drinks.

After we departed from the port of these *Ciawani*, we passed vp the riuer with the flood, and ancored the ebbe, and in this sort we went onward. The third daie that we entred the riuer our *Galley* came on ground, and stuck so fast, as we thought that euen there our discouery had ended, and that we must haue left 60 of our men to haue inhabited like rookes vpon trees with those nations: but the next morning, after we had cast out all her ballast, with tugging and hawling to and fro, we got her afloate, and went on: At fower daies ende wee fell into as goodlie a riuer as euer I beheld, which was called the great *Amana*, which ran more directlie without windings and turnings than the other. But soone after the flood of the sea left vs, and we enforced either by maine strength to row against a violent currant, or to returne as wise as we went out, we had then no shift but to perswade the companies that it was but two or three daies worke, and therfore desired them to take paines, euery gentleman and others taking their turns to row, and to spell one the other at the howers end. Euerie daie we passed by goodlie branches of riuers, some falling from the west, others from the east into *Amana*, but those I leaue to the description in the *Chart* of discouerie, where euerie one shall be named with his rising and descent. When three daies more were ouergone, our companies began to despaire, the weather being extreame hot, the riuer bordered with verie high trees that kept away the aire, and the currant against vs euery daie stronger than other: But we euermore commanded our Pilots to promise an end the next daie, and vsed it so long as we were driuen to assure them from fower reaches of the riuer to three, and so to two, and so to the next reach: but so long we laboured as many daies were spent, and so driuen to draw our selues to harder allowance, our bread euen at the last, and no drinke at all: and our men and our selues so wearied and scorched, and doubtfull withall whether we should euer performe it or no, the heat encreasing as we drew towards the line; for wee were now in fiue degrees[1].

The farther we went on (our victuall decreasing and the aire breeding great faintnes) we grew weaker and weaker when we had most need of strength and abilitie, for howerlie the riuer ran more violently than other against vs, and the barge, wherries, and ships bote of Captaine *Gifford,* and Captaine *Calfield,* had spent all their prouisions, so as wee were brought into despaire and discomfort, had we not perswaded all the companie that it was but onlie one daies worke more to attaine the lande where we should be releeued of all we wanted, and if we returned that we were sure to starue by the way, and that the worlde would also laugh vs to scorne. On the banks of these riuers were diuers sorts of fruits good to eate, flowers and trees of that varietie as were sufficient to make ten volumes of herbals, we releeued our selues manie times with the fruits of the countrey, and somtimes with foule and fish: we sawe birds of all colours, some carnation, some crimson, orenge tawny, purple, greene, watched, and of all other sorts both simple and mixt, as it was vnto vs a great good passing of the time to beholde them, besides the reliefe we found by killing some store of them with our fouling peeces, without which, hauing little or no bread and lesse drink, but onely the thick and troubled water of the riuer, we had been in a very hard case[2].

[1] This was a great mistake of Ralegh, and does not argue much for the astronomical skill of his observers and sailing-master. In lieu of being in 5°, he was then in about 9° north of the equator. The mouth of the Caroni was then supposed to be in latitude 4° north instead of 8° 8′ north.

[2] At the season when the fruit of the Manicole palm (*Euterpe*, spec.?) is ripe, the flocks of maccaws, parrots, marudis and powis surpass all description. The blue and yellow Maccaws (*Macrocercus Araraunа,* Auct.) are at that period the most numerous; and as they form an excellent soup, resembling hare-soup in taste, they were much sought after by us. The Powis (*Crax alector,* Linn.) is as large as a turkey, with more of game flavour. The Marudi (*Penelope cristata,* Gmel.) may be compared to a pheasant. But the most delicious eating is afforded by the Vicissi and whistling ducks

Our old Pilot of the *Ciawani* (whom, as I said before, we tooke to redeeme *Ferdinando*,) told vs, that if we would enter a branch of a riuer on the right hand with our barge and wherries, and leaue the *Galley* at ancor the while in the great riuer, he would bring vs to a towne of the *Arwacas* where we should find store of bread, hens[1], fish, and of the countrey wine, and perswaded vs that departing from the *Galley* at noone, we might returne ere night: I was very glad to heare this speech, and presently tooke my barge, with eight musketiers, Captain *Giffords* wherrie, with himselfe and foure musketiers, and Captaine *Calfield* whith his wherrie and as manie, and so we entred the mouth of this riuer, and bicause we were perswaded that it was so neere, we tooke no victuall with vs at all: when we had rowed three howres, we maruelled we sawe no signe of any dwelling, and asked the Pilot where the town was, he told vs a little farther: after three howers more the *Sun* being almost set, we

(*Dendrocygna viduata* and *D. autumnalis*), which visit the inundated savannahs in large numbers. The musk duck or Hefa (*Cairina moshata*, Flem.) is found on the trees bordering the river, and is in its wild state much superior to the domesticated musk duck, which is called improperly Muscovy. They make their nests on trees and rocks, and when the young are fledged the parent seizes the duckling with the bill by the neck, and carries it to the water below, where they are as nimble and dive with as much skill as if they had been reared on the surface of that element. We have never succeeded in discovering a nest among the reeds and rushes, and believe that they always build their nests on trees and sometimes on rocks, where we have found them ourselves. It may be conjectured how numerous the Vicissis and whistling ducks are during the season, when we observe that a single huntsman brought sometimes half a hundred as the result of a morning's excursion.

[1] We have met our domesticated hens from one end of Guiana to the other. The Indian rears poultry as a curiosity; he neither uses their eggs nor does he eat their meat. Our domestic fowls have been introduced by Europeans. When Pizarro anchored on the coast of Tumbez, he sent to king Guaynacapa a present of two hogs, four hens and a cock, which were regarded with the greatest astonishment. We have frequently met in Indian villages, deep in the interior of Guiana, a purely white breed of fowls. The Indian cares less for hens, but sets great value upon the cocks, the crowing of which (called tétong in the Macusi language) has taught him to judge of the time of the night.

began to suspect that he led vs that waie to betraie vs, for he confessed that those Spaniards which fled from *Trinedado,* and also those that remained with *Carapana*[1] in *Emeria,* were ioyned togither in some village vpon that riuer. But when it grew towardes night, and we demaunding where the place was, he tolde vs but fower reaches more: when we had rowed fower and fower, we saw no signe, and our poore water men euen hart broken, and tired, were ready to giue vp the ghost; for we had now come from the *Galley* neer forty miles.

At the last we determined to hang the Pilot, and if we had well knowen the way backe againe by night, he had surely gone, but our owne necessities pleaded sufficiently for his safetie: for it was as darke as pitch, and the river began so to narrow it selfe, and the trees to hang ouer from side to side, as we were driuen with arming swordes to cut a passage thorow those branches that couered the water. We were very desirous to finde this towne hoping of a feast, bicause we made but a short breakfast aboord the *Galley* in the morning, and it was now eight a clock at night, and our stomacks began to gnaw apace: but whether it was best to returne or go on, we began to doubt, suspecting treason in the Pilot more and more: but the poore olde Indian euer assured vs that it was but a little farther, and but this one turning, and that turning, and at last about one a clocke after midnight we saw a light, and rowing towards it, we heard the dogs of the village[2]. When wee landed we found few people, for the Lord

[1] The whole coast of Guiana between the Amazon and the Orinoco was called during the seventeenth and eighteenth centuries Caribania, or the Wild Coast. It is supposed that this region received the former name from its being the chief residence of the Caribs. (Hartsinck, Beschryving van Guiana: Amsterdam, 1770, vol. i. p. 1.) The letters *p* and *b* being frequently confounded by the Indians, it may have been changed into Carapana, or, what is more probable, Carapana into Caribania.

[2] It is a usual custom with the Indian to count distances according to reaches or hooks (Tesakung in Macusi). We have been frequently in a situation similar to that which is here so strikingly described by Ralegh, when, tired out by fatigue, we thought the last reach was never to come. It required then every encouragement to induce the worn-out crew to persist

of that place was gone with diuers *Canoas* aboue 400 miles of, vpon a iourney towards the head of *Orenoque* to trade for gold, and to buy women of the *Canibals*, who afterward vnfortunatly passed by vs as we rode at an ancor in the port of *Morequito* in the dark of night, and yet came so neer vs, as his *Canoas* grated against our barges: he left one of his companie at the port of *Morequito*, by whom we vnderstood that he had brought thirty yoong woomen, diuers plates of gold, and had great store of fine peeces of cotton cloth, and cotton beds. In his house we had good store of bread, fish, hens, and Indian drinke, and so rested that night, and in the morning after we had traded with such of his people as came down, we returned towards our *Galley*, and brought with vs some quantity of bread, fish, and hens.

On both sides of this riuer, we passed the most beautifull countrie that euer mine eies beheld: and whereas all that we had seen before was nothing but woods, prickles, bushes, and thornes, heere we beheld plaines of twenty miles in length, the grasse short and greene, and in diuers parts groues of trees by themselues, as if they had been by all the art and labour in the world so made of purpose: and stil as we rowed, the Deere came downe feeding by the waters side, as if they had beene vsed to a keepers call. Vpon this riuer there were great store of fowle, and of many sorts: we saw in it diuers sorts of strange fishes, and of maruellous bignes, but for *Lagartos* it exceeded, for there were thousands of those vglie serpents[1], and the people call it for

in paddling, when ultimately the barking of the dogs announced to our joy that we were approaching the desired spot.

[1] The Alligator (*Crocodilus sclerops*) and Cayman (*Crocodilus acutus*, Cuv.) are very numerous in the Orinoco. The former seldom reaches a greater length than six or eight feet, and does not prove dangerous to man. It is however otherwise with the latter, which is said to reach sometimes twenty-five feet in length. We have seen the skeleton of a Cayman which we found lying on the banks of the Rio Negro, twenty feet long. The largest animal of that description which we measured in the river Berbice was sixteen feet. The number of Indians along the banks of the Rio Orinoco, the Rio Negro, and other rivers in Guiana, who fall annually a prey to these monsters is very considerable.

the abundance of them the riuer of *Lagartos,* in their language. I had a *Negro* a very proper yoong fellow, that leaping out of the *Galley* to swim in the mouth of this riuer, was in all our sights taken and deuoured with one of those *Lagartos.* In the mean while our companies in the *Galley* thought we had beene all lost, (for we promised to returne before night) and sent the *Lions Whelps* ships bote with Captaine *Whiddon* to follow vs vp the riuer, but the next day after we had rowed vp and downe some fower score miles, we returned, and went on our way, vp the great riuer, and when we were euen at the last cast for want of victuals, Captaine *Gifford* being before the *Galley,* and the rest of the botes, seeking out some place to land vpon the banks to make fire, espied fower *Canoas* comming downe the riuer, and with no small ioy caused his men to trie the vttermost of their strengths, and after a while two of the 4 gaue ouer, and ran themselues ashore, euery man betaking himselfe to the fastnes of the woods, the two other lesser got away, while he landed to lay hold on these, and so turned into some by-creeke, we knew not whither: those *Canoas* that were taken were loden with bread, and were bound for *Marguerita* in the west Indies, which those Indians (called *Arwacas*) purposed to carrie thither for exchange: But in the lesser, there were three Spaniards, who hauing heard of the defeat of their gouernour in *Trinedado,* and that we purposed to enter *Guiana,* came away in those *Canoas*: one of them was a *Cauallero,* as the Captaine of the *Arwacas* after told vs, another a soldier, and the third a refiner.

In the meane time, nothing on the earth could haue been more welcome to vs next vnto gold, then the great store of very excellent bread which we found in these *Canoas,* for now our men cried, let vs go on, we care not how farre. After that Captaine *Gifford* had brought the two *Canoas* to the *Galley,* I tooke my barge, and went to the banks side with a dozen shot, where the *Canoas* first ran themselues ashore, and landed there, sending out Captaine *Gifford* and Captaine *Thyn* on one hand, and Captaine *Calfield* on the other, to follow those that were fled into the woods, and as I was creeping thorow the bushes, I saw an Indian basket hidden, which was the refiners basket, for I found in it, his quicksiluer, saltpeter, and diuers things for the triall of mettals, and also the dust of such ore as he had refined, but in those *Canoas* which escaped there was a good quantity of ore and gold. I then landed more men, and offered 500 pound to what soldier soeuer could take one of those 3 Spaniards that we thought were landed. But our labours were in vaine in that behalfe, for they put themselues into one of the small *Canoas*: and so while the greater *Canoas* were in taking, they escaped: but seeking after the Spaniards, we found the *Arwacas* hidden in the woods which were pilots for the Spaniards, and rowed their *Canoas*: of which I kept the chiefest for a Pilot, and carried him with me to *Guiana*, by whom I vnderstood, where and in what countries the Spaniards had labored for gold, though I made not the same knowen to all: for when the springs began to breake, and the riuers to raise themselues so suddenly as by no meanes we could abide the digging of anie mine, especially for that the richest are defended with rocks of hard stone, which we call the *White spar*, and that it required both time, men, and instruments fit for such a worke, I thought it best not to houer thereabouts, least if the same had been perceiued by the company, there would haue bin by this time many barks and ships set out, and perchance other nations would also haue gotten of ours for Pilots, so as both our selues might haue been preuented, and all our care taken for good vsage of the people been vtterly lost, by those that onely respect present profit, and such violence or insolence offered, as the nations which are borderers would haue changed their desire of our loue and defence, into hatred and violence. And for any longer stay to haue brought a more quantity (which I heare hath bin often obiected) whosoeuer had seene or prooued the fury of that riuer after it began to arise, and had been a moneth and od daies as we were from hearing ought from our ships, leauing them meanly mand, aboue 400 miles off, would perchance haue turned somewhat sooner than we did, if all the mountaines had been gold, or rich stones: And to say the truth all the branches and small riuers which fell into *Orenoque* were raised with such speed, as if wee waded them ouer the shooes in the morning outward, we were couered to the shoulders homewarde the very same daie[1]: and to stay to dig out gold with our nailes, had been *Opus laboris*, but not *Ingenij*: such a quantitie as would haue serued our turnes we could not haue had, but a discouery of the mines to our infinite disaduantage we had made, and that could haue been the best profit of farther search or stay; for those mines are not easily broken, nor opened in haste, and I could haue returned a good quantity of gold readie cast, if I had not shot at another marke, than present profit.

This *Arwacan* Pilot with the rest, feared that we would haue eaten them, or otherwise haue put them to some cruell death, for the Spaniards to the end that none of the people in the passage towards *Guiana* or in *Guiana* it selfe might come to speech with vs, perswaded all the nations, that we were men eaters, and *Canibals*: but when the poore men and women had seen vs, and

[1] The rising of the rivers in the interior of Guiana is sometimes so uncommonly sudden, that, as described by Ralegh, "if we waded them over the shoes in the morning outward, we were covered to the shoulders homeward." While ascending the river Rupununi in 1843 with the Boundary expedition, during the rainy season, we had encamped near the great cataract of that river; and while the crew were loading the canoes we ascended a small elevation, and, looking southward, saw the flood at a distance of a mile or two come rushing over the savannahs. We shall never forget that sight; there was something peculiar in seeing so great a mass of water, which threatened us with imminent danger. We hastened back to push our boats in the middle of the river, and profited by the sudden rise of ten feet and more to overcome the difficulty which the cataract otherwise would have offered to us. We were now able to row over the savannahs in a straight direction, avoiding the serpentine course of the river and its increased current. The expanse of water resembled an extensive lake. The snow-white Egrette in great numbers, the American stork, the stately Jabiru, cormorants, and large flocks of spurwing plovers, enlivened the surface above, while the tops of trees, granite blocks clothed in tropical vegetation, and here and there a small spot of elevated ground, alone remained visible.

that we gaue them meate, and to euerie one some thing or other, which was rare and strange to them, they began to conceiue the deceit and purpose of the *Spaniards*, who indeed (as they confessed) tooke from them both their wiues, and daughters daily, and vsed them for the satisfying of their owne lusts, especially such as they tooke in this maner by strength. But I protest before the maiestie of the liuing God, that I neither know nor beleeue, that any of our companie one or other, by violence or otherwise, euer knew any of their women, and yet we saw many hundreds, and had many in our power, and of those very yoong, and excellently fauored which came among vs without deceit, starke naked.

Nothing got vs more loue among them then this vsage, for I suffred not anie man to take from anie of the nations so much as a *Pina*, or a *Potato* roote, without giuing them contentment, nor any man so much as to offer to touch any of their wiues or daughters: which course, so contrarie to the Spaniards (who tyrannize ouer them in all things) drew them to admire hir Maiestie, whose commandement I told them it was, and also woonderfully to honour our nation. But I confesse it was a very impatient worke to keepe the meaner sort from spoile and stealing, when we came to their houses, which bicause in all I could not preuent, I caused my Indian interpreter at euery place when we departed, to know of the losse or wrong done, and if ought were stolen or taken by violence, either the same was restored, and the party punished in their sight, or els it was paid for to their vttermost demand. They also much woondred at vs, after they heard that we had slain the Spaniards at *Trinedado*, for they were before resolued, that no nation of *Christians* durst abide their presence, and they woondred more when I had made them know of the great ouerthrow that hir Maiesties army and flecte had giuen them of late yeers in their owne countries.

After we had taken in this supplie of bread, with diuers baskets of rootes which were excellent meate[1], I gaue one of the

[1] The root of the Cassava or Cassada (*Manihot utilissima*, Pohl.) forms

Canoas to the *Arwacas,* which belonged to the Spaniards that were escaped, and when I had dismissed all but the Captaine (who by the *Spaniards* was christened *Martin*) I sent backe in the same *Canoa* the old *Ciawan,* and *Ferdinando* my first Pilot, and gaue them both such things as they desired, with sufficient victuall to carie them back, and by them wrote a letter to the ships, which they promised to deliuer, and performed it, and then I went, on with my new hired Pilot *Martyn* the *Arwacan*: but the next or second day after, we came aground againe with our galley, and were like to cast hir away, with all our victuall and prouision, and so lay on the sand one whole night, and were farre more in despaire at this time to free hir then before, bicause we had no tide of flood to helpe vs, and therfore feared that all our hopes would haue ended in mishaps: but we fastened an ankor vpon the land, and with maine strength drew hir off: and so the 15 day we discouered a farre off the mountaines of *Guiana*[1] to our great ioy, and towards the euening had a slent of a northerly winde that blew very strong, which brought vs in sight of the great riuer of *Orenoque,* out of which this riuer descended wherein we were: we descried a farre off three other *Canoas* as far as we could discerne them, after whom we hastened with our barge and wherries, but two of them passed out

among all Indian tribes in Guiana the chief supply of food. It is a remarkable fact, that this root, which affords nourishment to millions in Guiana, Brazil and Venezuela, forms in its natural state a dangerous poison, which however appears to be so volatile, that by pressing the juice out and exposing the scraped root to the fire the latter loses this dangerous quality. We are nevertheless of opinion that it is unwholesome, and as it constitutes the principal article of food of the Indians, we may account it among those causes which undermine health and contribute to an early death. It exercises a very injurious effect upon the teeth, as we know by experience.

The Indians cultivate Yams (*Dioscorea sativa,* and *D. alata,* Linn.), Batatas or sweet potatoes (*Batatas edulis*, Chois.), Taniers (*Caladium sagittæfolium,* Vent.), and Eddas (*C. esculentum,* Vent.), in their provision-grounds, the roots of which plants are all nutritive and wholesome.

[1] These were probably the Sierra or mountains of Imataca, perhaps the peaks of Peluca and Paisapa, which are from sixteen hundred to two thousand feet high.

of sight, and the third entred vp the great riuer, on the right hand to the westward, and there staied out of sight, thinking that we meant to take the way eastward towards the prouince of *Carapana*, for that way the Spaniards keepe, not daring to go vpwards to *Guiana*, the people in those parts being all their enimies, and those in the *Canoas* thought vs to haue beene those Spaniards that were fled from *Trinedado*, and had escaped killing: and when we came so farre downe as the opening of that branch into which they slipped, being neere them with our barge and wherries, we made after them, and ere they could land, came within call, and by our interpreter tolde them what we were, wherewith they came backe willingly aboord vs: and of such fish and *Tortugas* egges as they had gathered, they gaue vs, and promised in the morning to bring the Lord of that part with them, and to do vs all other seruices they could.

That night we came to an ankor at the parting of three goodlie riuers[1] (the one was the riuer of *Amana* by which we came from the north, and ran athwart towards the south, the other two were of *Orenoque* which crossed from the west and ran to the sea towards the east) and landed vpon a faire sand, where we found thousands of *Tortugas* egges[2], which are very whol-

[1] It appears that Ralegh anchored to the east of the spot where San Rafael de Barrancas is now situated. The bed of the river is here divided by several islands, namely—nearest to the southern or right bank—by the great island Tortola or Guarisipa (Ralegh's Iwana); next to it follows the island of Yaya (Ralegh's Assapana), and closer in to the shore, where Barrancas is situated, are three smaller islands. The Caño Manamo, or as it is now usually called Brazo Macareo, flows off to the northward at a distance of about five miles east from Barrancas; this was the branch up which Ralegh came.

[2] The number of freshwater turtles which lay their eggs on the sandy islands in the Orinoco during the season is almost incredible. Humboldt considers that the number of turtles which annually deposit their eggs on the banks and sandy islands of the Lower Orinoco is near a million; and this relates only to one species, the Arrau (*Emys Arrau*, Humb.). Guiana possesses several species of freshwater turtles, but two kinds are chiefly abundant; the larger is called by the Indians Arraou, or more frequently Cassipan (Sparrey calls them Cassipam, see Purchas, iv. chap. 11); it

some meat, and greatly restoring, so as our men were now well filled and highlie contented both with the fare, and neerenes of the land of *Guiana* which appeered in sight. In the morning there came downe according to promise the Lord of that border called *Toparimaca*, with some thirtie or fortie followers, and brought vs diuers sorts of fruits, and of his wine, bread, fish, and flesh, whom we also feasted as we could, at least he dranke good Spanish wine (whereof we had a small quantitie in bottels) which aboue all things they loue. I conferred with this *Toparimaca* of the next way to *Guiana*, who conducted our galley and botes to his owne port, and carried vs from thence some mile and a halfe to his towne, where some of our captaines garoused of his wine till they were reasonable pleasant, for it is very strong with pepper, and the iuice of diuers herbs, and fruits digested and purged, they keepe it in great earthen pots of ten or twelue gallons[1] very cleane and sweete, and are themselues at their meetings and feasts the greatest garousers and drunkards of the world[2]: when we came to his towne

reaches a considerable size, and weighs sometimes from fifty to sixty pounds, and even one hundred pounds. The eggs of that kind are round, and the shell, although calcareous, is not quite firm. We have found from one hundred to one hundred and twenty eggs in one nest. The second kind is much smaller, being from fifteen to twenty inches in diameter, and weighing seldom twenty pounds. It deposits about eighteen eggs in a nest; these are somewhat larger than a pigeon's egg, which they resemble in form, and are much more delicate than those of the former kind. These turtles are called Terekaiba or Terekay (*Emys Terekay*, Humb.); they are not so numerous, but are met with in all the rivers of the interior. The eggs of the Cassipan are chiefly employed for preparing oil; they are likewise smoke-dried and kept for food. On the banks of the Orinoco, as well as on the Rio Negro, the turtle oil forms an article of trade.

[1] When it is remembered that the Indian women fabricate these huge pots without the potter's wheel, merely by the hand, their skill is to be admired. The form of most of their earthen vessels is almost classic, and approaches nearest to the Etruscan shape.

[2] The Indians prepare various intoxicating drinks; the most common of which is the Paiwa or Paiwori. The chief ingredient of this favourite drink is Cassada bread, which is baked of a greater thickness than for common purposes, and is especially charred upon a coal fire. The women

we found two *Cassiques*, whereof one of them was a stranger that had beene vp the riuer in trade, and his boates, people, and wife incamped at the port where we ankored, and the other was of that countrey a follower of *Toparimaca*: they laie each of them in a cotton *Hamaca*, which we call brasill beds[1], and two women

who prepare the beverage assemble around a large jar or other earthen vessel, and having moistened their mouths with fresh water, they commence chewing the bread, collecting in the vessel the moisture which accumulates in the mouth. This is afterwards put into a trough (called Canaua) or in large jars, in which a quantity of the charred bread has been broken up, over which boiling water is poured; and it is then kneaded, and portions which are not of an even consistency are again carried to the mouth, ground with the teeth, and returned into the earthen pot. This process is repeated several times, from the idea that it conduces to the strength of the beverage. The second day fermentation begins, and on the third the liquor is considered fit for use. We have seen a whole village, young and old, men and women, occupied in this disgusting process, when it was contemplated to celebrate our unexpected arrival among them; otherwise, for common use, the females alone employ themselves *ex officio* with the preparation. Their teeth suffer so much from this occupation that a female has seldom a good tooth after she is thirty years old. Thevet gives, in his 'Singularités de la France Antarctique,' p. 46, a representation of such a preparation for a feast, and observes that only virgins were permitted to prepare the beverage. This condition has been much modified, if in reality it formerly existed. The taste of the paiwori is very refreshing after great fatigue, and not unpleasant to the taste: if offered as the cup of welcome by the Indian, it would cause great offence to refuse it. The beverage to which Ralegh alludes appears to have been Cassiri, which is made of batatas or sweet potatoes, but which, being allowed to ferment, produces intoxication when drunk in large quantities.

[1] We have already observed that these hammocks are fabricated by the women either of cotton-thread, the fibres of the Mauritia palm, or of those of the Caraguata, a species of *Bromelia*. The hammocks manufactured by the Carabisi are much more durable than the Glasgow hammocks, and are sometimes as fine as these, though made only by the hand, and without machinery. The cotton-thread is spun by means of a primitive spindle. The Indians on the Uaupes, a tributary of the upper Rio Negro, manufacture hammocks from the fibre of a *Bromelia*, which are afterwards very tastefully ornamented with feathers of parrots, toucans, cocks of the rock, and other birds of splendid plumage.

On descending the Rio Negro in 1839, we saw upwards of twenty Indians occupied in San Gabriel manufacturing hammocks of the fibres of the Mauritia palm, under the direction of the commandant of that fort. The

attending them with six cups and a litle ladle to fill them, out of an earthen pitcher of wine, and so they dranke ech of them three of those cups at a time, one to the other, and in this sort they drinke drunke at their feasts and meetings.

That *Cassique* that was a stranger had his wife staying at the port where we ankored, and in all my life I haue seldome seene a better fauored woman: She was of good stature, with blacke eies, fat of body, of an excellent countenance, hir haire almost as long as hir selfe, tied vp againe in pretie knots[1], and it seemed she stood not in that aw of hir husband, as the rest, for she spake and discourst, and dranke among the gentlemen and captaines, and was very pleasant, knowing hir owne comelines, and taking great pride therein. I haue seene a Lady in England so like hir, as but for the difference of colour I would haue sworne might haue beene the same.

The seate of this towne of *Toparimaca* was very pleasant, standing on a little hill, in an excellent prospect, with goodly

hammock is the most indispensable article in an Indian house, or for an Indian's journey. On his travels, it is carried folded up and slung round his neck: the greatest precaution is used to prevent its getting wet. Where a halt is made, be it of ever so short a duration, the first object sought for is a convenient tree from which he can suspend it. It is a compliment paid to the stranger, if the host takes the hammock from him on entering the house, and slings it for his guest, and it is the duty of the wife to do this service for her husband. The common hammocks of the Indians are generally open (that is, not closely woven), and coloured red with roucou or arnotto.

[1] The beauty of the hair of the Indian females has frequently surprised us. We have in several instances seen the hair touch the ground. Some Carabisi or Caribs from the Rupununi accompanied us in 1836 to Georgetown, and among them a female, who had such beautiful hair that she excited the astonishment of every one. They anoint it daily, and chiefly use for that purpose the oil made from a nut called Carapa (*Carapa guianensis*, Aublet). The hair-dress of the Arawaak women is very tasteful, but it is more usual among the Guianians to allow the hair to fall over the shoulders. Among the Pianoghoto and Drio Indians the females generally wear their hair short, and the men in long tresses or queues. Although we have seen very old people among the Indians, we recollect but a few instances of hair turned white from age.

gardens a mile compasse round about it, and two very faire and large ponds of excellent fish adioyning. This towne is called *Arowacai*: the people are of the nation called *Nepoios*, and are followers of *Carapana*. In that place I sawe very aged people, that we might perceiue all their sinewes and veines without any flesh, and but euen as a case couered onely with skin. The Lord of this place gaue me an old man for Pilot, who was of great experience and trauell, and knew the riuer most perfectly both by day and night, and it shall be requisite for any man that passeth it to haue such a Pilot, for it is fower, fiue, and six miles ouer in many places, and twentie miles in other places, with woonderfull eddies, and strong currants, many great Ilands and diuers sholds, and many dangerous rocks, and besides vpon any increase of winde so great a billow, as we were sometimes in great perill of drowning in the galley, for the small botes durst not come from the shore, but when it was very faire.

The next day we hasted thence, and hauing an easterly wind to helpe vs, we spared our arms from rowing: for after we entred *Orenoque*, the riuer lieth for the most part east and west, euen from the sea vnto *Quito* in *Peru*[1]. This riuer is nauigable with ships little lesse than 1000 miles, and from the place where we entred it may be sailed vp in small pinaces to many of the best parts of *Nueuo reyno de granado*, and of *Popayan*: and from no place may the cities of these parts of the Indies be so easily taken and inuaded as from hence. All that day we sailed vp a branch of that riuer, hauing on the left hand a great Iland, which they cal *Assapana*, which may containe some fiue and twentie miles in length, and 6 miles in bredth, the great body of the

[1] This erroneous statement cannot surprise us at a period when the geography of these regions was so little known, and the river Meta was sometimes considered as the continuation of the Orinoco, instead of being merely a tributary. As far as the mouth of the river Apure the course of the Orinoco is on ascending west, but coming from the south it forms here its second great inflection. The first is formed at its confluence with the river Guaviare; its course has been previously from the south-east.

F 2

riuer running on the other side of this Iland: Beyond that middle branch there is also another Iland in the riuer, called *Iwana*, which is twise as big as the Isle of *Wight*[1], and beyond it, and betweene it and the maine of *Guiana*, runneth a third branch of *Orenoque* called *Arraroopana*[2]: all three are goodly branches, and all nauigable for great ships. I iudge the riuer in this place to be at least thirtie miles brode, reckoning the Ilands which diuide the branches in it, for afterwards I sought also both the other branches[3].

After we reached to the head of this Iland, called *Assapana*, a little to the westward on the right hand there opened a riuer which came from the north, called *Europa*[4], and fell into the great riuer, and beyond it, on the same side, we ankored for that night, by another Iland six miles long, and two miles brode, which they call *Ocaywita*: From hence in the morning we landed two *Guianians*, which we found in the towne of *Toparimaca*, that came with vs, who went to giue notice of our comming to the Lord of that countrey called *Putyma*, a follower of *Topiawari*, chiefe Lord of *Arromaia*, who succeeded *Morequito*, whom (as you haue heard before) *Berreo* put to death, but his towne being farre within the land, he came not vnto vs that day, so as we ankored againe that night neere the banks of another Iland, of bignes much like the other, which they call *Putapayma*, on the maine lande, ouer against which Iland was a very high mountaine called *Oecope*[5]: we coueted to ankor rather by these

[1] The island of Tortola, Ralegh's Iwana, is about thirty-three miles in length.

[2] This branch of the Orinoco is now called Caño Piacoa, from the town of the same name, which is situated on the right bank of the river. It has some trade with Demerara and Trinidad.

[3] The real breadth is from shore to shore, namely from Barrancas to Piacoa, about fourteen nautical miles.

[4] This is the Guarguapo; it is connected with several large lagunes, which for a distance of about twelve miles run parallel with the Orinoco.

[5] Perhaps the hills on which the fortresses San Francisco and El Padrasto were afterwards constructed. At a distance of about a mile south of these hills stood formerly Guayana Vieja. It is very remarkable that

Ilands in the riuer, than by the maine, because of the *Tortugas* egges, which our people found on them in great abundance, and also because the ground serued better for vs to cast our nets for fish, the maine banks being for the most part stonie and high, and the rocks of a blew metalline colour[1], like vnto the best steele ore, which I assuredly take it to be: of the same blew stone are also diuers great mountaines, which border this riuer in many places.

The next morning towards nine of the clocke, we weied ankor, and the brize encreasing, we sailed alwaies west vp the riuer, and after a while opening the lande on the right side, the countrey appeered to be champaine, and the banks shewed very perfect red: I therefore sent two of the little barges with captaine *Gifford*, and with him captaine *Thyn*, captaine *Calfield*, my cosen *Greenuile*, my nephew *Io. Gilbert*, captaine *Eynus*, master *Edw. Porter*, and my cosen *Butshead Gorges*, with some fewe soldiers, to march ouer the banks of that red land[2], and to discouer what maner of countrey it was on the other side, who at their returne found it all a plaine leuell, as farre as they went or could discerne, from the highest tree they could get vpon: And my old Pilot, a man of great trauell brother to the *Cassique*

Ralegh avoids most studiously mentioning the existence of this settlement, which Antonio de Berreo founded in 1591, consequently four years previous to Ralegh's arrival in the Orinoco. It is impossible to believe that the Indians should have neglected to inform him of its existence, and we are obliged to conclude that he omitted to mention it, as previously alluded to, for political reasons, as this priority in the occupation would have established the claim of the Spaniards to the country.

[1] The blackish gray or almost leaden colour of some of the rocks on the surface in the rivers of tropical countries has attracted the attention of scientific men without a proper solution having been come to. The coating, according to the analysis of Mr. Children, consists of oxide of iron and manganese. Humboldt thinks that it contains besides these two materials carbon and supercarburetted iron. The inhabitants of the Orinoco say that the exhalations of these rocks of "blue metalline colour" are injurious to health.

[2] The soil of the savannahs has generally a reddish colour from an admixture of iron.

Toparimaca told me, that those were called the plaines of the *Sayma*[1], and that the same leuell reached to *Cumana,* and *Carracas* in the west Indies, which are 120 leagues to the north, and that there inhabited fower principall nations. The first were the *Sayma,* the next *Assawai,* the third and greatest the *Wikiri,* by whom *Pedro Hernandez de Serpa* before mentioned was ouerthrowen, as he passed with three hundred horse from *Cumana* towards *Orenoque,* in his enterprize of *Guiana,* the fourth are called *Aroras,* and are as blacke as *Negros,* but haue smooth haire, and these are very valiant, or rather desperate people, and haue the most strong poison on their arrowes, and most dangerous of all nations, of which poison I will speake somwhat being a digression not vnnecessary.

There was nothing whereof I was more curious, than to finde out the true remedies of these poisoned arrowes, for besides the mortalitie of the wound they make, the partie shot indureth the most insufferable torment in the world, and abideth a most vglie

[1] Ralegh alludes here to those vast plains or llanos which extend from the delta of the Orinoco to the banks of the Apure, and in a northern direction to the chain of mountains of Cumana, occupying seven thousand two hundred square leagues. The savannahs of the Rupununi, Takutu, and Rio Branco, the site of Keymis's El Dorado, occupy fourteen thousand four hundred square miles. During the rainy season they present the aspect of a sea of verdure, but during summer they display a picture of desolation, and the full effects of a drought under the burning sky of the Tropics. In the word Sayma we recognise the Chaymas, an Indian tribe who inhabit the neighbourhood of Cumana, and of whom Humboldt has given a very perfect description. (Personal Narrative, English translation, vol. iii. chap. 9.) The Wikiri are the Guaiquerias or Guaikeries of the island of Margarita, and the peninsula of Araya, and a great number reside in a suburb of Cumana which bears their name. According to Humboldt a tribe of Aruros inhabit the Orinoco to the east of Maipures, and in a list of Indians in Cayenne a tribe called Arara is mentioned as living in the regions west of the Oyapoco. Ralegh observes that the Aroras were as black as negroes. The Waraus are generally of darker colour than the other Indian tribes, but the difference is not so great as to bear a comparison to negroes. The tribe of Assawais, whom he previously mentions, are perhaps the Accawais, a sister tribe of the Carabisi.

and lamentable death, somtimes dying starke mad, somtimes their bowels breaking out of their bellies, and are presently discolored, as blacke as pitch, and so vnsauery, as no man can endure to cure, or to attend them: And it is more strange to know, that in all this time there was neuer Spaniard, either by gift or torment that could attaine to the true knowledge of the cure, although they haue martyred and put to inuented torture I know not how many of them. But euery one of these Indians know it not, no not one among thousands, but their southsaiers and priests, who do conceale it, and onely teach it but from the father to the sonne.

Those medicines which are vulgar, and serue for the ordinarie poison, are made of the iuice of a roote called *Tupara*: the same also quencheth maruellously the heate of burning feauers, and healeth inward wounds, and broken veines, that bleed within the body. But I was more beholding to the *Guianians* than any other, for *Anthonio de Berreo* told me that he could neuer attaine to the knowledge therof, and yet they taught me the best way of healing as wel therof, as of al other poisons. Some of the Spaniards haue been cured in ordinary wounds, of the common poisoned arrowes with the iuice of garlike: but this is a generall rule for all men that shall heerafter trauell the Indies where poisoned arrowes are vsed, that they must abstaine from drinke, for if they take any licor into their body, as they shall be maruellously prouoked therunto by drought, I say, if they drink before the wound be dressed, or soone vpon it, there is no way with them but present death[1].

[1] The mystery respecting the arrow-poison of the Indians, although not entirely cleared up, is in a great measure removed. Neither snake's teeth nor stinging ants form the active principle, but the juice of a plant which we have described as *Strychnos toxifera*. (Hooker's Icon. Plant. t. 364 and 365; Journ. of Bot. vol. iii. p. 240.) This plant is only known to grow in three or four situations in Guiana, and is in its habit a ligneous twiner or bushrope (which kind of plants are called in the French colonies Liane, and by the Spaniards Bejuco). The Indians of the Macusi tribe are the best manufacturers of the poison, which is entirely composed of the juice

And so I wil returne again to our iourney which for this third day we finished, and cast ankor againe neere the continent, on the left hand betweene two mountaines, the one called *Aroami*, and the other *Aio*: I made no stay heere but till midnight, for I feared howerly least any raine should fall, and then it had beene impossible to haue gone any further vp, notwithstanding that there is euery day a very strong brize, and easterly winde. I

of plants. Previous travellers during the present century in Guiana never saw it prepared, nor did they see the plant growing of which it is made; and the accounts which they have given us of its preparation were perhaps imposed upon them by the Carabisis, but rest surely not upon personal experience, as they are so very erroneous. The Macusis call the plant Urari-yè, the poison itself Urari (read Ourahree), which the Carabisi, who constantly interchange the *r* and *l*, have corrupted into Urali and Ulari, of which Wurali has been made. The Caribs are not able to prepare the poison, and purchase it from the Macusis. It is surprising to us why a spurious name should have been substituted in England for the true one, since we find the proper name of the poison mentioned already by Keymis in Hakluyt (vol. iii. p. 687) in a table of names and rivers, &c., where under the head of poisoned herbs occurs the plant "Ourari." The author of these notes has given an unadorned account of the mode of preparing the poison in the Annals of Natural History, vol. vii. p. 407, and he has prepared it himself, by concentrating merely the infusion from the bark of the plant (*Strychnos toxifera*) which had been collected in his presence. It killed a fowl in twenty-seven minutes, although not sufficiently concentrated. Well-prepared poison, which is of a dark colour, shows its effects in the space of a minute, and kills a fowl in five minutes. Its effect is more or less sudden upon different animals, and the Indians say that monkeys and Jaguars are more easily killed with it than any other animals. We have been assured repeatedly by the Indians that there is no remedy against the Urari if it be good—salt and sugar are both considered antidotes against weak poison, but avail nothing where the Urari is strong. It has been related to us that, when wounded in wars, and salt is not to be had, the Indians resort to urine. The thirst which follows is described as almost intolerable, and certain death ensues if the thirst is quenched with water: the more the wounded person drinks, the greater becomes his thirst. Ralegh's relation is therefore perfectly correct in this respect. It has not been possible as yet to procure a perfect analysis of the Urari. The agent which destroys the vital powers in so short a period appears to be a new principle, hitherto unknown to chemists. Numerous experiments have recently been made with it in Berlin.

deferred the search of the countrie on *Guiana* side, till my returne downe the riuer. The next day we sailed by a great Iland, in the middle of the riuer, called *Manoripano,* and as wee walked a while on the Iland, while the *Galley* got a head of vs, there came after vs from the maine, a small *Canoa* with seuen or eight *Guianians,* to inuite vs to ankor at their port, but I deferred it till my returne; It was that *Cassique* to whom those *Nepoios* went, which came with vs from the towne of *Toparimaca*: and so the fift day we reached as high vp as the Prouince of *Arromaia* the countrey of *Morequito* whom *Berreo* executed, and ankored to the west of an Iland called *Murrecotima,* ten miles long and fiue brode: and that night the *Cassique Aramiari,* (to whose towne we made our long and hungry voiage out of the riuer of *Amana*) passed by vs.

The next day we arriued at the port of *Morequito,* and ankored there, sending away one of our Pilots to seeke the king of *Aromaia,* vncle to *Morequito,* slaine by *Berreo* as aforesaide. The next day following, before noone he came to vs on foote from his house, which was 14 English miles, (himself being 110 yeers old) and returned on foote the same daie, and with him many of the borderers, with many women and children, that came to woonder at our nation, and to bring vs down victuall, which they did in great plenty, as venison, porke, hens, chickens, foule, fish, with diuers sorts of excellent fruits, and rootes, and great abundance of *Pinas,* the princesse of fruits, that grow vnder the *Sun*[1], especially those of *Guiana.* They brought vs

[1] Who does not remember Thomson's description?—

> "Witness, thou best Anana! thou the pride
> Of vegetable life, beyond whate'er
> The poets imaged in the golden age:
> Quick let me strip thee of thy tufty coat,
> Spread thy ambrosial stores, and feast with Jove!"

We must give Ralegh the honour of having been the first who called this delicious production "the prince of fruits." It is related by Oldys, that when by a speedy voyage a pineapple was brought from America in great perfection, and King James tasted of it, he observed, that "it was a fruit too

also store of bread, and of their wine, and a sort of *Paraquitos*, no bigger than wrens, and of all other sorts both small and great: one of them gaue me a beast called by the Spaniards *Armadilla*, which they call *Cassacam*, which seemeth to be all barred ouer with small plates somewhat like to a *Renocero*, with a white horne growing in his hinder parts, as big as a great hunting horne, which they vse to winde in steed of a trumpet[1]. *Monardus* writeth that a little of the powder of that horn put into the eare, cureth deafnes.

After this old king had rested a while in a little tent, that I caused to be set vp, I began by my interpretor to discourse with him of the death of *Morequito* his predecessor, and afterward of the Spaniards, and ere I went anie farther I made him know the cause of my comming thither, whose seruant I was, and that the Queenes pleasure was, I should vndertake the voiage for their defence, and to deliuer them from the tyrannie of the Spaniards, dilating at large (as I had done before to those of *Trinedado*) her Maiesties greatnes, her iustice, her charitie to all oppressed nations, with as manie of the rest of her beauties and vertues, as either I coulde expresse, or they conceiue, all which being with great admiration attentiuely heard, and maruellously admired, I began to sound the olde man as touching *Guiana*,

delicious for a subject to taste of." We have met during our journeys in Guiana considerable extents of ground covered with pineapples; but in their wild state they are small, seldom larger than an apple, of a bright yellow; and though their smell is highly aromatic (surpassing in that regard the cultivated species), they are stringy, full of seeds, and rather acidulous in taste. It is only by cultivation that they acquire their superior flavour and their large size. The wild pineapple bears a different name among the Indian tribes from the cultivated, and we have our doubts whether it be not a different species.

[1] Ralegh's description of the armadillo is certainly amusing. We cannot conceive how he could describe an organ which by its situation and figure could not be mistaken except for what nature intended it, namely its tail, as "a great hunting horne," &c. The armadillo or cashikam (*Dasypus novemcinctus*) is very common in Guiana, and used as food by the Indians and by some of the Creoles.

and the state thereof, what sort of common wealth it was, how gouerned, of what strength and pollicy, how farre it extended, and what nations were friends or enimies adioining, and finally of the distance, and way to enter the same: he told me that himselfe and his people with all those downe the riuer towards the sea, as farre as *Emeria*, the Prouince of *Carapana*, were of *Guiana*, but that they called themselues *Orenoqueponi*[1], bicause they bordered the great riuer of *Orenoque*, and that all the nations betweene the riuer and those mountaines in sight called *Wacarima*, were of the same cast and appellation: and that on the other side of those mountaines of *Wacarima* there was a large plaine[2] (which after I discouered in my returne) called the valley

[1] The word *pona* signifies in the Macusi language 'upon.' In that sense it appears to be used likewise in this instance.

[2] The name of Wacaraima, or rather Pacaraima, is derived from the peculiar shape which several mountains of the sandstone chain bear to the form of an Indian basket called Pacara. Closely connected with the Sierra Parima is a chain of mountains which has appeared under the name of Pacaraima or Pacarinha in our modern maps. The author of these remarks has traversed that chain along its whole length, from the banks of the Corentyne to the shores of the Orinoco over more than nine degrees of longitude; and although it is interspersed with plains and valleys, its connection from the fifty-ninth degree of longitude (west of Greenwich) to the remarkable bifurcation of the Orinoco is easily recognised. It forms the division of those three great basins of the northern part of South America, namely, the gigantic Amazon, the mighty Orinoco, and its brother (so called by Keymis), the Essequibo. The most remarkable feature of the chain is a ridge of sandstone mountains, of which we trace the first on the banks of the Cuyuni in 6° 45′ north latitude and 61° west longitude: they are observed again at the banks of the Mazaruni, and their culminating eastern point is Mount Roraima (in 5° 9′ north latitude and 61° west longitude). This remarkable mountain rises to a height of about eight thousand feet above the sea, forming towards its summit a mural precipice fourteen hundred feet in height, from the summit of which several streams precipitate themselves to the foot of the wall-like cliff. Similarly formed, and nearly equal in height, is Cukenam, Marina, Wayatsipu, &c. The river Cukenam falls a height of from eleven to twelve hundred feet from the mural precipice of the same name, and forms one of the chief sources of the river Caroni. From the southern foot of the Pacaraima chain extend the great savannahs of the Rupununi, Takutu

of *Amariocapana*, in all that valley the people were also of the ancient *Guianians*. I asked what nations those were which inhabited on the further side of those mountaines, beyond the valley of *Amariocapana*, he answered with a great sigh (as a man which had inward feeling of the losse of his countrey and liberty, especially for that his eldest sonne was slain in a battel on that side of the mountaines, whom he most entirely loued,) that he remembred in his fathers life time when he was very old, and himselfe a yoong man that there came down into that large valley of *Guiana*, a nation from so far off as the *Sun* slept, (for such were his own words,) with so great a multitude as they could not be numbred nor resisted, and that they wore large coats, and hats of crimson colour[1], which colour he expressed, by shewing a peece of red wood, wherewith my tent was supported, and that they were called *Oreiones*, and *Epuremei*, those that had

and Rio Branco or Parima, which occupy about 14,400 square miles, their average height above the sea being from three hundred and fifty to four hundred feet. These savannahs are inundated during the rainy season, and afford at that period, with the exception of a short portage, a communication between the Rupununi and the Pirara, a tributary of the Mahu or Ireng, which falls into the Takutu, and the latter into the Rio Branco or Parima. Topiawari alludes to these plains as inhabited by the Epuremei, and after the return of Keymis they were considered the site of the fabulous lake Parima.

[1] Keymis and Marsham repeat the account of apparelled Indians, and Hartzinck, the author of the 'Beschryving van Guiana' (Amsterdam, 1770), observes, "The borders of Lake Parima are inhabited by numerous nations; some are clothed, and do not suffer strangers to come thither. In the year 1755, upon the relations of a certain Indian chief, the Spaniards undertook three expeditions into the interior to reach Lake Parima; but they were so much opposed by the Indians, chiefly during the third attempt, that they did not feel inclined to undertake another. They brought with them four prisoners of the clothed nation, which Mr. Persick of the Council of Justice of Essequibo, and others who were trading saw at that period." We have little doubt that the clothed Indians alluded to by Hartzinck were Kenicarus or half-civilized Indians, who came from the Rio Branco, which river Francisco Xav. de Andrade ascended as early as 1740; several Aldeas were established there soon after. Ajuricaba, a powerful chieftain of the Manaos, and an ally of the Dutch, scoured the Rio Branco and Rio Negro in 1720, and captured all the Indians he could secure in order to sell them as slaves.

slaine and rooted out so many of the ancient people as there were leaues in the wood vpon all the trees, and had now made themselues Lords of all, euen to that mountaine foote called *Curaa,* sauing onely of two nations, the one called *Iwarawaqueri,* and the other *Cassipagotos*[1], and that in the last battell fought betweene the *Epuremei,* and the *Iwarawaqueri,* his eldest son was chosen to carry to the aide of the *Iwarawaqueri,* a great troupe of the *Orenoqueponi,* and was there slaine, with al his people and freinds, and that he had now remaining but one sonne: and farther told me that those *Epuremei* had built a great town called *Macureguarai,* at the said mountaine foote, at the beginning of the great plaines of *Guiana,* which haue no end: and that their houses haue many roomes, one ouer the other, and that therein the great king of the *Oreiones* and *Epuremei* kept three thousand men to defend the borders against them, and withall daily to inuade and slaie them: but that of late yeeres since the Christians offred to inuade his territories, and those frontires, they were all at peace, and traded one with another, sauing onely the *Iwarawaqueri,* and those other nations vpon the head of the riuer of *Caroli,* called *Cassipagotos,* which we afterwards discouered, each one holding the *Spaniard* for a common enimie.

After he had answered thus far, he desired leaue to depart, saying that he had far to go, that he was old, and weake, and was euery day called for by death, which was also his owne phrase: I desired him to rest with vs that night, but I could not intreat him, but he told me that at my returne from the countrie aboue, he would againe come to vs, and in the meane time prouide for vs the best he could, of all that his countrie yeelded: the same night hee returned to *Orocotona* his owne

[1] The termination *ghiri* and *'ghoto* denote a tribe, people, &c., in the great Carib language. The Teutonic races are called Paranaghiri by all the Guianians, signifying people from beyond the sea (see *ante*, note at page 8). Ghoto implies likewise a tribe in the Carib language, as *e. g.* Puru 'ghoto, Piano 'ghoto, &c.

towne[1], so as he went that day 28 miles, the weather being very hot, the countrie being situate betweene 4 and 5 degrees of the *Equinoctiall*. This *Topiawari* is held for the proudest, and wisest of al the *Orenoqueponi*, and so he behaued himselfe towards me in all his answers at my returne, as I maruelled to finde a man of that grauity and iudgement, and of so good discourse, that had no helpe of learning nor breed.

The next morning we also left the port, and sailed westward vp the riuer, to view the famous riuer called *Caroli*, as well bicause it was maruellous of it selfe, as also for that I vnderstood it led to the strongest nations of all the frontires, that were enimies to the *Epuremei*, which are subiects to *Inga*, Emperor of *Guiana*, and *Manoa*, and that night we ankored at another Iland

[1] The occurrence of this word has been of great interest to us. It proves that the Orenoqueponi were a branch of the Macusi tribe, who now inhabit the savannahs of the Rupununi and Rio Branco. *Oroké* in that language signifies parrot; *touna*, water. But the occurrence of this name, as a singular instance, would scarcely induce us to come to such a conclusion, if there were not repeated instances in Ralegh's account which cannot be considered accidental. At page 57 (of the original edition) he speaks of the island Ocaywita; *Okai* is great, *iwotta* river, in that language. The great heron (a species resembling *Ardea cinerea*, Lath.) is called Wanure, hence Wanuretona (p. 65). The great town inhabited by the Epuremei is called Macureguarai. *Macuwari* is 'a sword,' *warai* the adjective 'like'; *Iconuru* signifies blue or bluish; it is that colour which the water in rivers with clayey bottom sometimes assumes, or in which distant objects seem to be enveloped: Ralegh mentions at page 93 a mountain called Iconuri. Iwana is a common name of men among the Macusis; Arowacai is the name of a Macusi village near the Cotinga. We have already alluded to the poetical signification of Yarico, the heroine of Addison's story (note at p. 40). We know from Ligon that she was carried away from the Spanish main. Even in the name of Toparimaca we might trace the Macusi language. *Eporimang* is the act of making others pleased; but to offer an example: in requesting a third person to try to conciliate a group of refractory Indians, we would tell him *topuremacka*, 'make them pleased' (or rather them make pleased). The analogy of these and other words is not merely accidental, but proves that the Macusis, or at least a branch of that tribe, formerly inhabited the Orinoco. They now live on the savannahs of the Rupununi and Rio Branco or Parima.

called *Caiama*[1], of some fiue or sixe miles in length, and the next day arriued at the mouth of *Caroli*[2], when we were short of it as low or further downe as the port of *Morequito* we heard the

[1] This island is now named Faxardo; it is about ten miles long, and lies in the Orinoco right before the mouth of the river Caroni. The island was formerly fortified, and a battery which Don Manuel Centurion erected about 1770 on the eastern point commanded both banks of the river. To judge from Keymis's relation, the Spaniards possessed fortifications on this island as early as 1596.

[2] The river Caroni is one of the largest tributaries which the Orinoco receives from the Sierra Parima. Its chief branch, the Yuruani, has its sources on the mountain Ayangcatsibang (literally, "Louse-comb mountain," from the jagged appearance of its mural precipice); the Cukenam, which joins the Yuruani, falls from the mountain Cukenam or Icukenama; from the point of junction of these two rivers, it is called Caroni. A short distance from its confluence with the Orinoco is the great cataract, or Salto, celebrated for its picturesque scenery. The river is said to fall over a bar from fifteen to twenty feet high. According to the description which Father Caulin gives of it, the noise of the cararact is heard at a distance of several leagues. Diego de Ordaz found in 1531–32 at the mouth of the Caroni a settlement called Caroao or Carao, which afterwards received the name of Santo Tomas de Guayana. The first missionaries who arrived on the Orinoco were the Jesuits Ignacio Llauri and Julian Vergara. They commenced their pious work in 1576; but after Santo Tomas was destroyed by the Dutch under the command of Captain Adrian Jansen in 1579, the inhabitants fled to the llanos of Cumana, where the greater number perished for hunger, and among them Father Llauri. (Caulin, lib. i. cap. 2.) The town having been rebuilt further eastward, as already related, was taken and burnt by Keymis in 1618. When Humboldt visited the Orinoco at the commencement of this century, there was in the neighbourhood of the great cataract a village called Aguacaqua or Caroni, with a population of seven hundred Indians. It is now entirely abandoned. The missions of the Catalonian Capuchins extended formerly from the eastern bank of the Caroni as far as the banks of the Imataca, the Curuma, and the Cuyuni. They consisted in 1797 of thirty-eight missions, with a population of sixteen thousand Indians, engaged in agriculture and the breeding of cattle. By the decrees of the Republic of Colombia of the 14th of December 1819, and the 28th of July 1821, these missions were suppressed, and at this time nearly all vestiges of their former existence are vanished, and the civilized Indians are greatly reduced in number. Codazzi assumes the number of civilized Indians in the canton of Upata, to which province formerly the missions belonged, at two thousand five hundred.

great rore and fall of the riuer, but when we came to enter with our barge and wherries thinking to haue gone vp some fortie miles to the nations of the *Cassipagotos*, we were not able with a barge of eight oares to rowe one stones cast in an hower, and yet the riuer is as broad as the Thames at Wolwich, and we tried both sides, and the middle, and euery part of the riuer, so as we incamped vpon the bankes adioyning, and sent off our *Orenoque-pone* (which came with vs from *Morequito*) to giue knowledge to the nations vpon the riuer of our being there, and that we desired to see the Lords of *Canuria*, which dwelt within the prouince vpon that riuer, making them know that we were enemies to the Spanyards, (for it was on this riuers side that *Morequito* slew the *Frier*, and those nine Spaniards which came from *Manoa*, the Citie of *Inga*, and tooke from them 40000 pesoes of Golde) so as the next daie there came downe a Lorde or *Cassique* called *Wanuretona* with many people with him, and brought all store of prouisions to entertaine vs, as the rest had done. And as I had before made my comming knowne to *Topiawari*, so did I acquaint this *Cassique* therewith, and howe I was sent by her Maiesty for the purpose aforesaid, and gathered also what I could of him touching the estate of *Guiana*, and I founde that those also of *Caroli* were not onely enemies to the Spaniardes but most of all to the *Epuremei*, which abounde in Gold, and by this *Wanuretona*, I had knowledge that on the heade of this riuer were three mighty nations, which were seated on a great lake, from whence this riuer descended, and were called *Cassipagotos*, *Eparagotos*, and *Arawagotos*, and that all those eyther against the Spaniards, or the *Epuremei* would ioine with vs, and that if wee entred the lande ouer the mountaines of *Curaa*, wee should satisfie our selues with golde and all other good things: hee told vs farther of a nation called *Iwarawaqueri* before spoken off, that held daily warre with the *Epuremei* that inhabited *Macureguarai* the first ciuill towne of *Guiana*, of the subiectes of *Inga* the Emperor.

Vpon this riuer one Captaine *George*, that I tooke with *Berreo* tolde me there was a greate siluer mine, and that it was neere the banckes of the saide riuer. But by this time as well *Orenoque, Caroli,* as all the rest of the riuers were risen fowre or fiue foote in height, so as it was not possible by the strength of any men, or with any boate whatsoeuer to rowe into the riuer against the streame. I therefore sent Captaine *Thyn,* Captaine *Greenuile,* my nephew *Iohn Gylbert,* my cosen *Butshead Gorges,* Captaine *Clarke,* and some 30 shot more to coast the riuer by lande, and to goe to a towne some twentie miles ouer the valley called *Amnatapoi,* and if they found guides there, to goe farther towardes the mountaine foote to another greate towne, called *Capurepana,* belonging to a *Cassique* called *Haharacoa* (that was a nephew to old *Topiawari* king of *Arromaia* our chiefest friend) because this towne and prouince of *Capurepana* adioyned to *Macureguarai,* which was the frontier towne of the Empire: and the meane while my selfe with Captaine *Gifford,* Captaine *Calfield, Edw. Hancocke,* and some halfe a dosen shot marched ouer land to view the strange ouerfals of the riuer of *Caroli,* which rored so farre of, and also to see the plaines, adioyning and the rest of the prouince of *Canuri*: I sent also captaine *Whiddon, W. Connocke,* and some eight shot with them, to see if they coulde finde any minerall stone alongst the riuers side. When we ronne to the tops of the first hils of the plaines adioyning to the riuer, we behelde that wonderfull breach of waters, which ranne down *Caroli*: and might from that mountaine see the riuer how it ran in three parts, aboue twentie miles of, and there appeared some ten or twelue ouerfals in sight, euery one as high ouer the other as a Church tower, which fell with that fury, that the rebound of waters made it seeme, as if it had beene all couered ouer with a great shower of rayne: and in some places we tooke it at the first for a smoke that had risen ouer some great towne[1]. For

[1] The description which Ralegh gives of the great cataract is highly graphic, and shows his power in depicting scenery. The constant moisture which prevails near cataracts imparts to the vegetation a livelier colour, and the surrounding trees are clothed with numerous orchideous plants,

mine owne part I was well perswaded from thence to haue returned, being a very ill footeman, but the rest were all so desirous to goe neere the said straunge thunder of waters, as they drew mee on by little and little, till we came into the next valley, where we might better discerne the same. I neuer saw a more beawtifull countrey, nor more liuely prospectes, hils so raised heere and there ouer the vallies, the riuer winding into diuers braunches, the plaines adioyning without bush or stubble, all faire greene grasse, the ground of hard sand easy to march on, eyther for horse or foote, the deare crossing in euery path, the birds towardes the euening singing on euery tree with a thousand seueral tunes, cranes and herons of white, crimson, and carnation pearching on the riuers side, the ayre fresh with a gentle easterlie wind, and euery stone that we stooped to take vp, promised eyther golde or siluer by his complexion. Your Lordships shall see of many sortes, and I hope some of them cannot be bettered vnder the sunne, and yet we had no meanes but with our daggers and fingers to teare them out heere and there, the rockes being most hard of that minerall sparre aforesaid, and is like a flint, and is altogether as hard or harder, and besides the veynes lie a fathome or two deepe in the rockes. But we wanted all thinges requisite saue onelie our desires, and good will to haue performed more if it had pleased God. To be short when both our companies returned, each of them brought also seuerall sortes of stones that appeared very faire, but were such as they found loose on the ground, and were for the most part but cul-

which prefer a moist situation. On descending the river Paramu, a tributary of the Upper Orinoco, in 1839, we observed one evening towards sunset, at some distance before us, what we at first mistook for clouds of white smoke from the fires which we supposed to have been kindled by some of our Indians, who had gone on before; but we were soon undeceived; it was a sheet of foam caused by a cataract which the river Kundanama forms at its junction with the Paramu. It would be difficult to describe the romantic scenery of this spot; the artist who accompanied our expedition has attempted to delineate it. (See Twelve Views in the Interior of Guiana, p. 19. London: Ackermann and Co.)

lored, and had not any gold fixed in them, yet such as had no iudgement or experience kept all that glistered, and would not be perswaded but it was rich because of the lustre, and brought of those, and of *Marquesite* with all, from *Trinedado*, and haue deliuered of those stones to be tried in many places, and haue thereby bred an opinion that all the rest is of the same: yet some of these stones I shewed afterward to a Spaniard of the *Caracas* who told me that it was *El Madre deloro*, and that the mine was farther in the grounde[1]. But it shall bee founde a weake pollicie in mee, eyther to betray my selfe, or my Countrey with imaginations, neyther am I so farre in loue with that lodging, watching, care, perill, diseases, ill sauoures, bad fare, and many other mischiefes that accompany these voyages, as to woo my selfe againe into any of them, were I not assured that the sunne couereth not so much riches in any part of the earth. Captaine *Whiddon*, and our Chirurgion *Nich. Millechap* brought me a kinde of stones like *Saphires*, what they may proue I knowe not, I shewed them to some of the *Orenoqueponi*, and they promised to bring me to a mountaine, that had of them verye large peeces growing Diamond wise[2]: whether it be Christall of the moun-

[1] The Caribs formerly brought small calabashes with gold-dust to the Dutch at the Essequibo, which they pretended to have collected at the Pacaraima mountains. Toward the end of the last century, an intendant of Venezuela, Don Jose Avalo, revived the idea of boundless mineral riches in Guiana, and, being imposed upon by some Mexican miners who declared that the rocks of the Caroni were auriferous, erected considerable works in the neighbourhood of the town of Upata. After large sums of the public money had been expended, it was found that the pyrites (Marquesite of Ralegh) contained no trace of gold whatever. Humboldt relates that not only was the mica-slate taken to the furnace, but strata of amphibolic (Hornblende) slate also were shown to him near Angostura, without any mixture of heterogeneous substances, which had been worked under the whimsical name of "oro negro" or black ore of gold.

[2] The stones here alluded to are rock-crystals, which are found in different situations in the Pacaraima mountains, but in the largest quantities on the banks of the Upper Cotinga, which has hence received the name of the Crystal River (Rio Cristaes) from the Portuguese. They are frequently very transparent, and consist of six-sided prisms, terminated by six-sided pyramidal points. The crystals are sometimes tinctured with colouring

taine, *Bristoll Diamond*, or *Saphire* I doe not yet knowe, but I hope the best, sure I am that the place is as likely as those from whence all the rich stones are brought, and in the same height or very neare. On the left hand of this riuer *Caroli* are seated those nations which are called *Iwarawakeri* before remembred, which are enemies to the *Epuremei*: and on the heade of it adioyning to the greate lake *Cassipa*, are situate those other nations which also resist *Inga*, and the *Epuremei*, called *Cassepagotos*, *Eparegotos*, and *Arrawagotos*. I farther vnderstood that this lake of *Cassipa* is so large, as it is aboue one daies iourney for one of their *Canoas* to crosse, which may be some 40 miles, and that therein fall diuers riuers, and that great store of graines of Golde are found in the summer time when the lake falleth by the banckes, in those braunches[1]. There is also another goodly riuer beyond *Caroli* which is called *Arui*, which also runneth thorow the lake *Cassipa*, and falleth into *Orenoque* farther west, making all that land betweene *Caroli* and *Arui* an Iland, which is

matter, so as to resemble amethysts, and we likewise found near Roraima some smoky opal. Ralegh's accounts are therefore fully borne out when he speaks of precious stones.

[1] The lake Cassipa has been shifted by successive geographers from place to place in the hydrographic system of the Orinoco, until recently, when its non-existence, like that of the lake Parima, has been sufficiently proved. There is little doubt that the great inundations of the river Paragua, (one of the chief tributaries of the Caroni, and which the missionaries of Piritu called a "laguna," from its extensive inundations and swampy nature,) together with the erroneous explanation which Ralegh received as to the purport of the information communicated by the Indians, gave rise to the account of the great lake of Cassipa, which he conceived to be forty miles long. Father Caulin expressly states that the river Paragua generally inundates the neighbouring country during the tropical winter (the rainy season), so that its real bed is then hardly discernible, for which reason it is called the Paragua, which means in the Caribbee language 'sea,' or 'great lake.' Ralegh observes that only the Caroli (Caroni) and the Arui (Rio Aro) issue from lake Cassipa; but in the maps of Sanson and D'Anville the Rio Caura flows likewise from lake Cassipa. This lake is still indicated in Jeffery's 'Chart of the Coasts of Caracas and the Mouths of the Orinoco,' published in 1794, where it approaches the right bank of the Orinoco within a few miles.

likewise a most beawtifull countrey. Next vnto *Arui* there are two riuers *Atoica* and *Caora*[1], and on that braunch which is called *Caora* are a nation of people, whose heades appeare not aboue their shoulders, which though it may be thought a meere fable, yet for mine owne parte I am resolued it is true, because euery child in the prouinces of *Arromaia* and *Canuri* affirme the same: they are called *Ewaipanoma*: they are reported to haue their eyes in their shoulders, and their mouths in the middle of their breasts, and that a long train of haire groweth backward betwen their shoulders[2].

[1] Between the rivers Aro (Arui) and Caura (Caora) the only stream of consequence is the Pao, which however must not be confounded with a larger river of that name which falls into the Orinoco on the left or northern bank. On the opposite shore, where the latter enters the Orinoco, and about fourteen miles to the west of the river Aro, is a place and small stream called Muitaco, to which Ralegh perhaps alludes under the name of Atoica. The Caora is the river Caura, sometimes called Coari in older maps.

[2] The account which Ralegh gives of the Indian tribes who have their eyes in their shoulders and their mouths in the middle of their breasts, has been charged as another proof of his attempt to deal in fables. Such accounts however have existed since the time of Pliny; and when Ralegh reported the wonderful tales, which he sufficiently proves were not the offspring of his own imagination, he merely related the common belief of the natives, not only at the period of his visit but up to this day. How frequently have we heard, in our ramblings, the most circumstantial accounts of the existence of tribes equally absurd in appearance as Ralegh's Ewaipanoma! Ctesias speaks of men with the head of a dog, and Pliny repeats Herodotus' relation of the Acephali, who, if the Libyans may be credited, "have their mouths in their breasts." Sir John Mandeville, speaking of the inhabitants of some southern islands, observes, "Alia insula habet homines aspectu deformes, nihil autem colli aut capitis ostendentes; unde et acephali nuncupantur: oculos autem habent ante ad scapulas, et in loco pectoris os apertum, ad formam ferri quo nostri caballi frænantur." We find therefore that Ralegh had several prototypes, and, as he himself observes, he grounded his belief of the existence of such a people upon the testimony of the natives.

We learn from Humboldt's narrative that the forests of Sipapo, where the missionaries place the nation of Rayas who have the mouth at the navel, are altogether unknown. (Vol. 5. p. 176.) An old Indian whom the great traveller met at Carichana, boasted of having seen these Acephali with his own eyes; and, absurd as these fables are, Humboldt observes that they have spread as far as the Llanos, "where you are not always permitted to doubt the existence of the Raya Indians." It is probable that Shakspeare,

The sonne of *Topiawari*, which I brought with mee into England tolde mee that they are the most mightie men of all the lande, and vse bowes, arrowes, and clubs thrice as bigge as any of *Guiana*, or of the *Orenoqueponi*, and that one of the *Iwarawakeri* tooke a prisoner of them the yeare before our arriuall there, and brought him into the borders of *Arromaia* his fathers Countrey: And farther when I seemed to doubt of it, hee tolde me that it was no wonder among them, but that they were as great a nation, and as common, as any other in all the prouinces, and had of late yeares slaine manie hundreds of his fathers people, and of other nations their neighbors, but it was not my chaunce to heare of them til I was come away, and if I had but spoken one word of it while I was there, I might haue brought one of them with me to put the matter out of doubt. Such a nation was written of by *Maundeuile*, whose reportes were held for fables many yeares, and yet since the East *Indies* were discouered, wee finde his relations true of such thinges as heeretofore were held incredible: whether it be true or no the matter is not great, neither can there be any profit in the imagination, for mine owne part I saw them not, but I am resolued that so many people did not all combine, or forethinke to make the report.

When I came to *Cumana* in the west *Indies* afterwards, by chaunce I spake with a spanyard dwelling not farre from thence, a man of great trauell, and after he knew that I had ben in *Guiana* , and so farre directlie west as *Caroli*, the first question he asked me was whether I had seene anie of the *Ewaipanoma*, which are those without heades: who being esteemed a most

having read Ralegh's Guiana voyage, makes use of his account of the Ewaipanoma, which he introduces in his Moor of Venice; and when Othello gave fair Desdemona a relation of the wonders he had seen, he included—

> "The cannibals, that each other eat,
> The Anthropophagi, and men whose heads
> Do grow beneath their shoulders."

Oldys supposes that this was done in compliment to Sir Walter Ralegh. Keymis certifies the existence of the headless men, and speaks, in a marginal note, of a sort of people more monstrous, "who have eminent heads like dogs, and live all the day-time in the sea, and they speak the Carib language." (Hakluyt, vol. iii. p. 677.)

honest man of his word, and in all thinges else, told me that he had seen manie of them : I may not name him because it may be for his disaduantage, but he is well known to *Monsier Mucherons* sonne of London, and to *Peter Mucheron* marchant of the *Flemish* shipp that was there in trade, who also heard what he auowed to be true of those people. The fourth river to the west of *Caroli* is *Casnero*[1] which falleth into *Orenoque* on this side of *Amapaia,* and that riuer is greater then *Danubius,* or any of *Europe*: it riseth on the south of *Guiana* from the mountaines which deuide *Guiana* from *Amazones,* and I thinke it to be nauigable many hundred miles : but we had no time, meanes, nor season of the yeare, to search those riuers for the causes aforesaid, the winter being come vppon vs, although the winter and summer as touching cold and heate differ not, neither do the trees euer senciblie lose their leaues, but haue alwaies fruite either ripe or green, and most of them both blossomes, leaues, ripe fruite, and green at one time : But their winter onelie consisteth of terrible raynes, and ouerflowings of the riuers, with many great stormes and gusts, thunder, and lightnings, of which we had our fill, ere we returned. On the North side, the first riuer that falleth into *Orenoque* is *Cari,* beyond it on the same side is the riuer of *Limo*[2], betweene these two is a great nation of *Canibals,* and their chiefe towne beareth the name of the riuer and is called *Acamacari*: at this towne is a continuall markette of women for 3 or 4 hatchets a peece, they are bought by the *Arwacas,* and by them solde into the west Indies[3]. To

[1] It is probable that Ralegh alludes to the river Cuchivero, which comes from the south and falls east of Caicara into the Orinoco. It is however a river of no such size as to be worthy of being compared with the Danube.

[2] The rivers Cari and Limo unite previous to their falling into the Orinoco.

[3] The sale of females is now almost entirely abolished among the Guianians, although it was formerly carried on to a great extent by the Caribs. The Macusis were accused of selling their female relatives, and even their daughters; and though we cannot vouch for the correctness of this asser-

the west of *Limo* is the riuer *Pao,* beyond it *Caturi,* beyond that *Voari* and *Capuri* which falleth out of the great riuer of *Meta,* by which *Berreo* descended from *Nueuo reyno de granada*[1]. To the westward of *Capuri* is the prouince of *Amapaia,* where *Berreo* wintered, and had so many of his people poysoned with the tawny water of the marshes of the *Anebas*[2]. Aboue *Amapaia,* towarde *Nueuo reyno* fall in, *Meta, Pato,* and *Cassanar*: to the west of these towardes the prouinces of the *Ashaguas* and *Catetios* are the riuers of *Beta, Dawney,* and *Vbarro,* and towardes the frontyer of *Peru* are the prouinces of

tion, we know instances where females have been sold during our visits from 1835 to 1844, and carried to Demerara. We recollect the trial of an official person in the criminal court of that colony, his dismissal from office, and his incarceration, for having purchased two Macusi girls, whom he was said to keep in slavery.

[1] It is not very evident which rivers Ralegh alludes to when speaking of the Caturi, Voari and Capuri. The latter is the Apure; but whether the Caturi is the Rio Manapire and the Voari the Guarico may be questioned. The proximity of the Apure, Arauca and Meta, and the numerous branches by which the two former are connected, give rise to great confusion. It is evident that Amapaia is the low swampy country between the Guarico and the Apure. The Casanare is one of the largest tributaries of the Meta, and is navigable up to the foot of the Andes of New Granada. The banks of the Rio Pauto, a tributary of the Meta, were formerly inhabited by Salivas. The Rio Negro, which falls into the upper river Meta, has its source within a few leagues of Santa Fé de Bogota. Indeed a fleet of flat-bottomed vessels may enter the Orinoco by the Boca de Navios and ascend that river to the mouth of the Rio Meta, entering which they might go up one hundred and seventy-two leagues till within twenty leagues of Santa Fé de Bogota. The communication with New Granada and Angostura by means of the Meta is not uncommon. These remarks of Ralegh sufficiently prove that he had a very good idea of the geography of these regions. The river Goavar is probably the Guaviare or Guabiari, which has its source on the eastern foot of the Andes, and flows through the savannahs of San Juan de los Llanos.

[2] The marshes of the Anebas are the extensive plains of Casanare. An Indian tribe, the Banibas or Manibas, inhabit at present the regions between the rivers Uaupes, Içana and the sources of the Rio Negro, a tributary of the Amazon; some are settled in the villages of the Rio Negro. Are they the descendants of Ralegh's Anebas, forced to emigrate from the Casanare further southward?

Thomebamba and *Caximalta*: adjoyning to *Quito* in the North of *Peru* are the riuers of *Guiacar* and *Goauar*: and on the other side of the saide mountaines the riuer of *Papamene* which descendeth into *Maragnon or Amazones* passing through the prouince of *Mutylones* where *Don Pedro de Osua* who was slayne by the traytour *Agiri* before rehearsed, built his *Brigandines*, when he sought *Guaina* by the waie of *Amazones*[1]. Betwene *Dawney* and *Beta* lieth a famous Iland in *Orenoque* now called *Baraquan* (For aboue *Meta* it is not knowne by the name of *Orenoque*) which is called *Athule*[2], beyond which, ships of burden cannot passe by reason of a most forcible ouerfall, and Current of waters: but in the eddy all smaller vesselles may be drawen euen to *Peru* it selfe: But to speake of more of these riuers without the description were but tedious, and therefore I will leaue the rest to the discription. This riuer of *Orenoque* is nauigable for ships little lesse then 1000 miles, and for lesser vessels neere 2000. By it (as aforesaid) *Peru, Nueuo reyno,* and *Popaian,* may be inuaded: it also leadeth to that great Empire of *Inga,* and to the prouinces of *Amapaia* and *Anebas* which abound in gold: his branches of *Cosnero, Manta, Caora* de-

[1] The Guiacar (Guayare or Canicamare) appears to be the Guayavero, a tributary of the Guaviare. The Papamene, or river of silver, is the Caqueta or Jupura, a tributary stream of the Solimoes or Upper Amazon, which Pedro de Ursua descended in 1560, to meet his death from the hands of the tyrant Aguirre.

[2] Ordaz affirms that the Orinoco, from its mouth to the confluence of the Meta, is called Uriaparia, but that above this river it is called Orinucu. Ralegh's evidence contradicts this, as he states expressly that above Meta it is not known by the name of Orenoque, and is from thence called Barequan. The Orinoco above the junction of the Guaviare is called by the natives Paragua, or great river, sea; and the erroneous interchange of *p* and *b*, so common among the Indians, may have given rise to Baraguan. The Rio Beta is a small stream which, near the Isla Solvaje, enters the Orinoco from the west; the Dawney, likewise frequently mentioned by Sparrey, is probably the Rio Tomo. The cataract Ature (called Athule by Ralegh and Sparrey) stops all further navigation in large boats during the dry season; but when the bed of the river is full, small sloops descend from the Cassiquiare to Angostura.

scend from the middle land and valley, which lyeth betweene the easter prouince of *Peru* and *Guiana*; and it falles into the sea betweene *Maragnon* and *Trinedado* in two degrees and a half, al which your Honors shal better perceiue in the generall description of *Guiana, Peru, Nueuo reyno,* the kingdom of *Popayan,* and *Roidas,* with the prouince of *Vensuello,* to the bay of *Vraba* behind *Cartagena,* westward: and to *Amazones* southward[1]. While we lay at ancor on the coast of *Canuri,* and had taken knowledge of all the nations vpon the head and braunches of this riuer, and had founde out so many seuerall people, which were enemies to the *Epuremei,* and the newe Conquerers: I thought it time lost to linger any longer in that place, especially for that the fury of *Orenoque* beganne dailie to threaten vs with daungers in our returne, for no halfe day passed, but the riuer began to rage and ouerflowe very fearefully, and the raines came downe in terrible showers, and gusts in greate abundance: and withall, our men beganne to cry out for want of shift, for no man had place to bestowe any other apparrell then that which he ware on his backe, and that was throughly washt on his body for the most part ten times in one day: and we had nowe beene well neare a moneth, euery day passing to the westwarde, farther and farther from our shippes. Wee therefore turned towards the east, and spent the rest of the time in discouering the riuer towardes the sea, which we had not yet viewed, and which was most materiall. The next day following we left the mouth of *Caroli,* and arriued againe at the port of *Morequito* where we were before (for passing downe the streame we went without labour, and against the winde, little lesse then 100 miles a day): As soon as I came to ancor I sent away one for old *Topiawari,*

[1] It does not appear that Ralegh ever executed his intention of giving a description of these regions; at least no trace is to be discovered of such a manuscript, which would have been of too great a value to have been passed over by his contemporaries and early biographers. The statement that the Orinoco falls into the sea in two degrees and a half must be a misprint, as he observes previously that the Caroni is in four degrees of latitude.

with whom I much desired to haue farther conference, and also to deal with him for some one of his countrey, to bring with vs into England, as well to learne the language, as to conferre withall by the way, (the time being now spent of anie longer stay there) within three howers after my messenger came to him, he arriued also, and with him such a rabble of all sortes of people, and euery one loden with somewhat, as if it had beene a great market or faire in England: and our hungrie companies clustered thicke and threefold among their baskets, euery one laying hand on what he liked. After he had rested a while in my tent, I shut out all but our selues, and my interpreter, and told him that I knew that both the *Epuremei* and the Spaniards were enemies to him, his countrey, and nations: that the one had conquered *Guiana* alreadie, and that the other sought to regaine the same from them both: And therefore I desired him to instruct me what hee coulde, both of the passage into the golden partes of *Guiana*, and to the ciuill townes and apparrelled people of *Inga*. Hee gaue me an aunswere to this effect: first that hee did not perceiue that I meant to goe onwarde towardes the Citie of *Manoa*, for neyther the time of the yeare serued, neyther could he perceiue any sufficient numbers for such an enterprize: and if I did I was sure with all my company to be buried there, for that the Emperour was of that strength, as that many times so many men more were too few: besides he gaue me this good counsell and aduised me to hold it in minde (as for himselfe he knewe, he coulde not liue til my returne) that I shoulde not offer by any meanes heereafter to inuade the strong partes of *Guiana* without the helpe of all those nations which were also their enemies: for that it was impossible without those, eyther to be conducted, to be victualled, or to haue ought carried with vs, our people not being able to indure the march in so great heate, and trauell, vnlesse the borderers gaue them helpe, to carry with them both their meate and furniture: For he remembred that in the plaines of *Macureguarai* 300 Spaniards were ouerthrowen, who were tired out, and had none of the borderers to their friendes, but meeting their enimies as they passed the frontier, were inuironed of all sides, and the people setting the long dry grasse on fire, smothered them so as they had no breath to fight, nor coulde discerne their enemies for the great smoke[1]. He told me farther that fower daies iourney from his towne was *Macureguarai*, and that those were the next, and nearest of the subiectes of *Inga*, and of the *Epuremei*, and the first towne of apparrelled and rich people, and that all those plates of Golde which were scattered among the borderers and carried to other nations farre and neare, came from the saide *Macureguarai* and were there made, but that those of the lande within, were farre finer, and were fashioned after the Image of men, beastes, birdes, and fishes. I asked him whether he thought that those companies that I had there with me, were sufficient to take that towne or no, he told me that he thought they were. I then asked him whether he woulde assist me with guides, and some companies of his people to ioyne with vs, he answered that he would go himself with all the borderers, if the riuers did remaine fordable, vpon this condition that I woulde leaue with him til my returne againe fiftie souldiers, which hee vndertooke to victual: I answerd that I had not aboue fiftie good men in all there, the rest were labourers and rowers, and that I had no prouision to leaue with them of powder, shot, apparrell, or ought else, and that without those thinges necessarie for their defence, they shoulde be in daunger of the Spaniardes in my absence, who I knew woulde vse the same

[1] Topiawari alludes here to Berreo's unfortunate expedition up the Caroni, of which Fray Simon gives a detailed description in his 'Setima Noticia historial de las Conquistas de Tierra firme.' The grass on the savannahs sometimes reaches a height of five to six feet. It is a common custom among the Indians to set it on fire during the dry season, and the aspect which such "a sea of fire" affords, especially at night, is certainly sublime, although not unconnected with danger; we recollect that we were repeatedly obliged to strike our tents and fly for our life, when by chance the wind had changed and the flames were approaching our camp; we have likewise witnessed the burning down of Indian settlements on such occasions.

measure towardes mine, that I offered them at *Trinedado*: And although vpon the motion Captaine *Calfelde*, Captaine *Greenuile*, my nephewe *Iohn Gilbert* and diuers others were desirours to staie, yet I was resolued that they must needs haue perished, for *Berreo* expected daily a supply out of Spayne, and looked also howerly for his sonne to come downe from *Nueuo reyno de Granada*, with many horse and foote, and had also in *Valentia* in the *Caracas*, 200 horse readie to march, and I coulde not haue spared aboue fortie, and had not anie store at all of powder, leade, or match to haue left with them, nor anie other prouision, eyther spade, pickeaxe, or ought else to haue fortified withall. When I had giuen him reason that I could not at this time leaue him such a company, he then desired me to forbeare him, and his countrey for that time, for hee assured me that I shoulde bee no sooner three daies from the coast, but those *Epuremei* woulde inuade him, and destroye all the remayne of his people and friendes, if hee shoulde any way eyther guide vs, or assist vs against them. Hee further alleadged that the Spaniards sought his death, and as they had alreadie murdered his Nephew *Morequito* Lorde of that prouince, so they had him 17 daies in a chaine before hee was king of the Countrey, and ledde him like a dogge from place to place, vntill hee had paide 100 plates of Golde, and diuers chaines of spleene stones for his raunsome, and nowe since hee became owner of that prouince that they had manie times laide waite to take him, and that they woulde be nowe more vehement when they shoulde vnderstand of his conference with the English, and because said hee, they woulde the better displant me, if they cannot lay handes on mee, they haue gotten a Nephew of mine called *Eparacano* whome they haue christened *Don Iuan*, and his sonne *Don Pedro*, whome they haue also apparrelled and armed, by whome they seeke to make a partie against mee, in mine owne countrey: hee also hath taken to wife one *Louiana*, of a strong familie, which are my borderers and neighbours: and my selfe beeing nowe olde and in the handes of death, am not able to trauell nor to shift, as when I was of younger years: hee therefore prayed vs to deferre it till the next yeare, when hee would vndertake to drawe in all the borderers to serue vs, and then also it woulde be more seasonable to trauel, for at this time of the yeare, we should not be able to passe any riuer, the waters were and would be so growen ere our returne. Hee farther told me that I could not desire so much to inuade *Macureguari*, and the rest of *Guiana* but that the borderers would be more vehement then I, for he yeelded for a chiefe cause that in the wars with the *Epuremei*, they were spoyled of their women, and that their wiues and daughters were taken from them, so as for their owne partes they desired nothing of the gold or treasure, for their labors, but onely to recouer women from the *Epuremei*: for he farther complayned very sadly (as if it had beene a matter of greate consequence) that whereas they were wont to haue ten or twelue wiues, they were now inforced to content themselues with three or fower, and that the Lords of the *Epuremei* had 50 or 100. And in truth they warre more for women, then eyther for gold or dominion. For the Lords of countries desire many children of their owne bodies, to encrease their races and kindreds, for in those consist their greatest trust and strength. Diuers of his followers afterwardes desired me to make hast againe, that they might sacke the *Epuremei*, and I asked them of what? they answered, of their women for vs, and their Golde for you: for the hope of many of those women they more desire the warre, then eyther for Golde, or for the recouery of their ancient territories. For what betweene the subiectes of *Inga*, and the Spaniards, those frontiers are growen thinne of people, and also great numbers are fled to other nations farther off for feare of the Spanyardes. After I receiued this aunsweare of the olde man, wee fell into consideration, whether it had beene of better aduice to haue entered *Macureguarai*, and to haue begunne a warre vpon *Inga* at this time, yea or no, if the time of the yere, and all thinges else had sorted. For mine own part (as we were not able to march it for the riuers, neither had any such strength as was requisite, and durst not abide the coming of the winter, or to tarrie any longer from our ships) I thought it verie euill counsell to haue attempted it at that time, although the desire of golde will aunswere many obiections: But it woulde haue been in mine opinion an vtter ouerthrowe to the enterprize, if the same should be hereafter by her Maiestie attempted: for then (whereas now they haue heard we were enemies to the Spaniards and were sent by her Maiestie to relieue them) they would as good cheape haue ioyned with the Spanyards at our returne, as to haue yeelded vnto vs, when they had proued that we came both for one errant, and that both sought but to sacke and spoyle them, but as yet our desier of gold, or our purpose of inuasion is not known vnto those of the Empire: and it is likely that if her maiestie vndertake the enterprize, they will rather submit themselues to her obedience then to the Spanyards, of whose cruelty both themselues and the borderers haue alreadie tasted: and therfore til I had known her maiesties pleasure, I woulde rather haue lost the sacke of one or two townes (although they might haue been very profitable) then to haue defaced or endaungered the future hope of so many millions, and the great good, and rich trade which England maie bee possessed off thereby. I am assured nowe that they will all die euen to the last man against the Spanyardes, in hope of our succoure and returne: whereas otherwise if I had either laid handes on the borderers, or ransommed the Lordes as *Berreo* did, or inuaded the subiects of *Inga*, I knowe all had been lost for hereafter. After that I had resolued *Topiawari* Lorde of *Aromaia* that I could not at this time leaue with him the companies he desired, and that I was contented to forbeare the enterprize against the *Epuremei* till the next yeare, he freely gaue me his onelie sonne to take with me into England, and hoped, that though he himselfe had but a short tyme to liue, yet that by our meanes his sonne shoulde be established after his death: and I left with him one *Frauncis Sparrow*, a seruant of captaine *Gifford*[1],

[1] The name of the person whom Sir Walter Ralegh left behind was

(who was desirous to tarry, and coulde describe a cuntrey with his pen) and a boy of mine called *Hugh Goodwin*, to learne the language. I after asked the manner howe the *Epuromei* wrought those plates of golde, and howe they coulde melt it out of the stone; he tolde me that the most of the gold which they made in plates and images was not seuered from the stone, but that on the lake of *Manoa*, and in a multitude of other riuers they gathered it in graines of perfect golde and in peeces as bigg as small stones, and that they put to it a part of copper, otherwise they coulde not worke it, and that they vsed a great earthen potte with holes round about it, and when they had mingled the gold and copper together, they fastned canes to the holes, and so with the breath of men they increased the fire till the mettell ran, and then they cast it into moulds of stone and clay, and so make those plates and Images. I haue sent your Honours, of two sorts such as I coulde by chance recouer, more to shew the manner of them, then for the value: For I did not in any sort make my desire of golde knowen, because I had neyther time, nor power to haue a greater quantitie. I gaue among them manye more peeces of Golde then I receaued of the new money of 20 shillings with her Maiesties picture to weare, with promise that they would become her seruants thenceforth[1].

I haue also sent your Honors of the oare, whereof I knowe

Francis Sparrey, as we see from the publication of his description of the "Ile of Trinidad, the rich countrie of Guiana, and the mightie river of Orenoco, written by Francis Sparrey, left there by Sir Walter Ralegh 1595, and in the end taken by the Spaniards and sent prisoner into Spaine, and after long captivities got into England by great sute. 1602." (Purchas, vol. iv. chap. 11.) It does not contain much additional information above what had already been told by Ralegh himself.

[1] The only use which the Indians of the interior, who have no intercourse with the coast, make of money is to wear it as an ornament round their neck. We have distributed many a shilling for such a purpose, and by barter between the tribes money finds thus its way to the most distant nations. We met among the Woyawais, a tribe inhabiting the sources of the Essequibo, a medal struck to commemorate the victory of Frederic the Great at Chottusitz on the 17th of May, 1742.

some is as rich as the earth yeeldeth anie, of which I know there is sufficient, if nothing else were to be hoped for[1]. But besides that we were not able to tarry and search the hils, so we had neither pioners, bars, sledges, nor wedges of Iron, to breake the ground, without which there is no working in mynes: but we sawe all the hils with stones of the cullor of Gold and siluer, and wee tried them to be no *Marquesite,* and therefore such as the Spaniards call *El Màdre del oro,* which is an vndoubted assurance of the generall abundance; and my selfe saw the outside of many mines of the white sparre, which I know to be the same that all couet in this worlde, and of those, more then I will speake of.

Hauing learned what I could in *Canuri* and *Aromaia,* and receiued a faithful promise of the principallest of those prouinces to become seruauntes to her Maiestie, and to resist the Spanyardes, if they made any attempt in our absence, and that they woulde drawe in the nations about the lake of *Cassipa,* and those *Iwarawaqueri,* I then parted from olde *Topiawari,* and receiued his sonne for a pledge betweene vs, and left with him two of ours as aforesaid[2]: To *Francis Sparrowe* I gaue instructions to trauell to *Macureguarai,* with such marchaundizes as I left with

[1] Oldys observes, that some of the ore which Sir Walter Ralegh brought from Guiana, and probably some of that which he brought at this time, had been so carefully preserved in his family, that he himself saw it in the possession of Captain William Elwes, who, with various communications relating to Sir Walter Ralegh, obliged him likewise with a sight of the ore. (Oxford edit. of Sir Walter Ralegh's Life, note at p. 221.)

[2] Topiawari expected the return of Sir Walter Ralegh for a considerable period. In the 'Relation of the Habitations and other Observations of the River Marwin,' to which we have already had occasion to allude (see *ante,* note at p. 38), the author mentions that the old Indian who came down the Salinama (Surinam), and who was born at the Orinoco, told him that Topiawari wondered much that he had not heard from Sir Walter Ralegh, according to his promise, and that "Topiawari had drawn in the Indians of Wariwackeri, Amiariocopana, Wickeri, and all the people that belonged to Wanuritona, Captain of Canuria, and Wacariopea, Captain of Sayma, against Sir Walter his coming, to have warred against the Yeanderpureweis, and as yet Wanuritono and Wacariopea do expect his coming." (Purchas, book vi. chap. 17.)

him, thereby to learne the place, and if it were possible to go on, to the great City of *Manoa*: which being done, we weyed ancor, and coasted the riuer on *Guiana* side, because we came vp on the north side, by the launes of the *Saima* and *Wikiri*.

There came with vs from *Aromaia*, a *Cassique* called *Putijma*, that commaunded the prouince of *Warapana*, (which *Putijma* slewe the nyne Spaniardes vppon *Caroli* before spoken of,) who desired vs to rest at the porte of his Countrey, promising to bring vs to a mountaine adioyning to his towne that had stones of the cullor of Golde, which hee performed: And after wee had rested there one night, I went my selfe in the morning with most of the Gentlemen of my campany, ouer lande towardes the saide mountaine, marching by a riuers side called *Mana*, leauing on the right hande a towne called *Tuteritona*, standing in the prouince of *Tarracoa*, of which *Wariaaremagoto* is principall: Beyond it lyeth another towne towardes the south, in the valley of *Amariocapana*, which beareth the name of the saide valley, whose plaines stretch themselues some 60 miles in length, east and west, as fayre grounde, and as beawtifull fieldes, as any man hath euer seene, with diuers copses scattered heere and there by the riuers side, and all as full of deare, as any forrest or parke in England, and in euery lake and riuer the like abundance of fish and fowle, of which *Irraparragota* is Lord[1].

From the riuer of *Mana*, we crost another riuer in the said beawtifull valley called *Oiana*, and rested our selues by a cleare lake, which lay in the middle of the said *Oiana*[2], and one of our

[1] It appears that the regions which Sir Walter describes are the plains of Upata and Piacoa, formerly the site of numerous missions. These savannahs are abundantly visited by a species of deer (called Beyou, Waiking, &c. by the Indians), the large antlers of which show that it is best adapted for open plains or savannahs. There is still great uncertainty respecting its specific distinction, but we suppose it to be the *Guazuti* of Azara, or *Mazama campestris* of Smith.

[2] The allusion to the lake leads us to suppose that this was the river Casacoima; the Mana would therefore be the river now called Supamo. The river Conoyoima has likewise a lake close to its bank; but from the relation which follows, it appears that Sir Walter had to row some di-

guides kindling vs fire with two stickes[1], we staied a while to dry our shirts, which with the heat hong very weete and heauy on our shoulders. Afterwards we sought the ford to passe ouer towards the mountain called *Iconuri,* where *Putijma* foretold vs of the mine. In this lake we saw one of the great fishes, as big as a wine pipe, which they call *Manati,* and is most excellent and holsome meate[2]. But after I perceiued, that to passe the saide riuer woulde require halfe a daies march more, I was not able my selfe to indure it, and therefore I sent Captaine *Keymis* with six shotte to goe on, and gaue him order not to returne to the port of *Putijma,* which is called *Chiparepare,* but to take leasure, and to march downe the said valley, as farre as a riuer called

stance before he reached Arriacoa, while the mouth of the Conoyoima is scarcely four miles from "where Orinoco deuideth it selfe into three great braunches."

[1] The skill of the Indians in kindling fire by means of two sticks is very surprising. None of us Europeans were able to imitate them in this art. The sticks are two different kinds of wood, one of which is softer than the other; the tree from which the softer is taken is called Hirihiri. A small notch having been made in the Hirihiri wood, it is kept by means of the great toe and its adjunct (by the bye the Indian uses his toes as skilfully as we do our fingers) firmly on the ground. He now takes the stick of harder wood, and applying the end of it to the notch, turns it rapidly round with a twirling motion; the friction enlarges the notch of the horizontal stick, and at its side appears a small heap of wood-dust, the result of the revolving motion, which ultimately, when the friction produces smoke, ignites like tinder. Meanwhile some dry grass and fine shavings of wood or the *bekersda* (a peculiar stuff which is found in ants' nests and serves as touch-wood) have been kept ready, which are put upon the burning embers, and the flame soon appears. It is now seldom that the Indians resort to their original mode of making fire; most of them possess a steel, and the red and blue jaspers of Roraima serve the same purpose as the best flints.

[2] The Lamantin or Manati (*Manatus americanus,* Cuv.) is very abundant in some of the rivers in Guiana. It affords a wholesome meat, of good flavour, intermediate between pork and veal; nevertheless, in consequence of some superstitious scruples, many of the Indian tribes do not eat it. As the animal is amphibious, the Catholics are permitted to use its meat during Lent and on other fast days. We know little of the anatomical structure of this animal, which is still a great rarity in our museums.

Cumaca[1], where I promised to meete him againe, (*Putijma* himselfe promising also to be his guide,) and as they marched, they left the townes of *Emparepana*, and *Capurepana*, on the right hande, and marched from *Putijmas* house, downe the saide valley of *Amariocapana*, and wee returning the same daie to the riuers side, sawe by the way many rockes, like vnto Golde oare, and on the left hand, a rounde mountaine which consisted of minerall stone.

From hence we rowed downe the streame, coasting the prouince of *Parino*; As for the braunches of riuers which I ouerpasse in discourse, those shal be better expressed in the description, with the mountaines of *Aio, Ara,* and the rest, which are situate in the prouinces of *Parino* and *Carricurrina*[2]. When wee were come as farre downe as the lande called *Arriacoa*, (where *Orenoque* deuideth it selfe into three great braunches, each of them beeing most goodly riuers[3],) I sent away Captaine

[1] Cumaca is an Arawaak word, and signifies Silk-cotton-tree (*Bombax Ceiba*, Linn.). A settlement called Cumaka is at present situated on the Aruka, a tributary stream of the river Barima. Ralegh probably alludes here to the river Tipurua.

[2] The word Carricurrina is a compound of *Carucuri* or *Carucuru*, which in the Tamanac and Carib dialects signifies gold; yellow, like a lemon, is called *tikire* in Carib, and *emuripo* in Macusi. It is very remarkable that the Indians of Guiana have no word for silver in their language. They have adopted the Spanish and Portuguese *plata* and *prata*; and in the eyes of the untutored natives a piece of silver has much greater value than a similar piece of gold. Humboldt considers it probable that *Carucuru* is a foreign word, which may have been introduced with this precious metal from the Cordilleras. "In the Peruvian or Quichua (lengua del Inga) gold is called *cori*, whence are derived *chichicori*, gold in powder, and *corikoya*, gold ore." (Humboldt's Personal Narrative, English translation, vol. v. p. 823.) Articles of brass, or any metal of a yellow colour, are expressed among the Guianese by a word which contains the radical *coru* or *cori*. Ralegh introduces Carricurrina, gold-land, with some ingenuity, the more since the observation that he "saw by the way many rocks like unto gold ore" had just before been stated.

[3] We have alluded to this division of the Orinoco on a former occasion (see *ante*, note at p. 63). The branch which Ralegh descended, and which he calls Cararoopana, is now known by the name of the Caño Piacoa, from a town of that name which lies on the right bank of the Orinoco, and

Henry Thyn, and Captaine *Greeneuile* with the Galley, the nearest way, and tooke with me Captaine *Gifford*, Captaine *Calfeild*, *Edward Porter*, and Captaine *Eynos* with mine owne barge, and the two wherries, and went downe that braunch of *Orenoque*, which is called *Cararoopana*, which leadeth towards *Emeria* the prouince of *Carapana*, and towards the east sea, as well to finde out Captaine *Keymis*, whome I had sent ouer land, as also to acquaint my selfe with *Carapana*, who is one of the greatest of all the Lordes of the *Orenoqueponi*: and when we came to the riuer of *Cumaca* (to which *Putijma* promised to conduct Captaine *Keymis*) I left Captaine *Eynos* and Master *Porter* in the said riuer to expect his comming, and the rest of vs rowed downe the streame towardes *Emeria*.

In this braunch called *Cararoopana* were also many goodly Ilandes, some of sixe miles long, some of tenne, and some of Twentie, when it grewe towards sunne sett, we entred a braunch of a riuer that fel into *Orenoque* called *Winicapora*[1], where I was enformed of the mountaine of Christall, to which in trueth for the length of the way, and the euill season of the yeare, I was not able to march, nor abide any longer vpon the iourney: we saw it a farre off and it appeared like a white Church towre of an exceeding height: There falleth ouer it a mightie riuer which toucheth no parte of the side of the mountaine, but rusheth ouer the toppe of it, and falleth to the grounde with a terrible noyse and clamor, as if 1000 great belles were knockt one against another[2]. I thinke there is not in the worlde so straunge

which constitutes the chief place of the canton of the Lower Orinoco or Piacoa.

[1] Winicapora is probably the river now called Caño José; its name is derived from the Arawaak language. *Wouin* signifies rain, *Wouiniabo* water, and *Cabara* (*capora*) a small river or brook. We meet frequently compounds of that description on the rivers Demerara and Berbice, the banks of which are mostly inhabited by Arawaaks; as for example Camicabara, Catchicabara, &c.

[2] The wonders of the mountains of Roraima and Cukenam, upon which one of the branches of the Caroni (the Cukenam) has its sources, are so famed among the Indians, that the author of these notes recognises in Ralegh's relation a description of these regions. We have already alluded

an ouerfall, nor so wonderfull to beholde: *Berreo* tolde mee that it hath Diamondes and other precious stones on it, and that they shined very farre off: but what it hath I knowe not, neyther durst he or any of his men ascende to the toppe of the saide mountaine, those people adioyning beeing his enemies (as they were) and the way to it so impassible.

Vpon this riuer of *Winecapora* wee rested a while, and from thence marched into the Countrey to a towne called after the name of the riuer, whereof the chiefe was one *Timitwara,* who also offered to conduct mee to the toppe of the saide mountaine called *Wacarima*: But when wee came in first to the house of the saide *Timitwara,* beeing vppon one of their feast daies, wee founde them all as drunke as beggers, and the pottes walking from one to another without rest[1]: we that were weary, and

to this remarkable mountain group of primitive sandstone, which extends about thirty miles in a north-west and south-east direction, and rises upwards of five thousand feet above the table-land, the uppermost fourteen hundred feet presenting a mural precipice of the most striking appearance. Down the face of these mountains rush numerous cascades, which eventually form tributaries to the three great rivers of the northern half of South America, namely the Amazon, the Orinoco and the Essequibo. (See *ante,* note at p. 75.)

[1] The scenes which occur during one of their drinking feasts surpass all description. The quantity of liquor drunk on such an occasion is enormous; and as there would not be a sufficient number of vessels in the largest household of an Indian chieftain to contain it, a canoe is generally taken from the river, rendered water-tight, and filled with their beverage. They do not stop until it is emptied; when it comes however to the dregs, the greater number lie senseless on the ground or in their hammocks. A friend has drawn our attention to a note in the 'Anglo-Saxon Dialogues of Salomon and Saturn,' edited by Mr. John M. Kemble, for the Ælfric Society (p. 176), in which the editor says:—"The ideas of cup and ship mingle singularly together in the old Norse expressions: thus in Hymisquida, § xxxiii., a large drinking vessel or cup is called Öl-Kiöl, *navigium cerevisiæ*:—

Þat er til costar	That may be tried
ef coma mættiþ	if ye can carry
ut or oro	out of our
Öl-Kiöl hofi.	dwelling the *beership.*

And in Haconarquida it appears that Winfar, or *vini navis,* also denotes a cup." Now we think that Öl-Kiöl has a more literal signification than

hotte with marching, were glad of the plenty, though a small quantitie satisfied vs, their drinke beeing very strong and heady, and so rested our selues awhile; after we had fedde, wee drewe our selues backe to our boats, vppon the riuer, and there came to vs all the Lordes of the Countrey, with all such kinde of victuall as the place yeelded, and with their delicate wine of *Pinas*, and with aboundance of hens, and other prouisions, and of those stones which wee call Spleene-stones. Wee vnderstoode by these chiefetaines of *Winicapora*, that their Lorde *Carapana* was departed from *Emeria* which was nowe in sight, and that hee was fledde to *Cairamo*, adioyning to the mountaines of *Guiana*, ouer the valley called *Amariocapana*, beeing perswaded by those tenne Spanyardes which lay at his house, that we woulde destroy him, and his countrey.

But after these *Cassiqui* of *Winicapora* and *Saporatona* his followers perceiued our purpose, and sawe that we came as enemies to the Spanyardes onely, and had not so much as harmed any of those nations, no though wee founde them to bee of the Spanyardes owne seruantes, they assured vs that *Carapana* woulde bee as readie to serue vs, as any of the Lordes of the prouinces, which wee had passed; and that hee durst doe no other till this daie but entertaine the Spanyardes, his countrey lying so directly in their waie, and next of all other to any enterance that should bee made in *Guiana* on that side.

And they farther assured vs, that it was not for feare of our comming that hee was remoued, but to bee acquited of those Spanyardes or any other that shoulde come heereafter. For the

as explained by Mr. Kemble: the custom of the Indians presents so remarkable a coincidence with this, that we consider the expression to have a deeper meaning than the mere convenience of so large a cup. We have already observed (see *ante*, note at p. 65) that the trough which forms generally a utensil in the houses of chieftains, for the purpose of containing the beverage during festivals, is called *Canaua* or Canoe, and this is the case in all the Guianian languages and dialects we are acquainted with. This vessel has the shape of a boat, and on occasions, as before referred to, a canoe is taken in addition out of the water.

prouince of *Cairoma* is situate at the mountaine foote, which deuideth the plaines of *Guiana*, from the countries of the *Orenoqueponi*: by meanes whereof if any shoulde come in our absence into his townes, hee woulde slippe ouer the mountaines into the plaines of *Guiana* amonge the *Epuremei*, where the Spanyardes durste not followe him without greate force.

But in mine opinion, or rather I assure my selfe, that *Carapana* (beeing a notable wise and subtile fellowe, a man of one hundred yeares of age, and therefore of greate experience) is remooued, to looke on, and if hee finde that wee returne strong, hee will bee ours, if not, hee will excuse his departure to the Spanyards, and say it was for feare of our comming.

We therefore thought it booteles to rowe so farre downe the streame, or to seeke any farther for this olde fox: and therefore frome the riuer of *Waricapana* (which lieth at the entrance of *Emeria*,) we turned again, and left to the Eastward those 4 riuers which fall from out the mountaines of *Emeria* and *Orenoque*, which are *Waracapari*, *Coirama*, *Akaniri*, and *Iparoma*[1]: belowe those 4 are also these braunches and mouths of *Orenoque*, which fall into the Est sea, whereof the first is *Araturi*, the next *Amacura*, the third *Barima*, the fourth *Wana*, the fift *Morooca*, the sixt *Paroma*, the last *Wijmi*: beyond them, there fall out of the land betweene *Orenoque* and *Amazones* 14 riuers which I forbeare to name, inhabited by the *Arwacas* and *Caniballs*.

It is nowe time to returne towardes the North, and we founde it a wearisome way backe, from the borders of *Emeria*, to re-

[1] The rivers here alluded to are probably the Socoroco (Waracapari), Imataca (Coirama), Aguire (Akaniri) and Carapo (Iparoma). The country which is watered by these rivers is called Emeria by Ralegh. The succeeding six rivers bear nearly the same names as mentioned by Ralegh; only the Wana is called Waini or Guainia, and the Paroma or Pawroma the Pomeroon. We cannot conjecture what Ralegh means by Wijmi, except he confounds it with the Waini already enumerated, as the only river of consequence which follows the Pomeroon is the Essequibo, which at that period was called Dissekebe or Divortia, as we learn from Keymis, or Araunama by the Arawaaks.

couer vp againe to the head of the riuer *Carerupana,* by which we descended, and where we parted from the galley, which I directed to take the next way to the Porte of *Toparimaca,* by which we entred first.

All the night it was stormie and darke, and full of thunder and great showers, so as we were driuen to keepe close by the bankes in our small boats, being all heartely afraid both of the billowe, and terrible Current of the riuer. By the next morning wee recouered the mouth of the riuer of *Cumaca,* where wee left Captaine *Eynus* and Edward Porter to attend the coming of Capatine *Keymis* ouer land: but when we entred the same, they had heard no newes of his ariuall, which bredde in vs a great doubt what might be become of him: I rowed vp a league or two farther into the riuer, shooting off peeces all the way, that he might know of our being there: And the next morning we hearde them answere vs also with a peece: we tooke them abord vs, and tooke our leaue of *Putijma* their guide, who of all others most lamented our departure, and offred to send his sonne with vs into England, if we could haue staide till he had sent backe to his towne: but our hearts were cold to behold the great rage and increase of *Orenoque,* and therefore departed, and turned towarde the west, till we had recouered the parting of the 3 braunches aforesaide, that we might put downe the streame after the Galley.

The next day we landed on the Iland of *Assapana,* (which deuideth the riuer from that braunch by which we went down to *Emeria*) and there feasted our selues with that beast which is called *Armadilla* presented vnto vs before at *Winicapora,* and the day following we recouered the galley at ancour at the port of *Toparimaca,* and the same euening departed with verie fowle weather and terrible thunder, and showers, for the winter was come on verie farre: the best was, we went no lesse then 100 miles a day, down the riuer: but by the way we entred, it was impossiblie to return, for that the riuer of *Amana,* being in the bottome of the bay of *Guanipa,* cannot be sayled back by any meanes, both the brize and currente of the sea were so forcible, and therefore we followed a braunch of *Orenoque* called *Capuri*[1], which entred into the sea eastward of our ships, to the end we might beare with them before the wind, and it was not without neede, for we had by that way as much to crosse of the maine sea, after wee came to the riuers mouth as betweene *Grauelyn* and *Douer*, in such boats as your Honours haue heard.

To speake of what past homeward were tedious, eyther to describe or name any of the riuers, Ilands, or villages of the *Tiuitiuas* which dwell on trees, we will leaue all those to the generall mappe: And to be short, when we were arriued at the sea side then grew our greatest doubt, and the bitterest of all our iourney forepassed, for I protest before God, that wee were in a most desperate estate: for the same night which we ancored in the mouth of the riuer of *Capuri*, where it falleth into the sea, there arose a mighty storme, and the riuers mouth was at least a league broad, so as we ran before night close vnder the land with our small boates, and brought the Galley as neere as we could, but she had as much a doe to liue as coulde be, and there wanted little of her sinking, and all those in her: for mine own part, I confesse, I was very doubtfull which way to take, eyther to goe ouer in the pestred Galley, there beeing but sixe foote water ouer the sands, for two leagues together, and that also in the channell, and she drew fiue: or to aduenture in so great a billow, and in so doubtfull weather, to crosse the seas in my barge.

[1] About four miles below Barrancas, the first of the branches which form the oceanic delta of the Orinoco separates from the principal trunk: it is at present known under the name of Brazo (arm or branch) Macareo. About fifteen miles from this point the Brazo Macareo divides into two branches, of which the left one, or western, is the Caño Manamo, and the right one, or eastern, the Caño Macareo, which Ralegh descended on the present occasion, and which he calls erroneously Capuri. This arm is generally selected by all vessels of no more than twenty or thirty tons burden when bound for Trinidad. The bay in which he passed the stormy night was the one in which the Macareo flows. The distance between the mouth of the Macareo and the south-western point of Trinidad is about seven leagues.

The longer we tarried the worse it was, and therefore I took Captaine *Gifford*, Captaine *Calfeild*, and my cosen *Greeneuile*, into my barge, and after it cleared vppe, about midnight wee put our selues to Gods keeping, and thrust out into the sea, leauing the Galley at ancor, who durst not aduenture but by day light. And so beeing all very sober, and melancholy, one faintly chearing another to shew courage, it pleased God that the next day about nyne of the clocke, we descryed the Iland of *Trinedado*, and stearing for the nearest part of it, wee kept the shore til we came to *Curiapan*, where we found our ships at ancor, then which, there was neuer to vs a more ioyfull sight.

Now that it hath pleased God to send vs safe to our ships, it is time to leaue *Guiana* to the Sunne, whom they worship, and steare away towardes the north: I will therefore in a fewe wordes finish the discouery thereof. Of the seuerall nations which we found vpon this discouery I will once againe make repetition, and how they are affected. At our first entrance into *Amana*, which is one of the outlets of *Orenoque*, we left on the right hand of vs in the bottome of the bay, lying directly against *Trinedado*, a nation of inhumaine *Canibals*, which inhabite the riuers of *Guanipa* and *Berreese*; in the same bay there is also a third riuer which is called *Areo*[1], which riseth on *Paria* side towards *Cumana*, and that riuer is inhabited with the *Wikiri*, whose chiefe towne vpon the said riuer is *Sayma*; In this bay there are no more riuers, but these three before rehearsed, and the fower braunches of *Amana*, all which in the winter[2] thrust so great abundance of water into the sea, as the same is taken vp fresh,

[1] The Areo is a tributary of the Amana, which river flows a short distance north of the Guanipa into a great laguna, out of which the river Guanipa alone issues and falls into the bay of Guanipa. We have already observed that Ralegh gives the Caño Manamo the name of the river Amana (see *ante*, note at p. 44). The only river which, besides the Guanipa, enters the bay is the Rio Chipa, a mere branch of the former. The river Guarapiche falls into the Gulf of Paria, twenty miles north-west of the Guanipa.

[2] It is scarcely necessary to observe that the rainy season is called the winter of the tropics.

two or three leagues from the land. In the passages towardes *Guiana*, (that is, in all those landes which the eight branches of *Orenoque* fashione into Ilandes,) there are but one sort of people called *Tiuitiuas*, but of two castes as they tearme them, the one called *Ciawary*, the other *Waraweeti*, and those warre one with the other.

On the hithermost part of *Orenoque*, as at *Toparimaca*, and *Winicapora*, those are of a nation Called *Nepoios*, and are of the followers of *Carapana*, Lorde of *Emeria*. Betweene *Winicapora* and the port of *Morequito* which standeth in *Aromaia*, and all those in the valley of *Amariocapana* are called *Orenoqueponi*, and did obey *Morequito*, and are nowe followers of *Topiawari*. Vpon the riuer of *Caroli*, are the *Canuri*, which are gouerned by a woman[1] (who is inheritrix of that prouince) who came farre off to see our nation, and asked mee diuers questions of her Maiesty, beeing much delighted with the discourse of her Maiesties greatnes, and wondring at such reports as we truely made of her highnes many vertues. And vpon the head of *Caroli*, and on the lake of *Cassipa*, are the three strong nations of the *Cassipagotos*. Right south into the land are the *Capurepani*, and *Emparepani*, and beyond those adioyning to *Macureguarai*, (the first Citie of *Inga*,) are the *Iwarawakeri*: all these are professed enemies to the Spanyardes, and to the rich *Epuremei* also. To the west of *Caroli* are diuers nations of *Canibals*, and of those *Ewaipanoma* without heades. Directly west are the *Amapaias* and *Anebas*, which are also marueilous rich in gold. The rest towardes *Peru* wee will omit. On the north of *Orenoque*, betweene it and the

[1] As the blood is thought to descend pure through the female line alone, the circumstance of a female standing at the head of a tribe is by no means uncommon. I found even the proud Carabisi in one of the settlements on the Corentyne under a female ruler. Ralegh perhaps imagined that the account of an Indian female chieftain in Guiana would prove of interest to Queen Elizabeth. In the Introduction, when speaking of the Amazons, we have pointed out the close similarity between the name Canuri and that of the river Canuriz, on the mouth of which, according to Father Acuña, Orellana met the female warriors.

west Indies are the *Wikiri*, *Saymi*, and the rest before spoken of, all mortall enemies to the Spanyardes. On the south side of the maine mouth of *Orenoque*, are the *Arwacas*: and beyond them the *Canibals*: and to the south of them the *Amazones*.

To make mention of the seueral beasts, birds, fishes, fruites, flowers, gummes, sweete woodes, and of their seuerall religions and customes, would for the first require as many volumes as those of *Gesnerus*[1], and for the rest another bundle of *Decades*. The religion of the *Epuremei* is the same which the *Ingas*, Emperors of *Peru* vsed, which may be red in *Cieca*, and other Spanish stories, howe they beleeue the immortalitie of the Soule, worship the Sunne, and bury with them aliue their best beloued wiues and treasure, as they likewise doe in *Pegu* in the east Indies, and other places. The *Orenoqueponi* bury not their wiues with them, but their Jewels, hoping to inioy them againe. The *Arwacas* dry the bones of their Lordes, and their wiues and friendes drinke them in powder. In the graues of the *Peruuians*, the Spanyards founde their greatest abundance of treasure: The like also is to be found among these people in euery prouince. They haue all many wiues, and the Lordes fiue folde to the common sort: their wiues neuer eate with their husbands, nor among the men, but serue their husbandes at meales, and afterwardes feede by themselues. Those that are past their yonger yeares, make all their breade and drinke, and worke their cotten beddes, and doe all else of seruice and labour, for the men doe nothing but hunte, fish, play, and drinke, when they are out of the wars[2].

[1] Conrad Gesner, an eminent physician and naturalist in Zurich, wrote numerous able works on different branches of natural history. His fame as a botanist was spread over Europe; but his greatest work was his 'Historia Animalium,' which procured him the appellation of the Pliny of Germany. He died in 1561.

[2] All the Indian tribes whom we have visited during our eight years' wanderings, bury with the dead the chief treasures which they possessed in life. The Arawaaks of the present day, although they no longer dry the bones of their chieftains and drink them in powder, celebrate at stated

I wil enter no further into discourse of their maners, lawes and customes: and because I haue not my selfe seene the cities of *Inga*, I cannot auow on my credit what I haue heard, although it be very likely, that the Emperour *Inga* hath built and erected as magnificent pallaces in *Guiana*, as his auncestors did in *Peru*, which were for their riches and rarenes most marueilous and exceding al in *Europe*, and I thinke of the world, *China* excepted, which also the Spanyards (which I had) assured me to be of trueth, as also the nations of the borderers, who being but *Saluaios*, to those of the Inland, do cause much treasure to be buried with them, for I was enformed of one of the *Cassiqui* of the valley of *Amariocapana* which had buried with him a little before our arriuall, a chaire of Golde most curiously wrought, which was made eyther in *Macureguarai* adioyning, or in *Manoa*: But if wee shoulde haue grieued them in their religion at the first, before they had beene taught better, and haue digged vppe their graues, wee had lost them all: and therefore I helde my first resolution, that her maiesty should eyther accept or refuse the enterprise, ere any thing shoulde be done that might in any sort hinder the same[1]. And if *Peru* had so many heapes of Golde, whereof those *Ingas* were Princes, and that they delighted so much therein, no doubt but this which nowe liueth

periods the death of their great men, by drinking-feasts and dances, during which they flagellate themselves most unmercifully with whips. Polygamy exists among all the Guianians, and the peculiar custom which forbids women to eat with the men still prevails. Some of the Caribs form an exception, and we have occasionally observed, when among that tribe, that the females take their meals with their husbands. The first wife generally conducts the domestic affairs, and though she possess no longer the love of her husband, she retains nevertheless the management of domestic matters.

[1] The resting-places of the dead are held most sacred, and it has cost us the greatest difficulty to procure the few skulls which we were able to collect during our journey. In order to hide our treasures of organic remains we have been obliged to secrete them among our wearing-apparel, and thus they have been unconsciously carried by Indians, whom, if the contents of their burden had been known to them, nothing in the world would have induced to place it upon their shoulders.

and raigneth in *Manoa*, hath the same humour, and I am assured hath more abundance of Golde, within his territorie, then all *Peru*, and the west Indies.

For the rest, which my selfe haue seene I will promise these things that follow and knowe to be true. Those that are desirous to discouer and to see many nations, may be satisfied within this riuer, which bringeth forth so many armes and branches leading to seuerall countries, and prouinces, aboue 2000 miles east and west, and 800 miles south and north: and of these, the most eyther rich in Gold, or in other marchandizes. The common soldier shal here fight for gold, and pay himselfe in steede of pence, with plates of halfe a foote brode, wheras he breaketh his bones in other warres for prouant and penury. Those commanders and Chieftaines, that shoote at honour, and abundance, shal find there more rich and bewtifull cities, more temples adorned with golden Images, more sepulchers filled with treasure, then either *Cortez* found in *Mexico*, or *Pazzaro* in *Peru*: and the shining glorie of this conquest will eclipse all those so farre extended beames of the Spanish nation[1]. There is no countrey which yeeldeth more pleasure to the Inhabitants, either for these common delights of hunting, hawking, fishing, fowling, and the rest, then *Guiana* doth. It hath so many plaines, cleare riuers, abundance of Phesants, Partridges, Quailes, Rayles, Cranes, Herons, and all other fowle: Deare of all sortes, Porkes, Hares, Lyons, Tygers, Leopards, and diuers other sortes of beastes, eyther for chace, or foode[2]. It hath a kinde of

[1] We must confess that this description is too highly coloured, even for the period at which Ralegh wrote; and we can only conjecture that it was intended for a lure to induce his countrymen to embark in his scheme for the conquest and colonization of Guiana. The author of "Newes of Sir Walter Rauleigh," who wrote that work to draw attention to the renewed schemes of Ralegh in 1617, avails himself of this passage to found upon it the best recommendation for embarking in the Guiana voyage.

[2] Ralegh's observations on animals and birds in his History of the World (lib. i. cap. vii. sect. 9) are very curious, but as naturalists we cannot agree with him on the identity of species in Europe, Asia and America. Nature would never change a young rook into a macaw, though it were

beast called *Cama*, or *Anta*, as bigge as an English beefe, and in greate plenty[1].

To speake of the seuerall sortes of euery kinde, I feare would be troublesome to the Reader, and therefore I will omitte them, and conclude that both for health, good ayre, pleasure, and riches, I am resolued it cannot bee equalled by any region eyther in the east or west. Moreouer the countrey is so healthfull, as 100 persons and more, which lay (without shift most sluttishly, and were euery day almost melted with heat in rowing and marching, and suddenly wet againe with great showers, and did eate of all sorts of corrupt fruits, and made meales of fresh fish without seasoning, of *Tortugas*, of *Lagartos*, and of al sorts good and bad, without either order or measure, and besides lodged in the open ayre euery night) we lost not any one, nor had one ill disposed to my knowledge, nor found anie *Callentura*, or other of those pestilent diseases which dwell in all hote regions, and so nere the Equinoctiall line[2].

reared in America from the first symptoms of life. Some species of the genus Ortyx resemble the European partridge, but they are not identical with it; the same may be said as to the pheasants, quails, &c. When enumerating pigs, hares, lions, tigers and leopards, Ralegh makes his comparisons from striking resemblances to these animals of the Old World. The pig kind is represented in America by the Peccari (*Dicotyles torquatus*, F. Cuv.) and the Poinka (*D. labiatus*, F. Cuv.), the hare by the Agouti (*Dasyprocta Ayuti*, Desm.), the lion by the Puma (*Felis concolor*, Linn.), the tiger by the Jaguar (*Felis onza*, Linn.), the leopard by some of the numerous spotted tiger-cats.

[1] This is the Tapir (*Tapirus Americanus*, Gmel.), the largest quadruped of tropical America. The meat is excellent in taste, but the Brazilians have a prejudice against it, and warned us repeatedly not to eat of it. We have never felt any ill consequences from eating it, and were highly delighted with our luck when we succeeded in replenishing our larder with such a large beast.

[2] During the eight years of our rambles through the thick forests over the hills and the extensive savannahs, though our night's lodging was often merely the shelter of an umbrageous tree,—though often drenched by rains and exposed to the heat of the tropical sun, our fare that of the Indians,—yet our health, after we had passed the first fevers in the commencement of the expedition, was seldom interrupted by disease. And

Where there is store of gold, it is in effect nedeles to remember other commodities for trade: but it hath towards the south part of the riuer, great quantities of Brasill woode, and of diuers berries, that die a most perfect crimson and Carnation: And for painting, al *France, Italy,* or the east Indies yeild none such: For the more the skyn is washed, the fayrer the cullour appeareth, and with which, euen those brown and tawnie women spot themselues, and cullour their cheekes. All places yeilde abundance of Cotten, of sylke, of *Balsamum,* and of those kindes most excellent, and neuer known in Europe: of all sortes of gummes, of *Indian* pepper: and what else the countries may afforde within the land wee knowe not, neither had we time to abide the triall, and search. The soile besides is so excellent and so full of riuers, as it will carrie sugar, ginger, and all those other commodities, which the west Indies hath[1].

this remark applies likewise to the Europeans who accompanied us. Indeed if we except the melancholy death of Mr. Reiss, by the upsetting of a boat in descending a cataract, we did not lose a single individual of our European companions by disease brought on by the climate or our hardships. It is otherwise however in the coast regions, where injurious miasmata render the sojourn frequently dangerous to Europeans.

[1] Few countries on the surface of the globe can be compared with Guiana for vigour and luxuriance of vegetation. A constant summer prevails; and the fertility of the soil, the humid climate, and congenial temperature ensure a succession of flowers and fruits. In a person accustomed to the sleep of nature in the northern regions, where during winter the trees are deprived of their greatest charms, the leafy crown and the fragrant blossoms, the appearance of the forest then clothed in the most lively green and covered with flowers cannot but raise astonishment and admiration. The dense and almost impenetrable forest of the interior offers inexhaustible treasures, not only for ship-building and architecture in all its branches, but likewise for the manufacture of furniture, and for many other purposes that minister to the restoration of health, or to the comfort and luxury of man. We know as yet but little of the medicinal properties of many of the numerous productions of this fertile province, which at present unheeded and unsought do not profit mankind, and may be considered as buried riches. The dye to which Sir W. Ralegh alludes is the Rocou, Arnotto, or Terra Orellana, prepared from the red pulp or pellicle which covers the seeds of a shrub called by Linnæus *Bixa Orellana.*

The nauigation is short, for it may bee sayled with an ordinarie wind in six weekes, and in the like time backe againe, and by the way neither lee shore, Enimies coast, rocks, nor sandes, all which in the voiages to the West indies, and all other places, wee are subiect vnto, as the channell of *Bahama*, comming from the West Indies, can not be passed in the Winter, and when it is at the best, it is a perillous and a fearefull place: The rest of the Indies for calmes, and diseases very troublesome, and the *Bermudas* a hellish sea for thunder, lightning, and stormes.

This verie yeare there were seuenteen sayle of Spanish shipps lost in the channell of *Bahama*, and the great *Phillip* like to haue sunke at the *Bermudas* was put back to Saint *Iuan de puerto rico*. And so it falleth out in that Nauigation euery yere for the most parte, which in this voyage are not to be feared: for the time of the yere to leaue *England*, is best in Iuly, and the Summer in *Guiana* is in October, Nouember, December, Ianuarie, February, and March, and then the shipps may depart thence in Aprill, and so returne againe into England in Iune, so as they shall neuer be subiect to Winter weather, eyther comming, going, or staying there, which for my part, I take to

The pigment called Caraweru or Chico is obtained from the leaves of the *Bignonia Chica*, and some other species of the genus *Bignonia*, which are macerated, and the colouring matter is found as a sediment in the form of a light powder. It is comparatively very costly among the Indians, and might be usefully employed in the arts as an excellent substitute for madder, which it surpasses as a colour. Of balsams and gums, we need merely mention the balsam of copaiva, umiri, elemi, acouchi, gum anime, gum lac, &c., all of which are derived from trees in the forests of Guiana. The Indian pepper is the fruit of *Capsicum baccatum*, Linn., and various other species and varieties supply indispensable condiments to the Indians. Ralegh's observations respecting the fitness of the soil for the cultivation of sugar have been amply realized: the colony of British Guiana exported in 1836 nearly one hundred and eight million pounds of sugar, and nearly five million pounds of coffee, besides other produce. This was the largest export it ever made since it was settled as a colony, nor is it likely that it will again export such a large quantity of produce.

be one of the greatest comforts and incouragments that can be thought on, hauing (as I haue done) tasted in this voyage by the west Indies so many Calmes, so much heate, such outragious gustes, fowle weather, and contrarie windes.

To conclude, *Guiana* is a Countrey that hath yet her Maydenhead, neuer sackt, turned, nor wrought, the face of the earth hath not beene torne, nor the vertue and salt of the soyle spent by manurance, the graues haue not beene opened for gold, the mines not broken with sledges, nor their Images puld down out of their temples. It hath neuer been entred by any armie of strength, and neuer conquered or possesed by any Christian Prince. It is besides so defensible, that if two fortes be builded in one of the Prouinces which I haue seen, the flood setteth in so neere the banke, where the channell also lyeth, that no shippe can passe vp, but within a Pikes length of the Artillerie, first of the one, and afterwardes of the other: Which two Fortes wilbe a sufficient Guard both to the *Empire* of *Inga*, and to an hundred other seuerall kingdomes, lying within the said Riuer, euen to the citie of *Quito in Peru*[1].

There is therefore great difference betwene the easines of the conquest of *Guiana*, and the defence of it being conquered, and

[1] These observations respecting the defence of the Orinoco are very judicious. A strong battery established at Punta Barima, where the Dutch had as early as 1660 a fortified outpost, would prevent any vessel from entering the Orinoco drawing more than eight feet water. Punta Barima, or Point Breme, as it was called by the Dutch, commands entirely the entrance of the Orinoco by the Boca de Navios; and when on a late occasion the right of possession to this point was the subject of discussion between the British Government and the Republic of Venezuela, Punta Barima was appropriately and emphatically styled "the Dardanelles of the Orinoco." There are at present two fortifications on the right bank of the Orinoco, near the site of Vieja Guayana, called "Los Fuertes de San Francisco de Asis" and "del Padrasto," which are quite neglected; the situation is however so well selected, that proper fortifications might prevent the ascent of any vessel or flat-bottomed boat entering the Orinoco by the Brazo Macareo or any other branch of the Bocas chicas. It is to this point and the island of Fajardo that Ralegh seems to allude in this paragraph.

the West or East Indies: *Guiana* hath but one entraunce by the sea (if it haue that) for any vessels of burden, so as whosoeuer shall first possesse it, it shall bee founde vnaccessable for anie Enimie, except he come in Wherries, Barges, or *Canoas*, or els in flatte bottomed boats, and if he do offer to enter it in that manner, the woods are so thicke 200 miles together vppon the riuers of such entraunce, as a mouse cannot sitte in a boate vnhit from the banke. By land it is more impossible to approch, for it hath the strongest situation of anie region vnder the Sunne, and is so enuironed with impassable mountaynes on euerie side, as it is impossible to victuall anye companie in the passage, which hath beene well proued by the Spanish nation, who since the conquest of *Peru* haue neuer left fiue yeres free from attempting this Empire, or discouering some way into it, and yet of 23 seuerall gentlemen, knights, and noble men, there was neuer anie that knewe which way to leade an armie by land, or to conduct shippes by sea, any thing neere the said countrie[1]. *Oreliano*, of which the riuer of *Amazones* taketh name was the first, and *Don Anthonio de Berreo* (whome we displanted) the last: and I doubt much, whether hee himselfe or any of his, yet knowe the best waie into the saide Empyre. It can therefore hardly be regained, if any strength bee formerly set downe, but in one or two places, and but two or three crumsters or galleys buylt, and furnished vpon the riuer within: The west Indies hath many portes, watring places, and landings, and nearer then 300 miles to *Guiana*, no man can harbor a ship, except he know one onely place, which is not learned in hast, and which I will

[1] According to the list of "names of those worthy Spaniards who have sought to discover and conquer Guiana," which is attached to Keymis's Voyage (Hakluyt, iii. pp. 687–692), he enumerates twenty attempts. This list, we are told, was taken from the 'Primeira parte de las Elegias de varones illustres de las Indias compuestas por Juan de Castellanos.' 4to. Madrid, 1589. The first part of this rare work is the only one which was printed; the author had composed a second and third part, which may still exist in some one of the libraries of Spain in manuscript, but have never appeared in print.

vndertake there is not any one of my companies that knoweth, whosoeuer hearkened most after it.

Besides by keeping one good fort, or building one towne of strength, the whole Empyre is guarded, and whatsoeuer companies shalbe afterwardes planted within the land, although in twenty seuerall prouinces, those shall bee able all to reunite themselues vpon any occasion eyther by the way of one riuer, or bee able to march by land without eyther wood, bog, or mountaine: whereas in the west Indies there are fewe townes, or prouinces that can succour or relieue one the other, eyther by land or sea: By lande the countries are eyther desart, mounteynous, or strong Enemies: By sea, if any man inuade to the Eastward, those to the west cannot in many months turne against the brize and easterwind, besides the Spanyardes are therein so dispersed, as they are no where strong, but in *Nueua Hispania* onely: the sharpe mountaines, the thornes, and poisoned prickels, the sandy and deepe waies in the vallies, the smothering heate and ayre, and want of water in other places, are their onely and best defence, which (because those nations that inuade them are not victualled or prouided to stay, neyther haue any place to friende adioyning) doe serue them in steede of good armes and great multitudes.

The west Indies were first offered her Maiesties Grandfather by *Columbus* a straunger[1], in whome there might be doubt of deceipt, and besides it was then thought incredible that there were such and so many lands and regions neuer written of before. This Empire is made knowen to her Maiesty by her own vassal, and by him that oweth to her more duty then an ordinary subiect, so that it shall ill sort with the many graces and

[1] Bartholomew Columbus brought the first sea-charts in illustration of his brother's theory respecting a western continent to England, and offered the services of Christopher Columbus to Henry the Seventh, which he is said to have gladly accepted; but previous to any further steps being taken, Columbus had attached himself to the service of Queen Isabella. (Fernando Colon, Vida del Amirante, cap. 10.) Ralegh is therefore in error when stating that the West Indies were offered to Henry the Seventh.

benefites which I haue receaued to abuse her highnes, either with fables or imaginations. The countrey is alreadie discouered, many nations won to her Maiesties loue and obedience, and those Spanyards which haue latest and longest labored about the conquest, beaten out, discouraged and disgraced, which amonge these nations were thought inuincible. Her maiestie may in this enterprize employ all those souldiers and gentlemen that are yonger brethren, and all captaines and Cheiftaines that want employment, and the charge wilbe onely the first setting out in victualling and arming them: for after the first or second yere I doubt not but to see in London a Contratation house of more receipt for *Guiana*, then there is nowe in ciuil [Seville] for the West indies[1].

[1] As on a former occasion, so again we must consider this passage written in that exaggerated and imaginative strain which Ralegh supposed necessary to awaken more interest in the discovery of Guiana than his journey had already produced. It does not behove us to judge the spirit of the times which might have dictated such a course, and induced him to employ a poetical dress for his statements; but in a general sense we have little doubt he fully believed the existence of these riches at a period when the most learned were still given to credulity; and that Ralegh possessed a great share of it is proved by his History of the World, where we find sober discussions whether paradise was in the moon, and whether the ark was lighted by a carbuncle. Yet, we might ask, with all our advances in morals and science, do not the printed inducements to emigrate to North and South America and Australia, which have been put forth during the last twenty or thirty years, bear comparatively as exaggerated a style as those of Ralegh, by which two centuries and a half ago he wished to promote his magnificent scheme of colonizing one of the most fertile provinces of the globe? His hope expressed to the effect to see in London a mercantile-house ("casa de la contratacion") of more receipt from that country than there was in Seville for the West Indies, proves that the story of gold was the glittering outside of a scheme which had for its object the establishment of commercial companies for the colonization of Guiana. The narrative continues to its end in a similar style, and we cannot help regretting that Sir Walter Ralegh should have employed such coarse flattery to induce Queen Elizabeth to lend a favourable ear to his ambitious projects. He had not yet passed through the ordeal of his long imprisonment, which tempered and refined his mind, and during which, by the publication of his History of the World, he proved

And I am resolued that if there were but a smal army a foote in *Guiana*, marching towards *Manoa* the chiefe Citie of Inga, he would yeeld her Maiesty by composition so many hundred thousand pounds yearely, as should both defende all enemies abroad, and defray all expences at home, and that he woulde besides pay a garrison of 3000 or 4000 soldiers very royally to defend him against other nations: For he cannot but know, how his predecessors, yea how his owne great vncles *Guascar* and *Atibalipa* sonnes to *Guanacapa* Emperor of *Peru*, were (while they contended for the Empyre) beaten out by the Spanyardes, and that both of late yeares, and euer since the said conquest, the Spanyardes haue sought the passages and entry of his countrey: and of their cruelties vsed to the borderers he cannot be ignorant. In which respects no doubt but he wil be brought to tribute with great gladnes, if not, hee hath neyther shotte nor Iron weapon in all his Empyre, and therefore may easely be conquered.

And I farther remember that *Berreo* confessed to me and others (which I protest before the Maiesty of God to be true) that there was found among prophecies in *Peru* (at such time as the Empyre was reduced to the Spanish obedience) in their chiefest temples, amongst diuers others which foreshewed the losse of the said Empyre, that from *Inglatierra* those *Ingas* shoulde be againe in time to come restored, and deliuered from the seruitude of the said Conquerors[1]. And I hope, as wee with these fewe handes haue displanted the first garrison, and driuen

more than by any other act that he possessed the fairest claim to literary immortality. Here the strength of his intellect and the enlargement of his philosophical views, which were developed by seclusion, kept his highly imaginative and poetical temperament subservient to his sounder reasonings, and gave to posterity a work which has classed him with the most conspicuous characters of that distinguished period.

[1] The singular fulfilment of this prophecy, certainly advanced with remarkable effrontery, has been witnessed in our days. England occupied in the course of the late war the whole territory between the Orinoco and the Amazon, and at the treaty of Paris in 1814, the colonies of Demerara, Essequibo and Berbice were finally ceded to Great Britain.

them out of the said countrey, so her Maiesty will giue order for the rest, and eyther defend it, and hold it as tributary, or conquere and keepe it as Empresse of the same. For whatsoeuer Prince shall possesse it, shall bee greatest, and if the king of Spayne enioy it, he will become vnresistable. Her Maiesty heereby shall confirme and strengthen the opinions of al nations, as touching her great and princely actions. And where the south border of *Guiana* reacheth to the Dominion and Empire of the *Amazones*, those women shall heereby heare the name of a virgin, which is not onely able to defend her owne territories and her neighbors, but also to inuade and conquere so great Empyres and so farre remoued.

To speake more at this time, I feare would be but troublesome: I trust in God, this being true, will suffice, and that he which is king of al kings and Lorde of Lords, will put it into her hart which is Lady of Ladies to possesse it, if not, I wil iudge those men worthy to be kings therof, that by her grace and leaue will vndertake it of themselues.

An Abſtract taken

out of certaine Spanyardes Letters concerning Guiana *and the Countries lying vpon the great riuer of* Orenoque*: with* certaine reportes alſo touching *the ſame.*

An Aduertiſement to the Reader.

Hose letters out of which the abstractes following are taken, were surprised at sea as they were passing for Spayne in the yeare 1594 by Captaine *George Popham*: who the next yeare, and the same that Sir *Walter Ralegh* discouered *Guiana*, as he was in a voyage for the west Indies, learned also the reportes annexed. All which, at his returne, beeing two monthes after Sir *Walter*, as also so long after the writing of the former discourse, hearing also of his discouerie: hee made knowne and deliuered to some of her Maiesties most honorable priuie Councell and others. The which seeing they confirme in some parte the substance, I meane, the riches of that Countrey: it hath beene thought fitte that they shoulde be thereunto adioyned. Wherein the Reader is to be aduertised, that although the Spanyards seeme to glorie much of their formall possession taken before *Morequito* then Lord of *Aromaya*, and others there aboutes, which thoroughly vnderstoode them not at that time, whatsoeuer the Spanyardes otherwise pretende: Yet, according to the former discourse, and as also it is related by *Cayworaco*, the sonne of *Topiawary* nowe chiefe Lorde of the saide *Aromaya*, who was brought into England by Sir *Walter Ralegh,* and was present at the same possession and discouerie of the Spanyardes mentioned in these letters; it appeareth that after they were gone out of their Countrey, the Indians then hauing farther consideration of the matter, and more then coniecture of their intent, hauing knowne and hearde of their former cruelties vppon their borderers and others of the Indians elsewhere: At their next comming, there beeing tenne of them sent and imployed for a farther discouerie, they were prouided to receiue and intertayne them in an other manner of sorte then they had done before; that is to say, they slewe them and buried them in the Countrey, they so much sought. They gaue them by that meanes a full and complete possession the which before they had but begunne. And so they are minded to doe, to as many Spanyardes as come after. Other possession they haue had none since. Neyther doe the Indians meane as they protest, to giue them any other. One other thing to bee remembred is that in these letters the Spanyardes seeme to call *Guiana* and other Countries neere it, bordering vppon the riuer of *Orenoque,* by the name of *Nueuo Dorado,* because of the greate plenty of Golde there, in most places to be founde. Alluding also to the name of *El Dorado* which was giuen by *Martines* to the greate Citie of *Manoa,* as is in the former treatise specified. This is all I thought good to aduertise. As for some other matters, I leaue them to the consideration and iudgement of the indifferent reader.

W. R.

LETTERS TAKEN AT SEA BY CAPTAINE GEORGE POPHAM 1594.

Allonso *his Letters from the* Gran Canaria *to his brother being commaunder of* S. Lucas, *concerning* El Dorado.

THERE haue beene certain letters receiued here of late, of a land newly discouered called *Nueuo Dorado,* frome the sonnes of certaine Inhabitantes of this citie, who were in the discouerie: they write of wonderfull riches to be found in the said *Dorado,* and that golde there is in great abundance, the course to fall with it is 50 leagues to the windwarde to the *Marguarita.*

Allonsos *letter from thence to certaine Marchantes of* S. Lucas *concerning the* Dorado.

SIRS, we haue no newes worth the writing, sauing of a discouery lately made by the spaniardes in a new land called *Nueuo Dorado,* and in two daies sailing to the windward of the *Marguarita,* there is golde in that abundance, as the like hath not beene heard of. We haue it for certaine in letters written from thence by some that were in the discouery, vnto their parentes heere in the City. I purpose (God willing) to bestow ten or twelue daies in search of the said *Dorado,* as I passe in voyage towards *Carthagena,* hoping there to make some good sale of our commodities, I haue sent you therewith part of the information of the saide discouery, that was sent to his Maiesty.

Part of the Coppy that was sent to his Maiesty of the discouery of Nueuo Dorado.

IN the riuer of *Pato* otherwise called *Orenoque,* in the principall part thereof called *Warismero,* the 23 of Aprill 1593.

Domingo de vera Master of the Campe and Generall for *Anth. de Bereo* Gouernour and Captaine generall for our Lorde the King, betwixt the riuers of *Pato* and *Papamene* alias *Orenoque*, and *Marannon*, and of the Iland of *Trinedado*, in presence of me *Rodrigo de Caranca* register for the sea, commanded all the soldiers to be drawne together and put in order of battaile, the Captaines and soldiers, and master of the campe standing in the middest of them, said vnto them; Sirs, Soldiers, and Captaines, you vnderstand long since that our Generall *Anth. de Berreo*, with the trauell of 11 yeares, and expence of more then 100000 pesoes of Gold, discouered the noble prouinces of *Guiana* and *Dorado*: Of the which hee tooke possession to gouerne the same, but through want of his peoples health, and necessary munition, he issued at the Iland of *Marguarita*, and from thence peopled the *Trinedado*. But now they had sente me to learne out and discouer the ways most easily to enter, and to people the saide prouinces, and where the Campes and Armies may best enter the same. By reason whereof I entend so to do in the name of his Maiesty, and the said gouernour *Antho: de Berreo*, and in token thereof I require you *Fran. Carillo* that you aide me to aduance this crosse that lieth here on the ground, which they set on end towardes the east, and the said Master of the Campe, the Captains and soldiers kneeled down and did due reuerence vnto the said crosse, and thereupon the Master of the Campe tooke a bole of water and dranke it of, and tooke more and threw abroad on the ground: he also drew out his sword and cut the grasse of the ground, and the boughs of the trees saying I take this possession in the name of the king *Don Phillip* our master, and of his gouernour *Antho: de Berreo*: and because some make question of this possession, to them I answere that in these our actions was present the *Casique* or pincipal *Don Antho.* otherwise called *Morequito*, whose land this was, who yeelded consent to the said possession, was glad there of, and gaue his obedience to our Lord the King, and in his name to the said gouernour *Antho: de Berreo*. And the said Master of the Campe kneeled downe being in his libertie, and all the Captaines and soldiers saide that the possession was wel taken, and that they would defend it with their liues, vpon whosoeuer would say the contrary. And the saide master of the Camp hauing his sword drawen in his hand said vnto me, register that art here present, giue me an instrument or testimoniall to confirme me in this possession, which I haue taken of this land, for the gouernour *Antho. de Berreo* and if it be needfull I wil take it a new. And I require you all that are present to witnes the same, and do further declare that I will goe on, taking the possession of all these landes wheresoeuer I shall enter. Signed thus.

Domingo de vera *and vnderneath, Before me* Rodrigo de Caranca, *Register of the Army.*

AND in prosecution of the said possession, and discouery of the way and prouinces, the 27 of April of the said yere, the Master of the Camp entred by little and little with all the Campe and men of warre, more then two leagues into the Inland, and came to a towne of a principall, and conferring with him did let him vnderstand by meanes of *Antho*: *Bisante* the Interpretor that his Maiesty and *Antho: de Berreo* had sent him to take the said possession. And the said fryer *Francis Carillo* by the Interpretor, deliuered him certain thinges of our holy Catholique faith, to al which he answered, that they vnderstood him well and would becom Christians, and that with a very good wil they should aduance the crosse, in what part or place of the towne it pleased them, for he was for the gouernour *Antho*: *de Berreo,* who was his Master. Thereupon the said master of the Campe tooke a great crosse, and set it on ende toward the east, and requested the whole Campe to witnesse it and *Domingo de vera* firmed it thus.

It is well and firmly done, and vnderneath, before me Rodrigo Caranca, *Register of the Army.*

The first of May they prosecuted the saide possession and discouery to the towne of *Carapana*. From thence the said Master of the Camp passed to the towne of *Toroco* whose principall is called *Topiawary* beeing fiue leagues farther within the land then the first nation, and well inhabited. And to this principall by meane of the interpretor they gaue to vnderstand that his Maiesty and the said *Corrigidor* commanded them to take the possession of that land, and that they should yeeld their obedience to his Maiesty, and to his Corrigidor, and to the Master of the Campe in his name, and that in token thereof he would place a crosse in the midle of his towne. Whereunto the said *Cassique* answered they should aduance it with a very good will, and that he remained in the obedience of our Lorde the King, and of the saide Gouernour *Antho: de Berreo* whose vassale he would be.

The fourth of May we came to a prouince about fiue leagues thence, of all sides inhabited with much people, the principall of this people came and mette vs in peaceable manner: and hee is called *Renato*, he brought vs to a very large house where he entertained vs well, and gaue vs much gould, and the interpreter asking him from whence that gold was, he answered from a prouince not passing a daies iourney off, where there are so many Indians as would shadow the sunne, and so much gold as all yonder plaine will not conteine it. In which Countrie (when they enter into the *Borachera*) they take of the said gold in dust and annoint themselues all other therwith to make the brauer shewe, and to the end the gold may couer them, they annoint their bodies with stamped hearbs of a glucnous substance: and they haue warre with those Indians. They promised vs that if we would goe vnto them they would ayd vs, but they were such infinite number as no doubt they woulde kill vs. And being asked how they got that same gold, they told vs they went to a certaine downe or plaine and pulled or digged vp the grasse by the roote, which done, they tooke of the earth, putting in greate buckets which they carried to wash at the riuer, and that which came in powder they kept for their *Boracheras* and that which was in peeces, they wrought into Eagles.

The eight of May we went from thence, and marched about fiue leagues: at the foote of a hill we founde a principall called *Arataco,* with 3000 Indians, men and women al in peace and with much victuall, as hens and venison in great abundance, and many sortes of wine. Hee intreated vs to goe to his house and to rest that night in his towne being of 500 houses. The interpretor asked whence he had those hens, he said they were brought from a mountaine not passing a quarter of a league thence, where were many Indians, yea so many as grasse on the ground, and that those men had the pointes of their shoulders higher then the Crownes of their heades, and had so many hens as was wonderfull, and if we would haue any we shoulde send them Iewes harpes for they woulde giue for euery one two hens, we tooke an Indian and gaue him 500 harpes, the hens were so many that he brought vs, as were not to be numbred. Wee said we woulde goe thither, they told vs they were now in their *Borachera* and would kill vs, we asked the Indian, that brought the hens if it were true, he said it was most tru. We asked him how they made their *Borachera,* he saide they had many Eagles of Gold hanging on their breasts and pearls in their eares, and that they daunced being al couered with Gold. The Indian said vnto vs, if we would se them, we should giue him some hatchets, and he would bring vs of those Eagles. The Master of the Camp gaue him one hatchet (he would giue him no more because they should not vnderstand we went to seeke gold) he brought vs an Eagle that wayed 27 pounds of good Gold. The Master of the Campe tooke it, and shewed to the soldiers, and then threw it from him, making shew not to regarde it. About midnight came an Indian and saide vnto him, giue me a pickaxe and I will tel thee what the Indians with the high shoulders meane to doe, the Interpretor told the Master of the Campe who commaunded one to be giuen him, he then told vs those Indians were comming to kill vs for our marchandize.

Hereupon the master of the campe caused his company to be set in order, and began to march. The 11 day of May, we went about 7 leagues from thence to a prouince, where we found a great company of Indians apparrelled, they tould vs that if we came to fight, they would fill vp those plaines with Indians to fight with vs, but if we came in peace, we should enter and be well entertained of them, because they had a greate desire to see Christians, and there they tould vs of all the riches that was. I doe not here set it downe, because there is no place for it, but it shall appeare by the information that goes to his Maiesty, for if it should here be set downe, fower leaues of paper would not conteine it.

The letter of George Burien Britton, *from the saide* Canaries *vnto his cosen a french man, dwelling in* S. Lucas, *concerning the* Dorado.

Sir, and my very good Cosen, there came of late certaine letters from a new discouered country not farre from *Trinedado,* which they writ, hath Gold in greate abundance, the newes seemeth to be very certaine, because it passeth for good amongst the best of this City. Part of the information of the discouery that went to his Maiesty, goeth inclosed in *Alonsos* letters, it is a thing worth the seeing.

The report of Domingo Martines *of* Iamica, *concerning the* Dorado.

He saith that in 93 being at *Carthagena* there was a general report of a late discouery called *Nueuo Dorado,* and that a little before him comming thither, there came a *Frigot* from the saide *Dorado,* bringing in it the portrature of a Giant all of Gold, of weight 47 kintals, which the Indians there helde for their Idol. But nowe admitting of Christianitie and obedience to the King of Spaine, sent their saide Idoll vnto him in token they were become Christians, and held him for their King. The company comming in the saide *Frigot* reported Golde to be there in most greate abundance, Diamondes of inestimable value, with greate store of pearle.

The report of a french man called Bountillier *of* Sherbrouk *concerning the* Trinedado *and the* Dorado.

He saith that being at *Trinedado* in 91. he had of an Indian there a peece of Golde of a quarter of a pounde in exchange of a knife, the saide Indian told him he had it at the heade of that riuer which commeth to *Paracoa* in the *Trinedado,* but said in the riuer of *Orenoque,* it was in greate abundance. Also in 93 being taken by the Spaniards; and brought prisoner into the Illand of *Madera* (the place for his prison) there came in this meane time a barke of 40 tunnes from a newe discouery, with two millions of Gold, the companie whereof reported Gold in that place to be in greate abundance and called it the *Nueuo Dorado.* This french man passed from Spaine in the barke, and hauing a cabben nere a gentleman, one of the discouerers that came from that place in the said barke had diuers times conference with him, and amongst other things, of the great abundance of Golde in the said *Dorado* being as they said within the riuer of *Orenoque.*

Reports of Certaine Marchants of Rio de Hacha, *concerning the* Nueuo Dorado.

They said (aduancing the kings great treasure in the *Indies*) that *Nueuo Reyno* yeelded very many Gold mines, and wonderful rich, but lately was discouered a certain prouince so rich in Gold as the report thereof may seeme incredible, it is there in such abundance, and is called the *Nueuo Dorado*: *Anthonio de Berreo* made the said discouery.

The report of a Spaniard Captaine with Berreo *in the discouery of* Nueuo Dorado.

That the information sent to the K. was in euery point truly said, that the riuer of *Orenoque* hath seauen mouths or outlets into the sea, called *Las Sciete bocas de drago,* that the said riuer runneth farre into the land, in many places very broad, and that *Antho : de Berreo* lay at *Trinedado* making head to goe to conquere and people the said *Dorado.*

APPENDIX.

Sir Walter Ralegh informs us in his voyage of discovery, that it had been his intention, on returning from Guiana, to land on the coast of Virginia, for the relief of the young colony which had been planted there under his auspices[1]. The unfavourable weather prevented him from executing this design; he coasted however Terra Firma, and anchored before Cumana. On the refusal of the inhabitants to furnish his fleet with provisions, he fired the town, and proceeded to St. Mary's and Rio de la Hacha, which he likewise laid under contribution; his course was from thence directed towards Cuba[2]. On the 13th of July, 1595, he fell in, off Cape St. Antonio, with Captains Preston and Sommers in the Ascension and the Gift, who were returning from their expedition against the Spaniards on Terra Firma. He sailed in their company until the 20th of July, when he lost sight of them, and returned "with honour and riches in the latter end of the summer 1595 to England[3]." We doubt whether the Guiana expedition proved advantageous to those who undertook it, but unhesitatingly adopt Roger Coke's opinion, that if Ralegh got nothing else by his voyage, "he got this advantage, that adding experience to his excellent theory in navi-

[1] See *ante*, p. 6.

[2] Birch's Works of Ralegh, vol. i. p. xxx. Camden's Elizabeth, Ann. 1595. Camden asserts that Ralegh carried away great booty from Cumana, which is not probable, as the inhabitants had already withdrawn their riches into the mountains at the approach of Preston towards the end of May.

[3] Birch's Works of Ralegh, *ibid.*

gation, he justly merited the applause of the best directors of sea affairs of his time[1]."

It is evident from the dedication and the address to the reader, prefixed to the publication of his voyage, that the intelligence which Ralegh brought of his discovery did not raise the interest which he expected. Many of the statements contained in this remarkable production were treated as fabulous, and his recommendation to secure the possession of these fertile regions to England as chimerical. The failure of the last expedition under Drake and Hawkins may have likewise contributed to lessen the enthusiasm of the English public for such enterprises. We have observed, that one of his plans was to carry a force to Guiana, of sufficient strength to induce the Inca of El Dorado to become the tributary and ally of England, and to establish commercial companies for colonizing Guiana. These propositions did not meet with support; indeed there are some doubts whether they were ever brought before her Majesty's ministers. It is more likely that the hazard of sending a large armament into so unhealthy a climate, prevented such a scheme from being taken under consideration at a period when the king of Spain seemed not to have given up his designs upon England. Beside which the jealousy and influence of Sir Walter's rivals were still too powerful to allow his project a favourable reception. Ralegh continued for some time after his return from Guiana in an apparent state of banishment from court; but we learn from a letter of Rowland Whyte to Sir Robert Sidney, that he lived in great splendour about London. This was an expediency which worldly wisdom dictated to him; it attracted the public eye, and caused the supposition that he lived from the fruits of his enterprize, and his new projects therefore were more likely to court favour.

To this period seems to belong a document, which, though extremely curious has hitherto been known only in manuscript. It bears the simple title, 'Of the Voyage for Guiana,' and is

[1] A Detection of the Court and State of England during the last four reigns, by Roger Coke: second edition, London, 1696, p. 55.

preserved among the MSS. of Sir Hans Sloane in the library of the British Museum. Although anonymous, it bears so many internal evidences, that we cannot doubt as to its being the production of Sir Walter Ralegh; it is written in that clear style so peculiar to him, and of which his Discovery of Guiana gives us so many instances. There are several paragraphs in this singular production which remove all doubts, if there should exist any, with regard to its genuineness. His allusion to the Amazons, who "with regarde of their sexe will be ready to ayde her majestie against the Spaniards"—the shortness of the voyage—his project of planting colonies, and speaking of the docility and mild manners of the Indians—the observation "wee ourselves in parte have had the like proofe"—are only some of the numerous circumstantial evidences which this production bears on its face. The artifice, based upon the knowledge of the Queen's weakness for flattery, in order to insure his project a favourable reception, coincides so fully with Ralegh's expedients on former occasions, that it forms a collateral proof that he was the author. Every word of the following passage bears the impress of Sir Walter: "It will add great increase of honor to the memorie of her majestie's name upon earth to all posterity, and in the end bee rewarded with an excellent starlike splendency in the heavens."

We have therefore not hesitated to add this piece to our present edition of Sir Walter Ralegh's Discovery of Guiana, as forming a connecting link between it and his last unfortunate expedition. This document, which was intended to remove any objections to his plan of occupying Guiana, and to enter into an alliance with the Inca of Manoa, is written with great clearness. His reasons and motives are most admirably set forth, and the answers to any probable objections stated with great perspicuity and force of argument. He was at that time fully aware that the plan proposed in his Discovery to carry a large force to Guiana, for the conquest of that empire, was considered impracticable, as such an armament could not be spared by England; he changes therefore his plan with much sagacity in this material point, and proposes now the novel measure of arming the Indians. He reasons that with their assistance an armament of four or five hundred men from England, containing among their number artificers and armourers, would be quite sufficient to execute his great designs, and agrees further that such an expedition would keep the Spaniards in their transatlantic possessions so occupied that "they would not hastily threaten us with any more of their invincible navies."

We notice in this document for the first time, in the literary productions of Sir Walter, a practice which he afterwards adopted to a much greater extent in his History of the World, namely, a reference to passages from the holy Bible, to compare and prove his deductions.

OF THE VOYAGE FOR GUIANA[1].

Touching the voyage for Guiana it is to be considered first, whether it bee to be vndertaken: secondly, the manner of subduing it: and lastely, the meanes howe to subdue it, and annex it to the Crowne Imperiall of the Realme of England.

The voyage [to][2] Guiana to [be] undertaken.

That it is to be vndertaken will appeare, if it be proued to bee (1) honorable, (2) profitable, (3) necessary, (4) and with no greate chardge, or difficultye accomplished.

It is honorable, both for that by this meanes infinite nombers of soules may be brought from theyr idolatry, bloody sacrifices, ignoraunce, and inciuility to the worshipping of the trve God aright to ciuill conversation, and also theyr bodyes freed from the intollerable tirrany of the Spaniards wherevnto they are already or likely in shorte space to bee subjected, vnlesse her excellent Majestie or some other christian prince doe speedily assiste, and afterward protect them in their jvst defensiue wars against the violence of vsurpers which if it please her highnes to vndertake, besids that presently it will stopp the mouthes of the Romish Catholickes, who vaunt of theyr great adventvres for the propogacion of the gospell[3], it will add greate increase of honor, to the memory of her Majesties name vpon earth to all posterity and in the end bee rewarded with an

[1] Sloane MSS., 1133, fol. 45.

[2] The edges of the manuscript having been cut too close, some of the writing is defaced. The words in brackets are inferred from the general sense of the paragraph.

[3] The desire of propagating the Roman Catholic faith influenced the Spaniards and Portuguese in their conquests, and served to give religious motives even to their cruelties, which they considered as being sanctified by the aims they had in view.

excellent starlike splendency in the heavens, which is reserved for them that turne many unto righteousnes, as the Prophet speaketh.

2. Likewise it is profitable, for heereby the Queens dominions may bee exceedingly enlarged, and this Realme inestimably enriched, with pretious stones, gold, silver, pearle, and other commodityes which those countryes yeald, and (God giuing good successe to the voiage) an entrance made thereby to many other Empyres, (which hapily may proue as rich as this) and it may bee to Peru it selfe and other Kingdomes of which the Spaniards bee now possessed, in those partes and else where.

3. Lastly, the necessity of attempting Guiana in regard of our owne security (albeit noe profite should redound thereby to the Indians, or to ourselves directly from those countryes) ought greatly to weigh with vs. For if the Spaniards by the treasure of those Kingdomes which hee hath already, be able to trouble the better parte of Christendome, what would hee doe if hee were once established in Guiana, which is thought to bee more rich then all other lands which hee enjoyeth either in the East or West Indies. Whereas if her Majestie weare seased of it, hee mighte bee soe kepte occupied in those prouinces that hee would not hastely threaten vs, with any more of his inuincible navies.

[Possib]ilities of [subd]ving the Guianians.

But although this voyage were never so honorable, profitable, or necessary for our estate to be undertaken, yet if we had not some possibility for the effecting of our purpose, it were more meete to strengthen our selues at home, then to weaken our forces in seeking to annoy our enemy abroad. But such opportunity and so many encouragements doe now offer themselves vnto her highnes that (I suppose) there is no prince in the world but hee would greatly strayne hymselfe, rather then to omitt the advantage of such a booty. Among others, these inducements are to bee weighed.

1. The Bordurers, who are sayd to bee naturalls, and to whom onely the Empire of Guiana doth of right apperteine, are already prepared to joyne with vs, having submitted themselves

to the Queen's protection both against the Spaniards and Emperor of Guiana who usurpeth upon them.

2. The Spaniards for theyr oppressions and usurpations, are detested and feared both by the Guianians and bordurers, by the former, beecause the Spaniards forced them to fly from theyr owne country of Peru, and by the latter, by experience of the Spanish dealing towardes themselves and theyr adjoyning neighbors. So as it is reported none doe assiste them save the Arwacans, a vagabond, poore, and small people. But it is like that all the countryes of the continent who are not yet inthralled to the Spaniards and have heard of their outrage and especially the Amazones in regarde of their sexe, will be ready to ayd her Majestie against the Spaniards.

3. The voyage is shorte being but 6 weekes sayling from England and the like backe againe, which may so bee contriued as going, abiding, and returning we may bestow an whole yeare without any winter at all by the way, no lee shore, no sandes, or enimies coast.

4. No chardge but onely at the first setting forth which need not be great, especially if the course layd downe in this treatise or some such like, be taken, considering the country yeeldeth store of corne, beasts, fowle, fish and fruit for victualls, and steele and copper for the making of armor and ordinance, and among the Amapagotos and Caraccas horses may be had and in short time manned for our service in the wars.

5. It is thought the passage to it may bee easely fortifyed by sea and the country by nature is defensed by land with mountaines and multitude of nations, that it is impossible in manner by land to bee evicted, beeing once attayned by vs.

6. Though we are not greatly to rely upon prophesies, yet if it weare found in Peru (as Don Anthonio de Berreo told Sir Walter Ralegh) among other prophesies that from Inglatiera the Inga should be restored to Peru, it may fall out to bee true (as many of theyr prophesies did both in Mexico and Peru which indeed foreshewed the altaration of those Empires) at least the pro-

phesy will greatly daunt the Spaniards and make them afrayd of the worst event in these imployments.

7. If it be remembred how the Spaniards haue without just title or any wrong at all donne to them by the harmelesse Indians, forceably enuaded and wrongfully deteyned their countryes aboute 100 yeares, committing barbarous and exquisite massacres to the distruction of whole nations of people (arising by estimacion of some of accompt among them and acquaynted with theyr proceedings in some few yeares to the number of 20 millions of reasonable creatures made to the Image of God and lesse harmefull then the Spaniards themselves) whereby more fruitfull land was layd wast and depopulated then is in all Europe and some parte of Asia, in reuenge wherof their owne religious men do make accompte that the just God in judgment will one day horribly chasten and peraduenture wholy subuert and root out the Spanish nation from the world. Againe if it bee noted that the Spaniards haue aboue 20 severall times in vayne sought the conquest of Guiana, and that it doth by the providence of the Almighty now (as it were) prostrate herselfe before her Majesties feet the most potent enemy that the Spaniards hath, not onely intreating but by vnualuable offers and vnanswerable reasons alluring, even urging and forcing her highnes to accept it vnder her alleigeaunce, who would not bee perswaded that now at length the great judge of the world, hath heard the sighes, grones, lamentacions, teares, and bloud of so many millions of innocent men, women, and children aflicted, robbed, reuiled, branded with hot irons, roasted, dismembred, mangled, stabbed, whipped, racked, scalded with hott oyle, suet, and hogsgrease, put to the strapado, ripped alive, beheaded in sport, drowned, dashd against the rocks, famished, deuoured by mastifes[1], burned

[1] The Spaniards made the first use of mastiffs against the Indians in Hayti. These fierce dogs were trained to scent the unfortunate natives, and to mangle their bodies if they offered resistance. The Spanish historians celebrate the prowess of one of these dogs called Bezzerillo, which was trained to stand sentinel during night, to watch against unexpected

and by infinite crueltyes consvmed, and purposeth to scourge and plague that cvrsed nation, and to take the yoake of seruitude from that distressed people, as free by nature as any Christian. In comtemplacion of all which things, who would not bee incouraged to proceed in this voiage, hauing in a maner none other enemyes but these Spaniards, abhorred of God, and man, being provoked by so many allvrements, occacions, reasons, and opportunityes, in a most just cause, the safety of our dread soveraigne, of our selves, and of a great part of the Christian world thereuppon depending.

Now having proued that the voiage for Guiana is to be vndertaken that there is a full hope of good successe therein with great honor and profytt to her Majestie and to her successors, and to all the subjects of her dominions: It cometh next to be discussed in what manner it is most convenient for vs to labor to haue the Empire of Guiana subdved and vnited to the crowne of England which must be either by expelling the vsurping Inga of Manoa from Guiana vnder the right and title of the naturalls, and their free election, taking possession of the Tassell royall, or whatsoever other tokens, or ensignes of the Empyre are retayned among them, to the vse of her Majestie and her successors, or else onely by way of composition to draw the Inga to doe homage, and to hold of her Majestie as her vassell, by reteyn services by way of honorable couenants vpon good consideracions heereafter in this Treatise to be expressed. The effecting of the former seemeth more profitable, but the latter more safe and more convenient as our case standeth which I doe gather by these reasons following.

The manner of subdving Guiana.

attacks or to guard prisoners. Bezzerillo was of such great service that his master drew for him a day's pay and a half as ranking with cross-bow men. When sent in pursuit of an Indian, on coming up with him, he rushed upon his victim and dragged him by the arm to the camp, or if he offered any show of resistance he tore him to pieces. The race of Bezzerillo was propagated from the island to the continent for the destruction of the unfortunate Indians on the main.

1. If wee doe seeke to depose the Emperor of Guiana then we shall loose the advantage of setting them on to attempt the recouery of Peru from the Spaniards or otherwise to inuade the Spanish dominions next affronting.

2. Yt is greately to be feared that notwithstanding we might by the helpe of the Bordurers overthrow hym, yet in the end hee would rather joyne with the Spaniards (who would be ready to win hym vnto them by fayre promises) then suffer vs to rest quiett in Guiana.

3. We shall bee much weaker and lesse able to resiste the puissance of the Spaniards if we haue not the assurance of the Guianians and their assistants.

4. By setting the Guianians against vs, we shall never reduce them to the obedience of the Gospell which ought to bee one principall respect in our endeavors.

5. Wee may haue sufficient profite both by the contynuall trafficke and by the sayd couenants to be agreed vpon by the Guianians, without the absolute conquest of Guiana.

6. And lastly, this agreeth best with the prophesy which the Spaniards haue among them for the recouery of Peru by the Inga.

The means of subdving Guiana.

Thus much of the manner of subdving the Guianians, the meanes of procuring this come nexte to bee considered, which ought to bee just before God according to our christian profession, and honorable among men according to the accustomed proceedings of our English nation. For it were farr better with the helpe of our confederates vnder the defence of the Almighty to strengthen ourselves in our owne countryes, then to purchase our securitye by assaulting Guiana by such practises as the Spaniards vsed in the conquest of the Indies. Therefore the president of their dishonorable actions may not serue for our instructions. For which purpose I lay downe this as a maxime (which yet upon better aduise I ame ready to retracte) that no Christians may lawfully invade with hostility any heathenish people not under their allegiaunce, to kill, spoile, and conquer them, only vpon pretence of their fidelity. My proses and reasons be these.

1. In the beginning God having made the world, reseruing the heauens for his throne of Majestie, gave the earth and all therein, with the benefytt yssuing from the sunne, the moone, and all the starrs, to the sonnes of men as is manifest by the blessing of God uppon Adam, afterwards renewed vnto Noah (Gen. 1. 28. Gen. 9. 1. 7.) and his discendaunts, confirmed in parte by God himselfe to the (Gen. 17. 20.) posterity of wicked Ismaell, after to Nebuchadnezer in these (Jerem. 27. 5.) words I haue made the Earth, man and the beast vpon the ground by my greate power, and haue giuen it to whom it pleaseth me: But now I have giuen all these lands into the hande of Nebuchadnezer the King of Babell my seruant &c. To the like effect sayth Daniel to Nebuchadnezer: (Dan. 2. 37.) O King, thou arte King of Kings, for the Lord of Heauen hath giuen thee a kingdome, power, strength, glory, &c. By all which it seemeth to me very liquid and cleare that by God's ordinaunce the beleuers are not the only Lords of the world, as beeing not able to people the 20th parte thereof, but that by the gift of God, Idolaters, pagans, and Godlesse persons bee intituled to the possession, and haue a capacity to take, and an ability to hold a property in lands and goods as well as they, which beeing manifested by the former allegacions, it is against the rules of Justice (which giueth to euery man his owen) to depriue them of their goods, lands, libertyes, or liues, without juste title therevnto.

2. When Jepthe by his Embassadors shewed to the King of (Judg. 11. 23. 24.) Amon the righte that the Israelites had of inuading the possessions of Amon, he maketh not his title from pretence of their Idolatry or Gentleisme, but because the God of Israel had giuen those lands vnto them. The God of Israel (sayth he) hath cast out the Amorites before his people of Israel, and wouldest thou possess it? wouldest not thou possess that which Chemosh thy God giueth thee to possess? So whomsoever the Lord God driueth out before vs, them will we possess. But God hath giuen no Christians any such warrant, therfor thei may not do the

like: as nether the good Kings of Israel or Juda vsed to doo unles upon just cause of wrongs from the Idolaters receved.

3. Christians are commaunded to doo good vnto all men, and to haue peace with all men; to doo as thei would be donn vnto; to giue none offence to one or other: and lastely Christ willed the disciples to pay tribute to Cæsar, an Infidell, he refused a worldly kingdome, as not apperteyning vnto hym, he reproued his Apostles when thei desired that fier might come from heauen
Luke 9. 56. to destroy the Samaritans, who refused to entertayn hym, saying, you know not what spirit you are of, the sonn of man is not come to destroy mens liues but to saue them. Therfor no christian Prince under pretence of Christianity only, and of forcing of men to receiue the ghospell, or to renounce their impietyes, may attempte the inuasion of any free people not vnder their vassaladge. For Christ gaue not that power to Christians as Christians, which he himselfe as soveraigne of all Christians, neither had, nor would take.

4. By the lawe of nature and nations we agree that Prescription or priority of possession only, giueth right vnto lands or goods, against all straungers, indefesibly by any but the true owners.

5. We ourselves hould it unreasonable that the Pope vpon cullor of religion only, should giue away, or that any prince should therfor presume to intrude vpon our dominions: or that any Protestant should incroch vpon the Papists, the Muscouits, or Turks, vpon the like occasion; or that an excommunicate person (whom Christ denounceth to be as an heathen) or a Mahumetist comming into our cuntry for traffique, or an alien Atheist (if any weare among vs) not seducing our people, should be assaulted in goods or person, by any priuate man, or other whosoever, under whose jurisdicion he is not placed. The like rule in proporcion is to be obserued for not inuading any Idolaters dominions.

6. To be shorte all sound Christians for the semblable practise do repute the Kings of Castile, and Portugall, meere usurpors

in Africke, and America. Among the Papists also Bellarmine[1] avoweth that Pope Alexander 6, nether did, nor could give to the foresayd kings the Indies to be conquered and possessed, but only to be conuerted to the faith by them. And the matter being called into question in Spayn, betwen the Lord Bishop of Chiapa and D. Sepulueda[2], the two vniuersities of Salamanca and Alcala and allso (if I mistake not mine author) the Lords of the Assembly who weare apointed to heare the controversy debated, did resolve that such kinde of inuasiue warrs vppon infidells could not be justified; howsoever the Spaniards (this notwithstanding) nether had, nor yet haue any minde to waive the possession which by violent intrusion they haue of the Indies.

De Rom. Pontif. l. 5. c. 2.

Thus much to confirme that opinion before deliuered that Christians may not warrauntably conquer Infidells vpon pretence only of their infidelity. But I hould it very reasonable and charitable to send preachers safely guarded if need bee, to offer Infidells the gladd tidings of the Gospell, which being refused by them (or peradventure the Infidells giving hard measure to the Preachers) this can ground no sufficient quarrell to ouerrunn their countryes. I neede to speake the lesse of this, because her Majestie is already inuited to take vpon her the Seignorie of Guiana by the naturalls therof, whose ancient right to that Empire may be followed if it be thought convenient. But because in my simple judgment (vpon the former reasons) it is more safe and commendable for vs rather to seeke to bring

[1] Cardinal Robert Bellarmino was born at Monte Pulciano in Tuscany in 1542, and entered the order of Jesuits in 1560. He distinguished himself by his erudition, and was made in 1599 a Cardinal and Archbishop of Capua. Bellarmino is the author of numerous controversial works, chiefly directed against the reformed religion. Boyle says of him, that he had the best pen for controversy of any man of his age.

[2] The Bishop of Chiapa was the celebrated Bartholomew De Las Casas, the generous and constant defender of the rights of the natives of South America. John Ginez de Sepulveda, historiographer to the emperor Charles the Fifth, rendered himself ignobly conspicuous as the author of a 'Vindication of the cruelties of the Spaniards against the Indians,' in opposition to the benevolent designs of Las Casas.

Guiana to become tributory, then to conquer it, I will pursue that conclvsion, shewing how with least charge, and greatest facility, we may best aduantage ourselves without conquest. This may be compassed by these 2 meanes. First by bringing the Bordurers and the Epireumei and Guianians to an unity among themselves. Secondly into a league with vs against the Spaniards, and their adherentes, if happely the adherentes can not be drawen from them, which greatly importeth to be laboured by vs.

1. By discrediting the Spaniards among them, which must be by acquainting them with the usurpacions, insolences, and tyrranyes of the Spaniards before remembred vpon their kindred in Peru, vpon their neighbors, and vpon whomsoever ether by fraud or force thei can fasten possession. For proofe whereof Bartol: de las Casas booke of the Spanish crueltyes with fayr pictures, or at least a large table of pictures expressing the particularityes of the crueltyes there specified (neatly wrought for the better credite of our workemanshipp, and their easier vnderstanding) would be sent to the Inga, and his Cassiques by some interpreters, that thei may publish them among their vassals, and to all the estates of the confining countryes rovnde about that thei may bee all (as much as is possible) conjoyntly linked, and exasperated against the Spaniards. And by informing them that the Spaniards doe holde their religion of the Pope, the great inchantor or cousner, and troubler of the world, who sent them first to invade those countryes, who teacheth them to breake all fayth, promises, oathes, couenantes with all such as bee not of their owne religion, so farr forth as may serue his and their turne, who giueth his followers dispensacions to steale, robb, rebell and murther; and likewise pardoneth for mony whatsoever wronges or villanyes, are by them committed.

2. On the other side thei may be wrought to affect vs by these allvrements. 1. By presents sente from her Majestie to the Emperor and principall cassiques. 2. By shewing them the commodityes of our countryes. 3. By due commending of her

Maiestie, and this state vnto them; as that She is a moste gratious, mercifull, and juste Princess, releeuing sundry distressed nations both in her owne and forrayn countries against the Spaniards in the Indies, Ireland, Spayn, Portugall, and ellswher: for illustracion wherof the maps containing Sr. Fran: Drakes exploites at Sto. Domingo &c. is to be showne vnto them[1]: furthermore that she is of great magnifficence and puissance, her countryes populous, rich, warlike and well provided of shippes as any state in the northern world, for manifesting of this the maps of the severall sheires in England, and the large map of the city of London[2], should bee conueyed vnto them. Also that her Majestie hath many mighty allies and confederates ready to ayde her against the Spaniards (if need were) as the Frenchmen, Germanes, &c. and the maps of their countryes to bee deliuered vnto them. That the King of Spayne made choise among all other Princes christned as a matter of high advancement to joyne in marriage with her Majesties sister and predecessor. And that her Majesties religion is farr differing from the Spanish, maynteining truth, justice, and faythfulnes, prohibiting all murders, treasons, adulteries, thefts, and whatsoever correspondeth not with equity and reason. 4. Lastly, their fauors are to be wonn by entring a league with them concerning condicions to be performed by them in consideracion of honorable performances by vs to be rendred and made.

[1] The work to which Ralegh here alludes is apparently "A Summarie and trve discourse of Sir Francis Drake's West Indian Voyage. Wherein were taken the Townes of Saint Iago, Sancto Domingo, Cartegena and Saint Augustine. With Geographicall Mappes exactly describing each of the Townes, with their situations, and the manner of the Armies approaching to the winning of them. Diligently made by Baptista Boazio. Printed London 1589."

[2] Christophorus Saxton's Atlas of the Counties of England was published in 1576–78. It is a splendid specimen of a collection of early maps. The large map of the city of London to which Ralegh alludes is Ralph Aggas's Plan of London in 1560. It was republished by Vertue, and is six feet by two feet three and a half inches. A copy of each of these works, in excellent preservation, is among the collections in the British Museum.

1 The condicions to be required of them are these. First to renounce their Idolatry, and to worship the only true God, vnto which vnlesse thei will yeeld it may be doubted whether we being Christians may ioyne with them in armes against the Spaniards or not. Some profes mouing this doubte I will briefly offer with submission to sounder judgment.

Jehosaphat hauing aided in battell an Idolatrous King was checked by a Prophet sent from God to hym saying, wouldst
2 Chron. 19. 2. thou helpe the wicked, and hate them that loue the Lord. Therefore for this thing the wrath of the Lord is vpon thee. Likewise Amaziah King of Judah, hired 100 thousand men Isralites (who had fallen from God by Idolatry) to ioyne with him in warrs against the Edomites, and a man of God came
2 Chron. 25. 7. vnto hym and sayd: Lett not the army of Israell go with thee, for the Lord is not with Israell &c. whereuppon Amaziah dismissed the Israellites and discomfited the Edomites.

1. Objection. Asa by the helpe of Idolaters vanquished his enemyes. 1 K. 15. 20.

Answeare. Asa is reproued for this notwithstanding it had pleased God to giue hym the victory. 2 Chro. 16. 7. The like is to be answered for Hernando Cortez and others who conquered by the helpe of some Indian Idolaters.

2. Objection. It will require great time to conuert them from their Idolatry.

Answeare. It shalbe sufficient at the first to assemble the Cassiques to persvade their people to abandon their Idolls and to surcease their bloudy sacrifices, also to take their promise to yeeld to the gospell (which should be summarily propounded as it was by the Bishop Vincent de Valverde to Attibaliba[1]) and to

[1] Francisco Vicente de Valverde, a Dominican monk, bishop and almoner to the expedition under Pizarro, approached Atahualpa, who came at the head of eight thousand Indians, with a crucifix and the breviary in his hand, and offered him peace. The bishop spoke to the Inca of the mysteries of the Christian religion, and of the partition which the Pope had made of the world among the Christian princes. Peru had been given, he said, to the emperor Charles, who had deputed Pizarro as governor. Atahualpa

draw their people thervnto, both now and heereafter further, as thei shalbe instructed.

3. Objection. Peraduenture thei will not condiscende to embrace our religion and abiure their owne.

Answeare. First being in distresse thei will rather yeeld to any condicion then be depriued of our protection, especially if wee shew vnto them that our God will not prosper vs if we should doe otherwise. Againe experience in other places giueth great hope that litle persvasion will serve to effect this matter. Wheresoever Cortez travelled in Mutezuma his countryes the people did at the first without contradiction giue hym leaue to demolish their Idolls; only (as I remember) in Thaxcallan for a tyme thei made some scruple of it. In China at the preaching of some fryers the people were redily persvaded to relinquish their Sodomitry and Idolatry, sauing thei durst not professe the Gospell openly fearing the Magistrates, who are jelious of inouations. When Pedrasuarez Cabrall[1], was sent into the East Indies by the King of Portugall, he hapned to discouer Brasill, wher the inhabitaunts seing the Portuguese kneeling at prayers, thei likewise kneeled after the same manner, making shew of prayeing. But of all other the Lord Bishop of Chiapa (who liued many yeares among the Indies) avowcheth that thei were teachable and capable of all good learning very apt to receaue the Catholic fayth, and to be instructed in good manners, hauing

indignantly denied such a claim, and asserted that Pachacama was the creator of the universe. Having taken the sacred book, which he was told contained the mysteries, out of the bishop's hands, and finding that it did not speak to him, he threw it to the ground. The Dominican cried vengeance on such a crime, and Pizarro's men commenced the onslaught upon the unarmed Indians, among whom the artillery made sad havoc. They were pursued by the cavalry until night; Atahualpa was made prisoner, two thousand of his followers lost their lives, and three thousand were taken captive. The Spaniards did not lose a single man during this cruel act. (Zarate, Hist. del Peru, lib. ii. cap. 5. Xeres, Conquista del Peru. Herrera, decad. iv. v. lib. 1. 2.)

[1] Pedro Alvarez de Cabral (or, as he is sometimes called, Pedraloez Cabral), a Portuguese navigator, discovered the coast of Brazil in April 1500.

lesse incombrances in attaining thervnto then any other, and that after thei once tasted of religion, thei were very much inflamed, ardent and importune to vnderstand the matter of fayth, deliuering their idols to the religious men to be burned, bringing their children to be baptised and chathechized, sending for them sometimes 50 Leagues, and receauing them as aungelles sent from heauen, which considered we may presvme the like of the Guianians. But if after deliberation it shall be found agreeable for vs to ioyne with them before their conuersion, then this first condicion and the objections thervpon arising, need lesse to trouble vs.

2 The 2 conditions should bee, that the Inga of Manoa by the consent of his Lords and Cassiques surrender the ensignes of his Empire to her Majestie to be retourned to him againe to be holden in cheife of the Crowne of England. Also her Majesties Lievetenantes to direct the Guianians in their conclusions both of warr and peace: Rendring yearely to her Majestie and her successors a great tribute allotting to her vse some rich mines and riuers of gold, pearle, siluer, rocks of pretious stones &c. with some large fruitfull countryes for the planting of her Colonyes.

3 Lastely for assvrance of these condicions they shall giue speciall hostages to be sent into England, which being ciuilled and conuerted heere, vpon there returne and receiving of others in their romes thei may be matched in marriage with English women. They shall also allow some choyse places for fortificacions; and moreover bynde themselues by the oathes and ceremonyes of their countryes, that thei will be loyall and faythfull in the premises and in all other thinges to her Majestie and her successors and to her and their highnes generalls for the time beeing.

The offers to be made vnto the Guianians, and performed on our partes may be these. 1. First that we will defend them their wiues, children and countryes against the Spaniards and all other intrvders. 2. Then that we will helpe them to recouer their country of Peru. 3. That wee will instructe them in liberall arts of civility behoofsfull for them that thei may be comparable to any christian people. 4. And lastly that we will teach them the vse of weapons, how to pitch theyr battells, how to make armor, and ordinance, and how to manage horses for seruice in the warrs.

This latter point (to say the truth) is the principall scope wherevnto in this Treatise I haue aymed, contayning in short a course of expedition most fitt to be followed (though never yet executed (so farr as I can heare or read of) in any of the conquests of the East or West Indies;) yet necessary to be now vsed by vs our case being farr different from the former enterprises in the New world. For wee are not to goe as Cortez, Pisarro, or the other conquerors against a naked vnarmed people (whose warrs are resembled by some to the childrens play called Iogo di Canne[1]). Butt we are to encounter with the Spaniards, armed in all respectes, and as well practised as ourselves. Therefore we must instruct the Indians in the vse and skill of making armor, and that for these causes.

1. We cannot spare a sufficient number to send to the conquest or at least having gott possession of Guiana wee cann not by the helpe of the naked Indians nor safely by the ayde of forreine forces to be hired, long inioye it. For the Spaniards will gather their strength from Spayn, Peru, Nova Hispania, Nueuo Regno de Granado, the Islands, and from other their dominions to disloge vs, we being farr from our supplies, which may be intercepted, or we so busied at home that wee cannot send any.

2. If we do not take this course it is not improbable that some other Potentate will at length thincke upon it, and vse it to our great trouble and too late repentance.

3. Besides if this policy be not vsed, we cannot set the Guianians on worke to inuade the countryes circumiacent posessed

[1] Juego de Cañas,—a sport formerly used not only by children, but likewise by gentlemen in Spain, imitating a skirmish, during which the players cast canes or reeds at one another instead of darts.

by the Spaniards which thing (vnder favor) would tend as much to our security, as any other, in reason to be deuised: neither can we haue conueniently sufficient armor and ordinance vnlesse we take the helpe of the Guianians to make some who haue brasse, and Iron[1] and many Goldsmiths of rare science (as may be thought) who would be very capable to receiue information from our Enginers, Armorers, and Artificers, which together with some ingenious persons (experimented for necessarye new inuentions) are to be carryed thether for that purpose.

1. Objection. But you will say we want armor to furnish them presently.

Answeare. It were not amisse at the first to aduenture somewhat extraordinary, seeing vpon our arriuall we may haue present payment for it, and also mony to send for more. And one of our armorers or gunmakers might with one labor teach 20 Guianians, who would quickly conceaue and imitate their actions.

2. Objection. If we arme and instruct them thei will expell vs, as able to defend themselues without vs.

Answeare. 1. The Indians for the most parte are a people very faythfull, humble, patient, peceable, simple without subtilty, mallice, quarrels, strife, rancor or desyer of reuengement, as meeke as lambs, as harmeles as children of 10 or 12 yeares. As the Bishop of Chiapa (a man as semeth of good credit) of his owne experience doth witnesse, and wee our selues in parte have had the like proofe of them. So as thei hauing receiued such great benefits as we shall confer vppon them, thei giuing also sufficient security by hostages, others &c. vnto vs, we cannot presume that thei will be so vngratefull as to rise against vs, or if some doe, doubtlesse we shall finde others that will sticke vnto vs. The history of the Tlaxcaltecas sayth fulnes to Her-

[1] The Indians were not acquainted with the use of iron until the conquest. It was even asserted that South America possesses no iron ore. This has been long since refuted: we have seen clay-iron-stone and bog-iron ore covering extensive districts in Guiana.

nando Cortez who had prepared 50000 men to send for his succor, beeing almost uanquished by the Mexicans, who came to meete hym in his returne providing 20 thousand men and women to bring his retinew and uictualle, who receiued hym with weeping, mourning and lamentacion, for the dammage donn unto hym by his enemyes, who enterteyned hym into their city, cherishing hym and his men being weake, weary, maymed, and almost famished, in better sort then thei could have found in their owne countryes, when the Tlaxcaltecas if thei had bene as faythles as many Christians are, might by deliuering him into the hands of the Mexicans haue purchased their peace and liberty: the history I say of these and such like kindnesses shewed vnto the mercilesse Spaniards, doe argue the great loue and faythfulnes of the poore Indian people where thei once have conceaued a good opinion.

2. Wee may make choise to arme and instructe such of them as we find most trusty and most prone to Christianity reseruing the powder and shott in our oween custody allowing them onely so much as will serue their present vse from tyme to tyme, concealing also the secret of making powder, or some other necessaryes from them till we haue full triall of their fidelityes, that thei may still stand in need of vs and of our counsell.

For the presente [we m]ay have the custo[dy of] all weapons in [our ow]en hands, giving [the w]orth ass well to [our m]en (for feare of [jealou]sy) as to the Indians [at the] tymes of tray[ning and] mustering, or [the] necessary use only [as ju]dging. Some cullor[able] and plausable reason [being given] vnto them.

3. Objection. By our example the Spaniards or some other civill people will arme the Indians and so displant us.

Answeare. We shall haue great aduantage in beginning this course before others. The Spaniards dare hardly trust any Indians with armor. In a short time the Guianians may be instructed, trayned and consequently armed, and we by them and thei by vs defended with greater facility (being in their owne country) then opugned by any others: as wee see the estates of Christendome can defend their owne dominions amid the forces of their armed aduersaryes.

Besids this easy and compendious way of possessing Guiana, by arming the inhabitants, there is speciall choise to be had in sending preachers of good discrecion and behauior for their con-

1 Cor. 14. 27. uersion (who may reviue the old order of Christian Churches in speaking by Interpreters) also of well gouernd souldiers and artisans, that will not wrong the Indians in their persons, women or possessions. To that end a seuerity of Martiall Discipline is to be vsed in the open presence of the Guianians (being made acquainted with the cause of the punishment) with full satisfaction for all iniuryes which by the ruder sort shalbe offered. This wilbe a singular meane to worke their conuersion to procure their louing affections, and to oblige them in assured loyalty to her Majestie. Otherwise if our men practise vpon them the Spaniards crueltyes (which God forbid) besids the wrath of God, and the vtter ouerthrow of the whole seruice to bee feared, it will fall out with the Guianians, as with the other Indians of the conquered nations, who cursed the God of the Spaniards mourning after their owne Idols, thinking them better then the Spanish God, whom thei held to bee the worst, the most vnjust, the most wicked of all Gods, because he had such seruants: and the Spanish king the most vnjust and cruell of all Princes, supposing that he did feed on humayne flesh and bloud, because he sent among them such ill subjects. As Barth: de las Casas expressely certified his Lordship the Emperor Charles the 5th in his suyte vnto hym for redresse of the horrible outrages perpetrated by his Spaniards against the Indians.

To conclude if it might seeme fitt to her excellent Majestie that 4 or 5 hundred men (whereof some to be Leaders, some casters of great ordinance, some gunners, some Armorers &c.) were landed by hundreds in seuerall places next confining to Peru, Noua Hispania, Castilia del Oro, Nueuo Regno, Terra Florida, or els where as shalbe most conuenient for prouision of armor and munition to furnish the people, with instruction to sett them to warr against the Spaniards, it is greatly to be hoped that in a short tyme the Spaniards should be so occupied with defending their Bordurs that we might rest more safely heere in England and in Guiana. And also further matter of such graunde consequence mighte be acomplished the like wherof haue not come to the knowledge of the world since the conquest of the Indies. Allwaies provided that this policy of arminge the Inhabitants, as a speciall secret, be discreetly carryed and concealed vntyll it be rypened and brought into open Action.

Ralegh's confidence in the soundness of his extensive views for the settlement of Guiana was not diminished by the coldness with which his plans were received. He planned a second voyage, and succeeded in inducing the lord-treasurer and Sir Robert Cecil to take an interest in it[1]. Strong solicitations were made about that period in his favour at Court, and he probably considered that by devoting himself personally to his interest he would be surer of success; he therefore entrusted Captain Laurence Keymis with the command of the expedition, which consisted of the Darling and the Discoverer. Keymis had accompanied Ralegh on his first voyage, and shared his firm belief in the wealth and capabilities of Guiana. He set sail in January 1596, and after his return in the following June published a narrative of this expedition, which he dedicated to his patron Sir Walter Ralegh[2]. Viewed as a literary production it is not without merit, but it bears the same exaggerated style as Ralegh's own production, whose infatuation seems to have been so great, that Keymis's report tended materially to confirm him in the belief of the mineral riches of the banks of the Orinoco, upon which he mainly built his designs of colonizing Guiana.

Ralegh was absent from England on the return of the expe-

[1] Rowland Whyte, in a letter to Sir Robert Sidney, observes, "His voyage goes forward, and my lord-treasurer ventures with him £500 in money: Sir Robert Cecyl ventures a new ship bravely furnished; the very hull stands in £800." (Sidney Papers, vol. i. p. 377.)

[2] A Relation of the Second Voyage to Guiana, performed and written in the year 1596 by Laurence Keymis, Gentl. London, 1596.

dition, and engaged in the memorable action at Cadiz. During the interval of Keymis's voyage he had been partly restored to favour, and appointed a member of the council of war to the expedition under the Earl of Essex and Lord Effingham. After his return from Cadiz he bethought himself anew of his Guianian project, which, if it could be said to have slumbered, was fully revived by Keymis's favourable account. For the purpose of enlarging these discoveries, and keeping up amicable relations between the Indians and the English, a pinnace was fitted out which had been in the late engagement off Cadiz, the command of which Ralegh gave to Leonard Berric. She sailed from Weymouth for Guiana on the 27th of December 1596, and returned after an absence of six months[1].

These expeditions, which were undertaken almost entirely at Ralegh's expense, prove that his projects regarding Guiana rested upon a full persuasion of ultimate success, and disarm the accusation of Hume and others that he stated deliberate falsehoods in his narrative to further his ambitious objects.

The public employments to which Ralegh was called, and his restoration to the favour of his sovereign, rendered it impossible for him to devote himself personally to the prosecution of his great colonial projects; it appears therefore that Guiana, for awhile at least, did not occupy the chief place in the machinations and workings of his restless mind.

His character offers so many contrarieties, that in following the different actions and events of his life one is perplexed to form an opinion of this great man. It is asserted by all the contemporary historians that the populace disliked Ralegh; and this feeling was reciprocal, as he never lost an opportunity of evincing his contempt for the lower orders. Nevertheless, in the short period of his intercourse with the natives, he succeeded in taking such a strong hold on their affection and respect, that years

[1] A narrative of this expedition, written by Master Thomas Masham, a gentleman of the company, is inserted in Hakluyt's Voyages, vol. iii. p. 692.

were not able to remove the remembrance of him. Dr. Southey speaks doubtfully of this attachment; we have however such strong evidence of the fact in the narratives of Leigh and Harcourt, who undertook expeditions to Cayenne in 1606 and 1608[1], that there remains no room for doubt, even were the circumstances that Topiawari permitted Ralegh to take his son to England, and that Harry the Indian lived with him two years in the Tower, not of themselves sufficient proofs. The respect with which he had contrived to impress the Guianian chiefs was so strong, that the tradition of his visit was still current in the middle of the last century. Bancroft says, that "the Caribs retain a tradition of an English chief, who many years since landed amongst them, and encouraged them to persevere in enmity to the Spaniards, promising to return and settle amongst them and afford them assistance; and it is said that they still preserve an English Jack, which he left there that they might distinguish his countrymen[2]".

It would be exceeding the proposed limits of the present publication, to follow Ralegh in that career which, during the last five years of Elizabeth's reign, distiguished him so preeminently as a warrior and a legislator, but which yet unhappily offers likewise many instances in which his conduct deserved censure. His good star seemed to have reached its zenith at the close of that glorious reign, when it began to decline.

Immediately after the death of Queen Elizabeth a meeting took place at Whitehall, for the purpose of proclaiming her successor, which was attended by the principal officers of the Crown and

[1] Robert Harcourt's Relation of a Voyage to Guiana. (Edition, London, 1626, p. 11.) The author of the 'Relation of the Habitations, and other Observations of the River Marwin' (Purchas's Collection of Voyages, book vi. cap. 17) expressly observes, that the Indian who came to visit him "spake very much of Sir Walter Ralegh," and that "Topiaiwarie wondered that he heard not from Sir Walter, according to his promise; and how Topiaiwarie did verily thinke that the Spaniards had met with him and slaine him."

[2] Bancroft's Essay on the Nat. Hist. of Guiana, p. 258. London, 1769.

men of standing then in London; Ralegh's name occurs among the signatures on this important occasion[1].

It is asserted by Aubrey that Ralegh proposed at this meeting, "to keep the staff of government in their own hands, and set up a Commonwealth, and not to remain subject to a needy and beggarly nation[2]". This astounding assertion is not confirmed by any other historian; but there appears to be little doubt that Ralegh entertained an opinion, that James's power of appointing the Scotch to places of trust and emolument in England ought to be subjected to some limitations. This sentiment was probably conveyed to the King, who had already been prejudiced against Ralegh by the Earl of Essex. Sir Robert Cecil seems to have feared Ralegh more than any one of those who, like him, aimed at power and places of honour; and in a secret correspondence which he carried on with the Scottish King previous to the death of Queen Elizabeth, he succeeded in impressing James with a belief that Ralegh was unfavourable to his succession, and intended to oppose him whenever the Queen's death should happen[3]. This tended to confirm Essex's designs, and we cannot wonder that the King took a dislike to Ralegh before he had set foot on English soil, which manifested itself soon after his arrival in London, in his dismissal as Captain of the Guard, which office was given to Sir Thomas Erskine. The prejudice against Ralegh was so strong, that all his actions were misinterpreted; and ere the King had been three months in England, Ralegh was charged with being implicated in the Spanish plot or Lord Cobham's treason, which had for its object to dispossess James of his crown, and to place his cousin, the Lady Arabella Stuart, upon the throne. Sir Walter was absurdly

[1] Carte, Hist. of Engl. vol. iii. p. 708.

[2] Letters written by eminent persons, from the MSS. of John Aubrey, &c., vol. ii. p. 519. London, 1813.

[3] Secret Correspondence of Sir Robert Cecil with James VI. king of Scotland; published by Sir David Dalrymple. Edinburgh, 1766. Cayley's Life of Ralegh, vol. ii. p. 2.

accused of having conspired with Lord Cobham for the purpose of effecting the Lady Arabella's succession, and having for that purpose sought pecuniary assistance from the King of Spain. Nothing seems to have grieved him so much as the accusation of a conspiracy with that power towards which he felt such a deep-rooted hatred, and at a period when, as he says in his letter to the Commissioners, he had made an offer to King James of raising at his own cost two thousand men to attack Spain in her American possessions[1].

Toward the end of July Ralegh was committed to the Tower, and indicted at Staines in Middlesex on the 21st of September, 1603; Cobham and Grey three days after, and all three returned prisoners to the Tower. The explorer whose energy and perseverance we have admired during his first Guiana voyage, the hero who headed the fleet at Cadiz and braved the batteries of the Spaniards, the leader who in spite of natural obstacles and difficulties stormed Fayal, appears now to have lost his manly courage and fortitude, and to have made an attempt upon his own life. "One afternoon," writes Lord Cecil to Sir Thomas Parry, ambassador in France, "while divers of us were in the Tower, examining some of the prisoners, he (Ralegh) attempted to have murdered himself. Whereof when we were advertised we came to him and found him in some agony, seeming to be unable to endure his misfortunes, and protesting innocency with carelessness of life[2]." The wound, Cecil asserts, was not severe, being rather a cut than a stab[3].

[1] His tract, 'A Discourse touching a War with Spain, and of the protecting of the Netherlands,' was written shortly after the King's accession, for the purpose of being presented to his Majesty. He endeavoured to show that Spain "hath begun of late years to decline; and it is a principle in philosophy," he says, "that *Omnis diminutio est preparatio ad corruptionem*. That the least decay of any part is a forerunner of the destruction of the whole." How true this proved with regard to himself!

[2] A copy of this letter is among the MSS. in the British Museum, Ayscough's Cat., No. 4176.

[3] In a letter of John Peyton, Lieutenant of the Tower, and dated the

This design upon his life seems not to have been the result of momentary impulse, but premeditation. In a letter written to his wife previous to the attempt, he says, "I can not live to think how I shall be derided, to think of the expectation of my enemies, the scorns I shall receive, the cruel words of lawyers, the infamous taunts and despites, to be made a wonder and a spectacle [1]."

The plague raged in London at the time when the prisoners were to be brought to trial, and the court sat at Winchester. Ralegh was conveyed to the castle at Winchester in his own coach, under the custody of Sir Robert Mansel. The public feeling was so strong against him, that on his way he was assailed with bitter speeches and execrations by the populace. "They threwe tobacco-pipes, stones and myre at hym, as he was caryed in the coache; but he neglected and scorned them, as proceeding from base and rascal people[2]."

Ralegh's trial took place on the 17th of November: he defended himself with eloquence, force and perspicuousness. He appealed to his acts during the former reign, which bore testimony that he had always condemned the Spanish faction, and had spent forty thousand crowns against that power.

30th of July, 1603, occurs the following passage: "Sir Walter Rawley his hurt will be within these two days perfectly whole: he does still continue perplexed as you left him; he is desirous to have Mr. Heriot [Hariot] come to him, wherein I can not conceive any inconvenience, if it shall so stand with the lords their honorable pleasure." (Memoirs of Sir Walter Ralegh by Mrs. A. F. Thomson, p. 488.)

[1] The letter from which the above paragraph is extracted is printed in Bishop Goodman's Court of King James the First, published by John Brewer, M.A., London, 1839, vol. ii. p. 93. It is a most remarkable production of this remarkable man, full of pathetic appeals and proofs of agonizing emotions. He recommends his lady to marry again, not for love but to avoid poverty; and with regard to the sinful action he is on the point of committing, he flatters himself in that deceptive hope, that though "it is forbidden to destroy ourselves," he trusts "it is forbidden in this sort, that we destroy not ourselves despairing of God's mercy."

[2] Letter of Michael Hickes to the Earl of Shrewsbury, in Lodge's Illustrations, vol. iii. p. 217.

Could it be supposed, he argued, that he, whose object it had so recently been to humble Spain to the dust, as he proved by the treatise he had written, should now espouse her cause? His defence was however vain; Sir Edward Coke, the Attorney-General, conducted the trial on behalf of the Crown in such a manner as was calculated, says Hume, to leave an indelible stigma not only upon Coke's character, but upon that of his age and country[1]. As if his presentiment of "the scorns he should receive, the cruel words of lawyers, the infamous taunts and despites," were to be fulfilled to the tittle, the Attorney-General assailed him with the epithets of traitor, monster, viper, and spider of hell; and when by the base subservience of the jury he was brought in guilty of high-treason, the Lord Chief Justice Popham, before pronouncing sentence, ungenerously accused him "with the defence of the most heathenish and blasphemous opinions." Ralegh, without deigning to make any remark, accompanied the sheriff to the prison "with admirable erection, yet in such sort as a condemned man should do[2]."

The injustice of this trial was so flagrant, that the great tide of popular feeling, which had hitherto run against Ralegh, now turned in his favour; his fate raised the deepest sympathy, and his conduct under the persecution of the court engaged general admiration.

Ralegh after his condemnation wrote to the King, sueing for his life with dignified submission; the result of this supplication was, that the Bishop of Winchester at the King's command waited upon him, to prepare him for death, which from that moment he expected daily. During that period he wrote the

[1] The trial is fully reported in Hargrave's State Trials, vol. i. p. 211. A detailed account of it was likewise printed "for S. Redmayne" in 1719. Cayley observes respecting these proceedings, "We shall wish, that this unsightly tissue of abuse, malevolence and oppression had never existed as such upon the records of our own country."

[2] Sir Thomas Overbury's 'The Arraignment of Sir Walter Rawleigh.' London, 1648, p. 25.

touching letter to Lady Ralegh which has been printed in the Remains, as asserted, copied "out of his own handwriting." It has since been reprinted by Birch and Cayley[1]. We shall not pause at the tragi-comedy which King James resorted to with respect to those implicated in the Cobham treason. Ralegh was reprieved with the rest, and committed to the Tower during his Majesty's pleasure[2].

It is one of the brightest traits in Sir Walter's character, that, his fate being decided, instead of giving way to further despondency, the activity of his mind was re-awakened; and we find that during his imprisonment his whole energy, intellectual and physical, was bestowed upon a subject which has earned him lasting fame in a field previously almost untrodden: we mean the conception and composition of his History of the World[3]. One of the particular features of this great production is the multiplicity of subjects he has introduced, touching upon war, navigation, politics, philosophy, and natural history, and illustrated by examples from his own experience. And it is here that we find so many reminiscences of his voyage to Guiana, and proofs that his imagination still revelled in the golden visions of El Dorado, or rather the inexhaustible riches of Guiana. His History is equally fruitful in episodes, reflections and maxims, interspersed with eloquent and most touching passages and graphic expressions. What a character would Ralegh have exhibited to posterity, did we know him only from

[1] Birch's Works, ii. p. 383; Cayley's Life of Ralegh, ii. p. 81.

[2] Sir Dudley Carleton in his letter to Mr. John Chamberlain, dated December 11th, 1603, observes, that Ralegh's turn for execution "is to come on Monday next," after the mock tragedy with the lords Cobham and Grey and Mr. Markham.

[3] We have read with very great pleasure the critical remarks in the Edinburgh Review (No. cxliii.) on the chief events in Sir Walter Ralegh's life and the tenour of his publications, to which we refer the reader for much useful information. It is the production of the late Professor Napier. An edition of Ralegh's works, with a life upon an extended scale, was one of Prof. Napier's early literary projects.

his martial actions and literary productions! In truth the motto "Tam Marte quam Minerva" would have found no worthier subject[1], and would have been equally appropriate as the one he himself selected.

The assertion by the author of the 'Curiosities of Literature,' that this great work was not the legitimate production of Sir Walter Ralegh, and that "the eloquent, the grand, and the pathetic passages interspersed" were alone his composition, has been ably met by Mr. Bolton Corney, in a publication which Professor Napier in the Edinburgh Review styles "one of the most learned and acute contributions to literary history that has appeared in our days[2]." Though Ben Jonson and Algernon Smith were of opinion that Ralegh had been assisted in his History of the World, the internal evidences which are adduced by Mr. Corney, Mr. Tytler, and the author of the critical remarks in the Edinburgh Review, leave little doubt that the entire work is the production of a single mind, and "wholly the composition of its reputed author[3]." Mr. Corney justly observes[4], "Sir Walter Ralegh was endowed with splendid abilities, but his abilities, without other qualifications, would not have produced the 'History of the World.' It is in the continued attachment to literature which he so especially evinced, and in the habit of assiduous application to his pursuits, that we read the secret history of its composition. I make the assertion with

[1] Ralegh's motto was "Tam Marti quam Mercurio." Prefixed to the 'Select Essays of Sir Walter Raleigh,' published by Moseley in 1650, and to the 'Maxims of State,' published by Shears, Jun. in 1656, are portraits of Ralegh, with his motto as a superscription.

[2] Edinburgh Review, No. cxliii. p. 69.

[3] Alexander Ross published, about the middle of the seventeenth century, 'Som Animadversions upon Sir Walter Raleigh's Historie of the World,' which display a great deal of learning, but are either hypercritical or argumentative.

[4] Bolton Corney, 'Curiosities of Literature illustrated.' Greenwich, 1837, p. 63. The aphorism quoted by Mr. Corney was written by Ralegh in an album of Captain Segar.

confidence, being enabled to prove its congeniality with his own sentiments: Opus peragunt labor et amor."

But few of Ralegh's literary productions were published during his lifetime[1]; and we have to regret the uncertainty which exists with regard to the genuineness of several works attributed to him[2].

During his confinement in the Tower he dedicated a considerable portion of his time to chemical inquiries and experiments. Cayley quotes the following passage from a letter of Sir William Wade, lieutenant of the Tower, to Sir Robert Cecil, dated the 19th of August 1605: "Sir Walter Ralegh hath like access (with Cobham) of divers to him. The door of his chamber being always open all the day to the garden, which indeed is the only garden the lieutenant hath. And in the garden he hath converted a little hen-house to a still-house, where he doth spend his time all the day in distillations[3]." We have seen a manuscript in Sir Walter's handwriting containing chemical processes, recipes and assays, among the latter of which we find an additional proof of his still unshaken faith in the richness of the Guiana ore. We extract the following passage:—

"I tried the oare of Guiana in this sort, I took of the oare

[1] We are aware of only two, namely, 'A Report of the truth of the Fight about the Isles of Azores this last Summer, betwixt the Revenge, one of her Majesty's ships, commanded by Sir Richard Grenville, and an Armada of the King of Spain.' 4to. 1591; and his 'Discovery of Guiana.'

[2] We abstain reluctantly from the inviting opportunity of dwelling in detail upon Ralegh's literary productions; our passing remarks in the Introduction, and in the course of this work, have directed attention to several of them, and for the rest we refer to Ralegh's works by Birch, and for a very complete list to Cayley's Life of Ralegh, vol. ii. p. 186.

[3] Cayley, vol. ii. p. 84. The little still-house is likewise alluded to in a note from Peter Turner, Doctor of Physic, who having been called in upon Ralegh's complaint of numbness, in consequence of his cold prison-room, recommends his removal to warmer lodgings, "that is to say to a little roome which he has bilt in the garden adjoyning to his still-house." This document, which is printed in full in Mrs. Thomson's 'Memoirs' (p. 495), is preserved at the State Paper Office, and is endorsed in Cecil's handwriting.

beaten small 12 graynes, of filled lead half an ownce, of sandever a quarter of an ownce. I beat the sandever small and then mixed all together and putt it into a crosett, covering it with another crosett that had a little hole in the topp and luted both together, then I covered all with good coal, and with two paire of ordenary bellowes we blew to it till all was melted down. Then we putt the lead uppon a test under a muffle till the lead was consumed and had of the 12 graynes a quarter of a grayn of gold"[1].

This curious manuscript, consisting of seventy folio pages, of which however only fifty-three are more or less filled, contains several other essays and experiments with ore, which we shall pass over; but we cannot dismiss it without alluding to the celebrated cordial which Ralegh invented[2], and which was in such high repute, that Anne, the queen of King James, took it herself; and when Prince Henry, her son, was in his last illness, she sent for some, but it had merely the effect of reviving for a short time the spark of life. Prince Henry died on the 6th of November 1612, in the nineteenth year of his age.

The prince's death was a severe stroke to Sir Walter Ralegh, who thus lost the patron of his studies, to whom he had dedicated his discourses on the Royal Navy and Sea Service. The latter piece contains an allusion to a previous discourse, on "a maritimal voyage, and the passages and incidents therein," which appears to be lost. These treatises on naval affairs seem

[1] Brit. Mus. MSS. Sloane, No. 359, fol. 52[b].

[2] It is inserted on page 63, with the superscription in his own handwriting, "Our great Cordiall." The exact composition of Ralegh's cordial is not known, in consequence of the original prescription merely stating the ingredients, and not the quantities. It may be a question, whether this was done by Ralegh from a selfish motive. It was so highly thought of in the reign of Charles the Second, that this monarch desired Nicholas Le Febure, the royal professor of chemistry and apothecary in ordinary to the King, to prepare a quantity in the exactest manner. Le Febure published a tract in 1665, 'Discours sur le grand Cordial de Sir Walter Ralegh,' which was translated into English while still in manuscript, and published by Peter Belon in 1664. (Cayley, vol. ii. p. 90.)

to have been the first of the kind in the English language. He likewise wrote, at the Prince's desire, a discourse upon the double alliance proposed by the ambassador of the Duke of Savoy, between the Princess Elizabeth, the eldest surviving daughter of King James, and the Prince of Piedmont; and, on the other hand, between Prince Henry and the eldest daughter of the Duke of Savoy. Ralegh, in his History of the World, alludes to a treatise on "the Art of War at Sea," which he had written "for the Lord Henry, Prince of Wales; a subject," he says, "to my knowledge never handled by any man, ancient or modern: but God hath spared me the labour of finishing it by his loss; by the loss of that brave prince of which like an eclipse of the sun, we shall find the effects hereafter"[1]. The death of the Prince of Wales materially influenced Sir Walter's fate, and we doubt whether Ralegh would have ended his days on the scaffold had the Prince lived.

The despondency which seized Sir Walter on this occasion was so great, that we have to ascribe to it the discontinuance of the other volumes of his History of the World. He says in the concluding words of that great work: "Beside many other discouragements persuading my silence, it hath pleased God to take that glorious Prince out of the world to whom they [his subsequent labours] were directed. Whose unspeakable and never-enough lamented loss, hath taught me to say with Job, versa est in luctum cithara mea, et organum meum in vocem flentium."

We have already alluded to an instance of despondency in

[1] History of the World, book v. cap. i. § 6. In the British Museum, under MS. Cotton, Titus, b. viii. art. 24, will be found the heads and chapters of this work in Sir Walter's handwriting, affording another proof that one of the subjects always uppermost in his mind was how to humble Spain. One of the intended chapters was, "Of the King of Spayne's weakness in the West Indies and how that rich trade [not *mine*, as erroneously quoted by Tytler] might be taken from him"; and, "Of his weakness in the East Indies and what places he holds in both." On the next folio (page 218) are written five names of ports and headlands; among these the name of Morocco attracted our attention, as there is a river of that name to the east of the Orinoco.

Sir Walter's life, produced by adversity, scarcely to be expected from a man whose character seemed endowed with such general strength and firmness of resolution. If the death of the Prince was really the principal cause of the discontinuance of his History, it affords an additional proof of this assertion.

His captivity had not diverted Ralegh from his Guiana projects. The voyages of Leigh and Harcourt, to which we have already referred, kept his interest awake. We learn from his apology, that he was every year, or every second year, at the charge of sending to Guiana, to keep the natives in hope of being relieved from the Spanish yoke[1]. The strongest proofs of attachment were shown by Harry the Indian, who shared Ralegh's captivity for two years. It appears from a document in the Harleian Collection, that in 1611 he made a most remarkable proposition to the Government; and as its tenour places Ralegh's firm belief in the existence of gold mines in Guiana beyond question, the publication of this paper is of high interest[2].

"An agreement betweene S^r^ Wa: Raleigh and the Lords for the journey of Guiana, to be performed by Captaine Keemish in Anno 1611.

"Your Lordshipps as I remember did offer to be att the charge to transport Keemish into Guyana with such a proportion of men in twoe shipps as should be able to defend him against the Spaniards inhabiting vpon Orenoke if they offered to assaile him (not that itt is meant to offend the Spaniards

[1] When Robert Harcourt arrived in 1608 at the Bay of Wiapoco (Oyapoke), the Indians came on board, and "Carasana, and one or two more of them were attired in old cloaths, which they had gotten of certaine Englishmen, who by the direction of Sir Walter Raleigh had traded there the yeare before." (Harcourt's Voyage of Guiana, Allde's edition of 1626, p. 10.)

[2] We met with this document in the Harleian Collection, (MSS. Harl. 39. fol. 340–350,) previous to our knowledge that a short extract from it had been published in the Edinburgh Review.

there or to beginne any quarrell with them except themselves shall beginne the warre).

"To knowe what number of men shall be sufficient may itt please your Lordshipps to informe your selves by Captaine More, a servant of Sir John Watts, who came from Orenoke this last spring, and was oftentimes ashore att St. Thome, where the Spaniards inhabite, which numbers made knowne to your Lordshipps and to the Captaines which you shall please to imploy with Keemish those Captaines shall be able to judge with what force they will vndertake to secure Keemishes passage to the Mine which is not above five miles from the navigable River taking the neerest way.

"Now your Lordshipps doe require of mee that if Keemish live to arrive and shall be guarded to the place and shall then faile to bring into England halfe a Tunne or as much more as he shall be able to take upp of that slate Gold ore whereof I gave a sample to my Lord Knevett That then all the charge of the journey shall be laid vpon mee and by mee to be satisfied whereto I willingly consent, and though itt be a difficult matter of exceeding difficulty for any man to find the same acre of ground againe in a country desolate and overgrowne which he hath seene but once and that sixteene yeares since which were hard enough to doe vpon Salisbury Plaine yett that your Lordshipps may be satisfied of the truth I am contented to adventure all I have (but my reputacion) vpon Keemishes memory, hoping that itt may be acceptable to the Kings Majestie and to your Lordshipps soe to doe considering that if Keemish misse of his marks my poore Estate is vtterly ouerthrowne, and my wife and children as utterly beggared.

"Now that there is noe hope after the Tryall made to fetch any more riches from thence I have already given your Lordshipps my reasons in my former letter and am ready vpon a Mappe of the Country to make demonstracion thereof if itt shall please your Lordshipps to give me leave, but to the kings Maiesties wisdome and your Lordshipps I submitt myselfe.

"But that which your Lordshipps doe promise is That halfe a Tunne of the former oare being brought home that then I shall have my Libertie and in the meane while my free pardon vnder the greate Seale to be left in his Maiesties hands till the end of the Journey."

This paper is of great importance; in the first place it relieves Ralegh from any charge of practising deception with the slate-gold-ore of which he had given a sample; how otherwise would he have offered to be at the risk of sending Keymis on such an errand? and, in the next place, it shows that he apprehended at that early period an interference of the Spaniards "inhabiting upon Orenoke:" he even informs their Lordships of the existence of the very town which was afterwards destroyed by Keymis: hence the Government were fully informed that there was a Spanish settlement in the district where he considered the mine to be situate[1]. We must therefore dismiss the accusation that he had concealed this fact, under the supposition that he would not have been permitted to undertake his second voyage had the Government been aware of it.

His proposition was not accepted at that period. The death of Cecil, which occurred six months previous to that of Prince Henry, had given Ralegh new hopes of regaining his freedom. We learn from a letter which he wrote about that time to the Queen, that he was as closely locked up as on the first day[2].

[1] This sentence refutes Dr. Southey's accusation, that Ralegh deceived the King by concealing from him that the Spaniards had any footing in Guiana; and thus, "deceiving and deceived, began in an unhappy hour his miserable voyage." We cannot help expressing our astonishment that such a strong case for his defence should have been overlooked by his biographers.

[2] A letter from Sir William Wade to Lord Cecil, dated December 9th, 1608, explains the reason of his strict confinement. It appears he "shewed himself upon the wall in his garden to the view of the people, who gaze upon him, and he stareth on them. Which he doth in his cunning humour, that it might be thought his being before your Lordship was rather to clear than to charge him." Which made Sir William "bold

Neither the interference of the Queen nor of the King of Denmark in his favour produced any effect, except that in 1614 the liberty of the Tower was allowed to him. Sir Ralph Winwood, no friend of the Spanish interest, had succeeded Lord Cecil as Secretary of State, and Ralegh addressed a letter to him in July 1615, in which he renews his proposition of a journey to Guiana, and refers to his former offer to Lord Cecil. He concludes this epistle with the following strong expression, "to die for the King and not by the King is all the ambition I have in this world[1]." In a previous letter to the Queen he proffered the same service, not actuated by personal interest in the matter, but solely to approve his faith to his Majesty, and "to do him a service such as hath seldom been performed for any King[2]."

What neither the intercession of the Queen and the late Prince Henry, nor the request of the King of Denmark could produce, was effected, after the disgrace of Car, Earl of Somerset, by a bribe to the uncles of the new favourite, Villiers, afterwards Duke of Buckingham. It is very probable that the idea of the existence of a mine, from which great benefits might be reaped, induced the needy King to lend a favourable ear to Villiers' intercession; and the gates of the Tower, so long closed on Ralegh, were now opened, on the 17th of March, 1615–16[3]. The bribe which had been paid to Sir William St. John and Sir Edward Villiers (half-brothers to the Lady Villiers, mother to the new favourite) was fifteen hundred pounds. It was asserted by Carew Ralegh, that an additional bribe of fifteen hundred pounds would have procured a full pardon, which assertion receives some confirmation from the author of "the Observations on Saunder-

to restrain him again and meet with his indiscreet humour." (Cayley's Life of Ralegh, vol. ii. p. 86.

[1] Brit. Mus. Harleian MSS., xxxix. Plut. 50 C. fol. 351.

[2] Memoirs of the Life of Sir Walter Ralegh, by Mrs. A. T. Thomson, p. 493.

[3] Camden fixes the date three days later; but according to a letter which Ralegh wrote on his liberation to Sir George Villiers, returning him thanks for his intercession, it was on the day above named.

son's history of Mary and James," who says that the uncles of Villiers offered for an additional seven hundred pounds not only full pardon to Ralegh, but "liberty not to go his voyage if he pleased." This would be a strong proof, if it could be substantiated, of Ralegh's entire confidence of success, and that the Guiana voyage was a condition of his release. The offer was declined. Carew Ralegh, in a letter to James Howell, gives as reason, that his father consulting Lord Bacon whether the commission the King had given him did not imply his pardon, received an opinion in the affirmative, accompanied by his advice rather to apply that sum towards the outfit for his expedition.

Sir Walter had no sooner obtained his freedom than he made every preparation for his voyage, and so high was the opinion entertained of his wisdom and the soundness of his scheme, that in the face of former failures, many offered to become associates in the enterprize, either in person or in gold. It was generally known that Ralegh intended to embark his remaining fortune in the undertaking; and this, united with the great reputation he had acquired in naval affairs, induced many merchants, both in England and abroad, to contribute to the adventure. The alluring picture of a gold-mine, or the advantages of Guiana as a colony, were too seducing to permit sounder reflections. Through the influence of Sir Ralph Winwood, Ralegh obtained a commission for the voyage, under the great seal as alleged by some, and directed, "Dilecto et fideli meo Waltero Raleigh militi[1];" but, as asserted in the Royal Declaration and in Rymer's Fœdera, only under the privy seal, without those expressions of trust and grace[2]. This commission, which was dated Westminster, the 26th of August 1616, empowered him

[1] Roger Coke: 'A Detection of the Court and State of England during the last four reigns.' Second edition. London, 1696, pp. 55, 57. Rapin Thoyras, in his 'Histoire d'Angleterre,' vol. vii. p. 120, observes that the King "lui accorda la commission qu'il demandoit, adressée, A notre amé et féal Walter Rawleigh," &c.

[2] Rymer's Fœdera, vol. xvi. p. 789.

to proceed to the south, and to such parts of America as were unappropriated by other states, and to search for all such articles and commodities therein as might be useful to commerce.

While these preparations were going on, the Spanish ambassador, Don Diego Sarmiento de Acuña (afterwards Count de Gondomar) did not remain a silent spectator. Ralegh's former voyage to Guiana, and his deep-rooted enmity to Spain, raised his apprehension that this expedition was intended for something more than the working of a mine or the settlement of colonies. Gondomar, who possessed already at that period great influence over the weak-minded monarch, failed not to complain of Ralegh's expedition, which he designated as hostile and piratical to King Philip and his subjects. So great an armament, as he had informed himself was going on, could never have for its object the working of a mine; and he offered, if Ralegh would proceed with one or two ships only, to induce the King of Spain to give him a safe convoy back, with any quantity of gold he might have procured in Guiana, and that he, the ambassador, would remain a pledge for his safety. As this offer was refused, Gondomar was fully warranted in mistrusting Ralegh's pacific assurances. Sir Ralph Winwood, upon the King's command, had exacted from Ralegh a statement of the number of his men, the burthen and armament of his ships, and the country and river which he was to enter. This statement was communicated to the Spanish ambassador, who forwarded it to his court; and Philip in consequence sent a royal "cedula" to the governors at Puerto Rico, Trinidad and New Granada, ordering them to take the necessary precautions and prepare for an attack[1].

[1] It is not probable that Ralegh's original letter which contained the statement was found in the governor's archives at San-Thomè, as asserted by his son Carew Ralegh. Father Simon states however that the royal cedula, which warned the governor Don Diego Palomeque of Ralegh's hostile intentions, was dated Madrid, the 19th March, 1617. (Fray Simon, Noticias historiales de las Conquistas de tierra firma, Setima Noticia, cap. xxiii. p. 636.)

Seven vessels lay ready equipped in the Thames in the commencement of March. We extract from the scarce publication entitled "Newes of Sir Walter Rauleigh" the following list of the vessels, which has not been published in that detailed form either by Oldys or Birch[1].

"A view and survey of such ships as were in the river of Thames, ready to goe to sea, vnder the command of Sir Walter Rauleigh, Knight, and of their names, tonnage and number of men, taken by certaine Gentlemen appointed therevnto by the Right Honourable Charles Earle of Nottingham, Lord high Admirall of England, the 15th of March 1616[2].

"THE DESTINY of London, of the burthen of 440 tons, whereof Sir Walter Rauleigh goeth Generall, Walter Rauleigh the younger, Captaine, Robert Burwick master, 200 men, whereof 100 saylers, 20 watermen, 80 Gentlemen, the rest Servants and Labourers; 36 pieces of Ordnance.

"THE STARRE alias THE JASON of London, of the burthen of 240 tons, John Pennington Captain, George Cleuingham, master; 80 men, one Gentleman and no more; 25 pieces of Ordnance.

"THE ENCOUNTER of London, of the burthen of 160 tons, Edward Hastings Captaine, Thomas Pye master; 17 pieces of Ordnance.

"THE JOHN AND FRANCIS alias THE THUNDER of the burthen of 150 tonnes; Sir William Sentleiger, Knight, Captaine, William Gurden, master, 60 souldiers, 10 land-men, 6 Gentlemen, 20 pieces of Ordnance.

"THE FLYING JOANE of London of the burden of 120 tons,

[1] Cayley observes that this list is not to be found in the copy of the tract which he possessed. A copy which is bound up in a volume of manuscripts in the British Museum (Ayscough's Cat. No. 3272) contains the list at the end.

[2] This is evidently a misprint and ought to be 1617.

John Chidley Captaine, William Thorne master, 25 men, 14 pieces of Ordnance.

"THE HUSBAND alias THE SOUTHAMPTON of the burthen of 80 Tonnes, John Bayley Captaine, Philip Fabian master, 25 mariners, 2 Gentlemen, 6 pieces of Ordnance.

"A pinnace called THE PAGE of 25 Tonnes, James Barker Captaine, Stephen Selby master, 8 saylers, three Rabnets[1] of brasse."

The following manuscript note is added to this list:—

"Sum total 1215 Tonnes—Men 431—Ordnance 121. There is no more men sett downe in the Encounter, but only 2, viz. the Captayne and Master."

The superscription of this document is of great importance, as imparting to it an official character, and proving undeniably that James' ministers had full notice of the magnitude of this armament; it is therefore evident that they winked at consequences which they must have foreseen.

The assembling of such a fleet could not fail to raise great curiosity, and it was visited by all the ambassadors resident in London,—among the rest by Count Desmarets, the ambassador of France. In some dispatches which this diplomatist forwarded to his court[2], he asserts that he had visited Sir Walter Ralegh's ship the Destiny several times[3], and had entered with him into conversation, during which Ralegh showed himself highly discontented, representing himself as having been unjustly imprisoned, and stripped of his estate—in a word, most tyrannically used, and as having on that account *resolved to abandon his*

[1] Robinet, a small piece of ordnance, about two hundred pounds in weight and an inch and a quarter within the mouth.

[2] As far as we know the first allusion to these despatches occurs in that masterly article in the Edinburgh Review, to which we have already had occasion to refer.

[3] Ralegh protests in his apology that he saw Desmarets only once on board of his vessel.

country, and to make the King of France the first offer of his services and acquisitions, if his enterprize, from which he confidently expected great results, should succeed.

If this assertion of Count Desmarets be founded on truth, it is distressing that we must look upon the man, whose life presents so many events which excite our admiration, as an unscrupulous hypocrite, alike destitute of principle and patriotism. In his letter to the Queen, he protests by the everliving God that his main object in the voyage was to approve his faith and to serve the King; and when ultimately on the point of departure for effecting his plans, he offers to transfer the results of his voyage to a foreign monarch. Fortunately for the memory of Sir Walter Ralegh, there is one point which gives room for doubt in the correctness of Desmarets' information, and we readily give the benefit of that doubt to Ralegh. The dates of these dispatches are respectively the 12th of January, 17th and 30th of March and the 24th of April, 1617, and it is asserted in the Edinburgh Review that the words in italics are translated from the last dispatch. Sir Walter sailed from the Thames on the 26th of March[1]; it is therefore remarkable that, if the proposal was made by Ralegh during the visit of the ambassador on board the Destiny, he should not have communicated it in his dispatch of the 30th of March, but have permitted a whole month to pass over before he reported it.

We do not wish to represent Ralegh's character as wholly free of blemish: we meet but too frequently occurrences in his eventful life that require all our charity, and the indulgence which the age he lived in may claim, in judging him; but we cannot bring ourselves, merely from the evidence which these dispatches contain, to consider him so deceitful a traitor to his king and country as they represent him.

[1] According to Camden's Annals of James the First, he sailed on the 28th of March.

The expedition anchored at Plymouth, where Ralegh was joined by the following vessels :

The Convertine, commanded by Laurence Keymis.
The Confidence, commanded by Wollaston.
The Flying Hart, commanded by Sir John Ferne.
The Chudley.
A Fly-boat, commanded by Samuel King.
Another, commanded by Robert Smith.
A Carvel.

On the 3rd of May Ralegh published, from "Plymouth in Devon," his orders to the fleet, which, having been reprinted by Birch and Cayley from the tract already referred to, we pass over, adding only the following observation of the author of the 'Newes:' "I will acquaint you with some particulars touching the general government of the fleet, which, although other men doubtless in their voyages in some measure observed, yet all in the great volumes which have been written touching voyages, there is no precedent of so godly, severe, and martial government, which not only in itself is laudable and worthy of imitation, but also fit to be written and engraven in every man's soul that covets to do honour to his king and country in this or like attempts[1]." Can we imagine, after this protestation, that the framer of these rules meditated deception and treason? is it not more likely that the zeal of Desmarets led him to exaggerate or misrepresent the truth?

Ralegh gives in his apology an account of the various difficulties he had to overcome ere he could sail from Plymouth, which did not take place until the end of June or beginning of July. He encountered a strong gale to the westward of Scilly, in which the Flying Joane nearly sunk and was obliged to put into Cork; and it was the 19th of August before he could proceed on the fatal voyage, which eventually cost him his life.

The question has frequently occurred to us, while contem-

[1] Newes of Sir Walter Rauleigh, p. 17.

plating this eventful period in Ralegh's life, when he had staked his whole happiness as it were upon the cast of a die, whether his mind never misgave him respecting the success of this expedition. His faith in the existence of the gold-mine must have been implicit, or how could he have persuaded his faithful and attached wife to part with all she possessed to raise money for the outfit of this fatal expedition? The sum of eight thousand pounds, given by the King as a compensation for Sherbourne, and which had been lent to the Countess of Bedford, had been called in, and Lady Ralegh consented to the sale of an estate belonging to her at Mitcham, for which she received £2500. This sacrifice sufficiently proves Lady Ralegh's confidence in the practicability of her husband's scheme, as she was now almost reduced to beggary, being obliged to subsist upon the four hundred pounds which had been granted to her in lieu of jointure, a part of which she had even pledged at the departure of her husband. This is proved by a letter from Lady Ralegh to Sir Julius Cæsar, in which she complains of delays in the payment of her annuity, and which we insert, as we are not aware of its having been published previously. The letter is as follows: "I make no doubt but you will see me satisfied and relieved in this my just desire being agreable to his Majesty's expresse commandment that I should receiue my payment without molestation or delay which I am daily put off by Mr. Byngley. I should have received £200. at Michelmas, most of it being due to poor men from Sir Walter for his necessaries, and the rest to maintain me till our Lady day; but I have not receiued one penny from the Exchequer synce Sir Walter went[1]".

We have hitherto only been made acquainted with the incidents of the voyage from Cork to Guiana by some passages in his Apology, though a journal of his second voyage in his handwriting exists in the British Museum, in the collection of his friend Sir Robert Cotton. After having perused this journal

[1] Lansdowne MSS., No. 142, fol. 292.

with care and attention, we cannot but express our astonishment that it was not published by Birch, or in the Oxford collection of Ralegh's works. Although there are some parts of the journal which consist of a dry enumeration of courses sailed and distances made, it is so replete with interesting remarks on meteorological phænomena and currents, to say nothing of the incidents of the voyage, that these are alone of sufficient importance to warrant their publication. Moreover it contains some explanations which throw light upon Ralegh's actions. It has been asserted that the journal is so full of blanks as to be unfit for publication; but in reality the few blanks which occur are of little importance, and we are inclined to think that the author of such an assertion did not peruse the document with sufficient attention. We do not hesitate therefore to insert the journal literally from the manuscript, expressing only our regret that the weight of misfortune which befell Ralegh prevented his continuing it after, probably, the news of the loss of his son had reached him at Trinidad.

SIR WALTER RALEGH'S JOURNAL OF HIS SECOND VOYAGE TO GUIANA.

Printed from the original Manuscript in the British Museum.[1]

THE 19th of August [1617] att 6 a clock in the morninge having the winde att N.E. we sett saile in the river of Corck where we had attended a faire winde 7 weekes. 19 day.

From 6 in the morning till 10 att night we ran 14 Leagues S. by W. from 10 att night till 10 in the morning we had no winde, so as between 10 in the morning and 4 att afternoone we made not above 2 L.[2] 20 day.

Att 4 the 20th day the winde began to fresh, and we stired away S. S. W. keiping a westerly course fering the westerly windes, and from 4 to two a clock after midnight being the morninge of the 21 day we rann 13 L.

From 2 in the morning of the 21 day being thursday till 8 in the same morning being 6 howres we ran 6 L: S. b. W. Then the winde came to the W. and W. by S. very little winde till one a clock the winde betweene the west and the S. and wee rann not in that time above 2 L. At one the winde began to sheft up att N. E. and presently to the N. W. and blew strong so as by 4 we ran 6 L. 21 day.

From 4 to 8 we ran 7 L. from 8 to 12 other 7 L. from 12 to 4 being friday morning 6 L. from 4 to 8. 6 L. the course S.S.W. from 8 to 12 other 6 L. S.S.W. and taking the hight, we found our selves in 48 Degrees wanting 10 minutes, we then stearde away S. by W. and so from 12 on friday the 22 day to 22 day.

[1] Cotton MSS.; Titus, B. VIII. fol. 153.

[2] L. signifies throughout leagues, of which there are twenty to a degree, D. degrees, M. minutes.

23 d. 8 in the morning being saterday the 23 day we ran neere 24 L. S. by W. the winde being att N.N.E.

From 8 on Saterday morning to 8 on Sunday morning being
24 d. Bartelmeie day and the 24 we ran 35 L. S. by W.

25 d. Then it grew calme and we ran not above 10 L. from Sunday the 24 to Monday the 25.

Att 8 in the morning the wynde fayled and blew but a little gale att S.E. Munday night it blew strong at S. and it fell back from the S. to the S.S.W. and overblew so as we could ly but W. northerly, and so continewed all twesday the 26 day the
26 d. winde falling back at one a clock of the same day to the S.W. we cast about and lay S.E. the other way that night [for][1] a try.

27 d. Wensday morning the 27 we sett saile and lay S.S.E. and then S. by E. the wind att W.S.W. then changed to the W.N.W. and N.W. so as from 5 the wensday morning to 12 a clock of the same day we ran some 7 L. and brought the north part of cape Finister est.

From 12 we steerd away S. and S. by E. to recover agayne
28 d. our falling from our course towards the W. till 12 the next day being the 28 when as we found ourselves in 42 D. wanting 10 m.

29 d. From 12 the 28 to 12 the 29 having the winde att N. we ran 35 L. and were in 40 [D.] wanting 30 m.

30 d. From 12 the 29 to 12 the 30 day we ran on 30 L. S: and brought Lisborne E. northerly.

Att 12 the same 30 day we discovered 4 sailes and giving them chase and ran W.S.W. till 7 att night, then leaving the chase we stood S.S.E till 12 att night, and then S. so as by 8
31 d. a clock Sunday morning we had gon 18 L. and were 20 L. short of the Cape Saint Vincent. These 4 shipps were french and came from cap Blanck laden with fishe and traine oel and were bound as they pretended for Civile[2] in Spayne, but because they should not give knowledge that I was then past by ioined

[1] This word is partly effaced in the original and not quite legible.

[2] Seville in Spain.

them with me 100 leagues to the southward and then buying of them a pinnes of 7 toone and 3 pipes of traine oel, for which I gave them in reddy monie 61 crownes I dismissed them. It is trew that I had arguments enough to perswade me that they had not fishe but robd the Portugals and Spaniards att cap Blanck, for they were not only provided and furnished like men of warr but had in them store of Spanish apparell and other things taken ther. But because it is lawfull for the french to make prise of the Spanish Kings subjects to the south of the Canares and to the west of the Assores and that it did not belong to mee to examine the subjects of the french King, I did not suffer my companie to take from them any peneworth of their goodes greatly to the discontentment of my companie who cried out that they were men of warr and theeves, and so in deed they were, for I mett with a Spanierd afterward of the gran Canares whom they had robd.

From 8 sunday morning to 12 munday being the 1 of September we rann 40 L. and were in 35 D. lacking 8 m. and made our way S. by E. 1 Sep.

From 12 on Munday to 12 on twesday the 2 day we rann 30 L. having lien by the lee 4 howres and were in 33 [D.] and half. 2 Sep.

From 12 on twesday to 12 on wensday the 3 day we ran 30 L. 3 Sep.

From 12 on wensday to 12 on thursday the 4 of Sep. we ran but 14 L. S. by E. Friday the 5 and Saterday the 6 day we ran with a good gale and made Lancerota[1] on saterday before nowne, but on Saterday night we stood of till midnight and then stood in and on Sunday the 7 day came to ancor neere the shore of Lancerota wher we landed our men to strech their leggs. The people fearing that we had bine the same fleet of Turckes which had spoyled Porta Sancta[2] putt them selues in arms and came to the sea side with a flag of trewes. The Governoure being 4 Sep. 5 & 6 Sep.

[1] Lanzarota, one of the Canary Isles, in lat. 28° 57′ N., long. 13° 33′ W.

[2] Porto Santo, one of the Madeiras.

desirus to speake with mee to which I yeilded taking with mee[1]
Bradshew with each of vs a sword and the Governour with one of his so armed came into the playne to meet mee, our troopes staying att equall distance from vs. After he had saluted mee, his first desire was to know whether we were Christians or Turckes, wherof being satisfied, he demanded what I sought for from that miserable and barren Iland peopled in effect all with Moriscos, I answered him that although I landed many men to refresh them, I had no purpose to invade any of the Spanish Kings territories having receiued from the King my master express commandment to the contrary, only I desired for my monie such fresh meat as that Iland yeilded, and because he should not doubt of what nation we were I willed him to be informed by the Inglish Marchant whose ship lay by vs and whom we found in his port, att our arivall trading with him and others of the Iland and had lately brought them wine from Tenerife and stayd for his lading of corne, wheruppon he prayed me to sett down in writing what I desired and it should be furnished the next day, promising to send me that night some few muttons and goates for myself and the Captaines. In the morning being
8 Sep. munday the 8 day the Inglish Marchants man came to me by whom I sent him a noate for a quantitie of wheat, goates, sheep, henns and wine for which the Marchant should make the prise, and to whom I would deliver so much redy moni or other truck as it amounted vnto, promising him that my companies should not go from the sea syde aboue a mile or two; nor offend any of the inhabitants. I stayd the next day but nothing came which day we spent in trayning and mustering our companies on the sea shore, the next he wrate me a letter in Spanish wherin he protested on the faith of a Cabaliro that he would send the prouisions the 3 day being the 11 of September and sent me the Inglish marchant which lay aboue att his towne with 2 french

[1] A similar blank in the original, which in the Apology for his last Voyage, is filled up with Lieutenant.

factors to assure me, whom he abused by protesting as much to them. For myne owne part I never gave faith to his words for [I] knew he sought to gayne tyme to carry the goods of the towne being 7 miles from vs into the mountaynes. My companie prest me that they might march towards the towne, but besyds that I knew that it would offend his Majesty I am sure that the poore Inglish Marchant should have byne ruined whose goods he had in his hands, and the way being mountenous and most extreeme stonie I knew that I must have lost 20 good men in taking a towne not worth two groats for they were 300 men wherof 90 musketiers uppon a ground of infinite advantage. When the 3 day was past I sent the marchants man with a letter charging him with his promise and faith given, and that did I not know that it would offend the King my soveraine, I would pull his Moriscos out of ther towne by the eares, and by the marchants man I sent some 20^{s} to buy some henns and other trifles, by whom he returned awnswere that we were the same Turcks which had taken and destroyed Porta Sancta[1] and therfore he was resolved to stand vpon his garde and were we Inglish yet if he gave vs any releife he was sure to be hanged; taking the monie from the marchants man and beat him for offring to buy any thing for vs without his leaue. I sent back the marchants man and wrote vnto him that because he was a poore fellow and neided apparell, if he would send back the marchants I would send him 40 riall more to buy him a dublet to his hose, and for the rest it was enough for mee to know his masters disposition who notwithstanding the peace with our King, yet he had given order, that no releife should be given to any of his subjects, and that evening departed and came the next day att

[1] It appears almost as if the Governor of Lanzarota had a presentiment of the fate which was to befall the island next year. A fleet of Turks and Algerians, consisting of sixty sails, under the command of Taban Arraez and Soliman, landed on the 1st of May 1618 five thousand men, stormed and sacked the town, and led nine hundred Christians into captivity. (Noticias de la Historia General de las Islas de Canaria, por Don Joseph De Viera y Clavijo, vol. ii. p. 364.)

night to the Gran Canares, and from the south part sent a Spaniard which was a fisherman of that Iland with a letter to the Governour to whom the other Ilands were subject as to the supreme audience with the coppie of the Governour of Lancerota his letter to me and mine to him, and how I had no intent to invade any of those Ilands nor to offend any of the Spanish Kings subjects, but only sought for water, and for fresh meate for my monie, praying the Governor to take knouledge that I had it in commandment from the King my master not to offer any violence, nor to take any places belonging to the Spanish King, only I desired from him to know if any such commandment were given to the governoure of Lancerota not to trade with vs but to offend vs in all he could, or whether himself being the Kings Leiuetenant of all the Ilands, had any such order; in the meane while landing to gett a little water which I did with great difficultie the quantitie being not half a tonne, I thought it perilous to stay in those extreme hott calmes my companie in all the shipps falling extremely sick wherof many died for want of water, I did therfore determine to stay but one day more for the Governours awnswere wher being on the land with a few men I sett 2 or 3 sentenels doubting the people might come downe on the suddayne, the Ilanders finding a centenel of 2 of our companie somewhat fare of from the rest they crept neere them by the favor of the trees and on the sunday ran vpon them, our musketier shooting of, gave vs the alarum our pick being charged with 3 of them receiued 3 wounds being one Smith a master mate of Sr J. Fernes shipp[1] but behaued himself so well as he slew one of them and recovored his pike, Cap. Thornehurst being a viliant and active man hasted to their reskew and with a horsmans peece shott another of them, Mr Hawton with his pick wounded the thyrde, so as all three died in the place, the rest taking their heeles. Wee were now out of their debts, for att Lancerota by the vanitie and madness of a sergeant who standing

[1] The Flying Hart.

centenel would needs force the governours centenel from his ground, they being 20 and ours but 3 wherof we lost two[1].

From the calmes of the great Canares wher att this time of the yeere (the springs being dried vp ther was no water to be had,) we set saile the[2] of September and stood for Gomera wher some of our companie assured vs ther was water enough; but we fell to leeward of it that night, the next day being thursday the[3] wee turn'd it vp and recovered the port, being the best of all the Canares, the towne and castell standing on the very breach of the sea, butt the billowes do so tumble and overfall as it is impossible to land vppon any part of the strand but by swimming, sauing in a cove vnder steep rocks wher ther can pass towards the towne but one after another and could they pass 10 men in frunt yet from the steep mountayne of rock over the way they were all sure to be beaten in peeces with massy stonns. Before we were att ancor they shott att vs from those rocks and wee to lett them know, that we had good ordenance gave them some 20 demiculverin thorow their howses and then forbeare, I then sent a Spanierd on shore to the Count Lord and Governour of the Iland and wrate unto him that I came not thither as the Hollanders did, to sack their towne and burne their churches as the Hollanders did in the yeere[4] but being in necessitie of water, for it only, and therfore as he had begvn the warr in shooting first, so it should be his fault to continew it by denying vs to relieue our selves wherevnto wee were

[1] The following paragraph from De Viera apparently refers to Ralegh's fleet: "Tambien se sabe que otra Esquadra de 14 buques batio infructuosamente aquel Puerto en Septiembre de 1617 durante algunos dias." (Noticias de la Historia General de las Islas de Canaria, vol. iii. p. 40.)

[2] A similar blank in the original.

[3] A similar blank in the original; it was apparently, to judge from what follows hereafter, the 18th of September.

[4] A similar blank in the original. Ralegh probably alludes to the great expedition under Peter van der Doez, consisting of seventy-six vessels manned with ten thousand men; they attacked Gomera on the 13th of June 1599, but were ultimately obliged to re-embark with great loss, as reported by Joseph De Viera. (Noticias de la Historia de Canaria, vol. iii. p. 39.)

maynly constraynde. To this he made awnswere in writing and in faire termes that he was advertised from the other Ilands that we were the same Turcks which had taken Porta Sancta, otherwise he would be reddy to do me seruice, I answered that he receiued that aduertisement from the Morisco of Forteventura, but to putt him altogether out of doubt I would send him 6 other Spaniards of the Gran Canares, taken on Affrica syde in a small barck who should resolue him that we were Christians and the vassalls of the King of Great Brittaine in perfait league and amitie with the King of Spaine. This being done wee made an agreement that his soldiers and others to the number of 300 should quitt their trenches vppon the landing places wher they were so well assured by divers redoubtes one above another as the Hollanders were forst to land their armie six mile from this port when they tooke it as aforesayd, and wher in passing the mountayns they lost 80 soldiers; and I for my part should promise on the faith of a Christian not to land above 30 mariners without weapons to fill water we were within a pistoll shott of the wash of the sea, myself farther promising that none of those should enter their houses nor their gardens. Vppon this agrement I sent my bote ashore with my baricos aduenturing but two poore saylers ashore and 4 to keip the boate which had in her head 2 good murderers and for the more saufty, and brought six shipps with their brod sydes towards the towne which I would haue beaten down in 10 howres if they had broken the agrement.

By the Spanierd which carried my letter to the Count, I sent his Ladie 6 exceeding fine handkerchers and 6 paire of gloves, and wrate vnto her that if ther were any thing worthy of her in my fleet she should command it and me. She sent me awnswere that she was sorry that her barren Iland had nothing worthy of mee, and with her letter sent mee 4 very great loaves of suger, a baskett of Lemmons which I much desired to comfort and refresh our many sick men, a baskett of oranges, a baskett of most delicate grapes, another of pomegranetts and of figgs, which trifles were better welcome vnto me than a 1000 crownes could have bine. I gave her sarvants 2 crownes to each, and answering her letter in the fairest termes I could, because I would not rest in her debt, I sent her 2 ovnces of amber greece, an ovnce of the delicate extract of amber, a great glass of rose water in high estimation here, and a very excellent picture of Mari Magdalen, and a cuttworck ruff. These presents were receiued with so great thancks, and so much acknowlegdment of debt as could be exprest, and vppon saterday there was sent mee a baskett of dellicate white manchett, and 2 dussen of fatt henns with divers frutes. In the mean while, friday, saterday and part of Sunday we filde 240 pipes of water, and the sunday evening we departed without any offence given or received to the valew of a farthing, for testimonie wherof the Earle sent his Friar abord my shipp with a letter to D. Diego Sarmiento ambassador in Ingland witnesing how noble we had behaued ourselves, and how justly we had delt with the inhabitants of the Iland.

Being reddy to sett saile we deliuered the Spanish fisherman his barck, and discharged another small barck taken here att our first arual with all their furniture, and directed our course from Gomera on the same sunday fortnight (being the 21 of September) which we arived att Lancerota, having spent 14 dayes among these Ilands. The provost Marshall Steed died.

From sunday att 4 att after nowne to munday att 4 being the 22 day we ran 20 L. for we caried a slack saile for some of our fleet which were not reddy to way with us. 21 Sep. 22 Sep.

From 4 on munday to twelve att nowne on twesday being the 23 we ran 25 L. S.W. by S. with the brises at N.E. 23 Sept.

From 12 on twesday to 12 on Wensday being the 24 of September we made 6 L. a wach, drawing att our sterne alonge boat of 14 toonne fastned with 2 great cabletts which hunge deipe in the way and greatly hindred our saylinge, holding the same south W. by S. course the winde constant. We had att this time 50 men sick in our shipp. 24 Sep. Whitney died. Daniel died.

From 12 on wensday to 12 on thursday the 25 day the brises 25 Sep.

continewing but not so strong, we rann about 33 L. S.W. by W. and found our selves in 23 [D.] and 17 minutes.

26 Sep. From Thursday 12 to friday 12, being the 26 day we brought ourselues into 22 [D.] northerly the winde continewing, and the course S.S.W. for wheras we resolued to fall with the wethermost Iland of Cap: de Vert, called S[t] Antoine, being informed that the same was desolate and could yeild vs no refreshing and that we had 60 men sick abord us, we determined to tuch att Bravo where I was told that ther were people and fresh meat.

27 Sep. From 12 the 26 to 12 the 27 we ran 38 L. and were in 19 D. 20 min: the course S. by W.

28 Sep. From 12 the 27 to 12 the 28 being Sunday we had a few hours calme and ran but 27 L. and were at 12 a clock in 18 D.

Nubal the M[r] Surgent died, Barber died, the Saile maker died.

Munday att noone we found our selues in 16 D. and 20 min: and Munday night by the starr we found our selues in 15 D. and half, and then we lay att hull from 8 att night to 6 in the morning when as wee saw the Iland of Stiago[1] faire by vs.

29 Sep. Munday being Michelmas day ther died our Master Surgent Mr. Nubal to our great loss, the same day also died Barber one of our quarter masters, and our saile maker, and we had 60 men sick and all myne owne sarvants amongst them that I had none of myne owne but my pages to serue mee.

last Sep. Twesday night we stood of because we ment to water att Bravo four leages to the westward of fridgo fuego[2] being 12 le: to the W. of Stiago. Holcroff the Sergeant of my sonns companie died.

That night the pinnes that was Cap: Barkers having all her men asleap, and not any one att the wach, drave under our bowspreet and sunck but the men were saved though better worthy to have binn hanged then saved.

Octob. 1. Wensday we stood back with Bravo but found very inconve-

[1] St. Jago, one of the Cape Verde Islands; Brava or St. John, previously alluded to, is one of the most southern of the group.

[2] Fuego or Fogo, another of the Cape Verde Islands.

nient Ancoring, and rough ground, and that night having the Viceadmirall with me att supper, my self being newly come from the shore to feel out a better rode, a hurlecano fell vppon vs with most violent rayne, and brack both our cabells att the instant greatly to the damage of the Shipp, and all our lives, but it pleased God that her head cast from the shore and drave of. I was myself so wete as the water ran in att my neck, and out att my knees, as if it had bine powred on me with pailes. All the rest of our fleet lost their cables and ancors, 3 of our small men that ridd in a cove, close under the land, had like all to have perished; Cap: Snedul grated on the rocks; Wulleston and King[1] scapt them not their ships lenght.

Thursday wee stood vp vppon a tack to recover the Iland, for 2 Oct. I had sent of my skiff to fish not half a quarter of an hower before the hurlecan, and I gave her lost and 6 of my men in her to my great discumfort, having had so great mortalitie, but I thanck my God I found them in the morning under the shore and recovered them, but I lost another of my pinneces called the 50 crownes (because I payd 50 crownes to the french men for her) in this storm.

Fryday one of my trumpeters and one other of the Coockrome died.

Finding that the raynes and stormes were not yet past in this place and finding no faire grovnd to ryde in, I resolved rather to leiue the Iland and the refreshing we hoped for here, then to indanger our shipps, the most of them having lost a cable, and ancor and myself two. This Iland of Bravo standeth in[2]

a little Iland but frutfull, having store of Goates, cattle, maize, figgs, and water; it hath on the north syde little Ilands and broken grovnds, which doth as it were impale it; on the west

[1] Captain Wolaston commanded the Confidence and Captain Samuel King a Fly-boat. (Newes of Sir Walter Rauleigh.)

[2] A similar blank in the original. The geographical position of Brava Road is lat. 14° 48′ north, longitude 24° 44′ west.

syde it hath an excellent watring place in a coue [1] in which ther may ride a dussen shipps if they come either before or after the raines and storms which beginn in the middle of Julie and end in the middle of August, and in this cove and all alongst the west syde aboundance of fish. There is a currant which setts very strong from the south to the north and runns in effect all wayes so[2]. This night Cap: Pigott's Leiuettenant, called Allen died.

3 Oct. Thursday night I stood of a league and then lay by the lee the most part of the night to stay for some of our shipps that were in the cove to take water so as by 12 on friday we were about 10 L. of the Iland. On friday morninge being the 3 of
4 Oct. October our Cape Marchant Kemishe died. Friday att noone we lay agayne by Lee to stay for King who was in my flibote, and lay so till saterday having sent back Cap: Barker in the carvell to seek him, but hering of neither wee filed our sailes att 12 and stood away a thwart the ocean steering away towards the coast of Guiana S.W. by W.

5 Oct. From Saterday 12 to Sunday 12 we made 30 L.

6 Oct. From Sunday 12 to Munday 12 we made 28 L. this Munday morninge died Mr. John Haward, Ensigne to Cap: North, and

[1] This appears to be the bay called Furna or the Oven, where by hauling in near the rock there is water enough for a first-rate man-of-war, and being land-locked from all winds, affords a safe anchorage.

[2] This remarkable observation of Ralegh's has since been confirmed. In no part of the ocean have mariners been more perplexed in accounting for currents than near the equator, chiefly between the meridians of twenty-five degrees and forty degrees west. The effect of the African monsoon, if the periodical wind prevailing during the changes of the season may be called so, is to divert a great portion of the equatorial stream to the north, north-north-east, and north-east, even beyond the Cape Verde islands. The American Exploring Squadron, which left Madeira on the 25th of September, 1838, after passing the parallel of the Canary Islands, met a north-easterly current of about half a mile an hour, where a current in a south-westerly direction is generally supposed to prevail. This passage in Ralegh's journal confirms our high opinion of the acuteness of his observations of whatever related to seamanship; hence no wonder that he rose to a reputation as a navigator which, after the death of Drake and Hawkins, was enjoyed by very few of his contemporaries.

Leiuetenant Payton and Mr. Hwes fell sick. Ther also died to our great greif our principall refiner Mr. Fowler [1].

From Munday att 12 to twesday the 7th of October we made but 4 L. a wach and in all 24 L. by the high not so much, for twesday att noone we found ourselves but in 12 D. and 30 min: and then the currant sett us half a poynt to the westward of the S.W. by W.[2] We found ourselves att 12 this Munday in 13 D. and 7 min. Oct. 7.

From 12 uppon twesday to 12 on Wensday the 8th of October we had little winde and made but 22 L. and we found ourselves in a leven deg: and 39 min: this eveninge my sarvant [3] Oct. 8.

Crabb died so as I had not any one left to attend me but my pages.

From 12 on Wensday to 12 on Thursday we had a fresher gale and made 30 L. but all this day wee bare little sayle the weather being rainy with gusts and much winde as it is commonly in these parts att the small of the moone. Oct. 9.

From 12 on thursday to 12 on friday we had nothing but Oct. 10.

[1] The Attorney-General Yelverton reproached Sir Walter Ralegh during his examination before the Commissioners, that the opening of a mine had never been the object of his last voyage, otherwise he would have made better arrangements for such a purpose. A similar charge is contained in the Royal Declaration. The regret which Ralegh expresses in his journal at the death of Mr. Fowler the refiner, proves the importance which he attached to this person; and at the examination before the Commissioners, he positively asserted that he had laid out two thousand pounds in providing the necessary materials. (Brit. Mus. Lansdowne MSS. 142, fol. 412.)

[2] The great current from the north-west changes immediately after passing the Cape Verde Islands; it becomes first southerly and sets afterwards to the west. Captain James Grant, R.N., observes, that on getting clear of the Cape Verde Islands, he found a strong current setting to the south. This merges ultimately in the great equatorial current, or, to use a term better known to navigators, the central drift. (See the Editor's remarks on the currents of the Caribbee Islands in the Journal of the Royal Geographical Society, vol. ii. p. 166.)

[3] A similar blank in the original. The death of Crab is likewise mentioned in Sir Walter's letter to Lady Ralegh. (See MS. copy in the Harleian Collection, 39 Plut. 4. C., and Sir Walter Ralegh's Remaines, edition of 1656, p. 163.)

raine and not much winde, so as we made but 4 L. a wach to witt 24 L. and the neerest that we could observe the sonn shining but little and by startts, was 10 Deg. and 8 min: but in the afternoone it clered up which we hoped that God would have continewed for we were all drownd in our cabins butt about 4 a clock ther rose a most fearfull blackness over the one half of the sky and it drave agaynst the winde which threatned a turnado and yet it pleased God that it brake but into raine and the evening agayne hopefull but ther blew no winde att all so as we lay becamed all the night, and the next day, at 12 on Saterday we observed and found our selves in 10 degrees and 10 minutes,
Oct. 11. and had not made from noone to noone above 5 L.

Oct. 12. From Saterday the 11 day at 12 to Sunday att 12 we had all calmes as before, and the little breath which we sometimes had was for the most part south and to the westward, which hath seildome bine seene in this passages and clymate so as we made not above 6 L. W. by S: in the afternowne the winde tooke vs a stayes and blew a little gale from the N.N.W.

This sunday morning died Mr. Hwes[1] a very honest and civile gentleman having lyen sick but 6 dayes. In this sort it pleased God to visite vs with great sicknes and loss of our ablest men both land men and sea men; and having by reason of the turnado att Bravo fayled of our watering we were att this time in miserable estate not having in our shipp above 7 dayes water, 60 sick men and nearly 400 leagues of the shore, and becalmed.

We found our selves this day at noone in 10 Deg. and so we had raysed since saterday noone butt 10 minutes.

Oct. 13. From sunday noone to munday noone we made not above 12 L. observe we could not for the darck weather, a lamentable 24 houres it was, in which we lost Captayne John Pigott my Leiutenant G: by land; my honest frinde Mr. John Talbote one that had liued with mee a leven yeeres in the tower, an

[1] In the letter to Lady Ralegh, enumerating the persons who died, he calls him "my cousin Mr. Hews." (See the manuscript copies in the Harleian Collection.)

excellent generall skoller and a faithfull trew man as lived[1]. We lost also Mr. Gardner and Mr. Mordent two very faire conditioned gentlemen, and myne owne cooke Francis.

From Munday att 12 to Twesday att 12 having in the night a fresh gale with much raine, we ran some 26 L. I observed this day, and so I did before, that the morning rainbow doth not give a faire day as in Ingland, but ther followed much raine and winde[2] and that we found the windes here for 6 or 7 dayes to geather to the Southward of the East as att South-est and south S.E. and allwayes raine and gusts more or less. Oct. 14.

Wensday morninge we saw another rainebowe and about 10 a clock it began to gather as black as pich in the south and from thence ther fell as much raine as I have seene but with little wind. Oct. 15.

From Twesday 12 to 12 this wensday we ran not above 14 leages, observe we could not neither munday, twesday nor wensday for the darckness of the skye which is very strange in these parts, for most of the afternoone wee stered our shipp by candellight.

From wensday 12 to thursday 12 we had all calmes sauing some few howers in the night and from 7 in the morning till 10 and the winde we had was so weake as we made not above 6 Lg; about 10 in the morning it began to raine and it continewed Oct. 16. Thursday morning a windfall in the North

[1] John Talbot was one of those who had permission to remain in the Tower with him. (See Brit. Mus. MSS., Ayscough's Cat. No. 4160, cxxi., where there is a list of "Persons permitted to have access to Sir Walter Ralegh.") The way in which he mentions Talbot's death proves how highly he valued him, and how severely he felt his loss. In his letter from Caliana to Lady Ralegh, after naming several of those who fell victims to the disease, he says: "but to mine inestimable grief Hammon and Talbot."

[2] A rainbow in the early part of the day is generally considered a prognostic of changeable weather under the tropics; hence the doggrel so common in the mouth of the mariner:

"A rainbow in the morning
Sailor take warning;
A rainbow towards night
Is the sailor's delight."

and within one houre a dubble rainebowe[1]. strong till 2 att after dinner, the effect of the morning rainebow. About 3 the winde the little that it was, blew att west S.W. which hath not often bine seene. Captain Jennings died and many fell sick.

Oct. 17. From thursday 12 to friday 12 we could make no reckning, for the winde changed so often betweene the S. and the west, as after the changing of the tack divers times we found it best to take in all our sailes and ly att hull, for the winde that blew was horrible with violent raine, and at S.W. and S.S.W. and so it continewed all night and so it doth continew this saterday morning and thinck that since the Indies were discovered never was the like winde found in this high, which we gess to be about 9 Deg: for we could not obserue since munday last[2].

Oct. 18. Saterday morning it cleared vp and att noone we found our selves in 9 Deg. and 45 Min: as we supposed, but the winde directly contrary as well in the stormes as in the soonn shininge, and liing att hull we drave to the north W. and fell altogether to leeward, we sett saile after dinner and stoode by a winde to the Eastward but could ly but S. E. and by E.

The night proved altogether calme, so as we moved no way,

[1] The internal principal rainbow is seldom seen under the tropics without the secondary or external one. We have seen in those latitudes on two occasions a supernumerary bow, and to such a phenomenon Ralegh seems to allude when speaking further on of a third rainbow.

[2] Captain Cook, in his second voyage, met with similar weather in these latitudes, where we suppose Ralegh was at the period to which his journal alludes. Captain Flinders in the Investigator, in 1801, after having passed on the 15th of August St. Antonio, the north-westernmost of the Cape Verde Islands, found the wind to dwindle into a calm. For three days afterwards it was light and variable, between north and south-east, after which it sometimes blew from the north-west and south-west, and sometimes from the eastward. Those variable winds, with every kind of weather, but most frequently with rain, continued until the 23rd of August in latitude 11° north. De la Perouse experienced similar winds during his passage in September 1785, which proves that this changeable weather is by no means uncommon between the months of August and October, a period during which the greater number of hurricanes occur in the West Indies.

but we hoped that vppon the change of the moone, which changed Sunday about aleven a clock, that God would send vs the longe looked for brise. This night died my cusen Payton Leiuetenant of my sonns companie.

Sunday proved also starck calme and extreeme hote, so as betweene saterday noone and sunday noone we could not recken that we had gon a leage, but that we had driven somewhat to the northward for we found ourselves on Saterday in 9. deg: and 45. min: and sunday att noone in 9. D. and 50. min. The evening proved exceeding faire and clere round about the horizon, and the sonn sett so faire, it being also the day of the change as we all hoped for exceeding faire weather, but the rules and signes of weather do not hold in this climate, for att midnight the sky was overcast and it began to gust agayne, but the winde good, the Munday morning was also exceeding darck, and it blew and did raine violently, towards 12 it cleered vp with a fresh gale att est and by S. so as I make accompt that we rann from 12 on Sunday to 12 on munday some 16 Leg: Octob. 19.

Munday between 6 and 7 att night we had a stronge gust with so much winde and raine as we were forst to lye att hull till midnight, and then wee sett saile, in the morning wee had much raine and winde, and that fearfull and resistless fall of a cloude called a spoute, and it fell blessed be God some 2 mile from [us] to windward[1]. Oct. 20.

From munday 12 to twesday 12 we had hardly aduanced 13 L. for we found ourselves att 12. but in 9. deg: twesday night proved faire and the winde till midnight att E.N.E. after midnight it fell slack and so continued till 12 on Wensday.

[1] Waterspouts are very frequent during the hot season in the West Indies; while residing at Tortola, one of the Virgin Islands, we saw as many as five at once in the channel between Thatch Island and Jost van Dyke. It is however singular that Ralegh should observe one between the Cape Verde and Windward West India Islands, where scarcely any of these electrical appearances are ever seen. The West Indians consider this phenomenon a prognostic of rain, which generally takes place within twenty-four hours of its appearance.

Oct. 22. Wensday we observed and found ourselves but in 8. D. and 12 min: and had not made above 22 Le: for the currant that setts here strongly to the N.W, took vs in the weather boow and duld our way, alwayes thrusting vs to leeward.

This Wensday morning we saw a thyrd rainebowe; of the two former we had the effect of foule weather, it also lightned the most part of these 2 nights which they say foreshewes raine and so we have found it hetherto. Wensdayes rainebowe gave us but one gust att night all the rest of the night being faire about 8 a clock we saw Magellans Cloude rovnd and white which riseth and setteth with the stares[1].

Oct. 23. Thursday morning was faire and we obserued and found ourselves in 7 Deg: and 40 Min: from Wensday noone to Thursday noone wee made vppon a course S.W. and by S. 18 leages. We had on thursday evening a rainebow, and ther followes a foule night, and a dark friday till noone with a winde att S.S.E. so bare as we could not lye our course, and so longe we have had those windes southerly agaynst the very order of nature in this navigation as we have cause to feare that we shall not be able to fech our port but be putt to seeward[2].

[1] The Magellanic clouds are of a darker appearance than the bright Milky Way, and are seen in the heavens towards the South Pole. They consist of three clusters, two of them near each other. The largest lies far from the South Pole, but the other two are not more remote from it than the first splendid star at the foot of the Southern Cross. These nebulosities are objects of as high an interest as the Southern Cross, the Luci Sante of Dante (Purg. i. 37), and were first distinctly described after the voyage of the great navigator whose name they bear. As Ralegh rightly observes, they have the same apparent motion as the stars, and are now considered to consist of a dense collection of stars at an immeasurable distance from our planet. See Humboldt, 'Examen Critique de l'Histoire de la Géographie du nouveau Continent,' vol. iii. p. 132; vol. iv. pp. 316–335; vol. v. p. 226.

[2] The experience of more than two centuries and a quarter has made us better acquainted with the peculiar changes of these latitudes, which Ralegh considers as anomalies. It has been assumed by meteorologists that a zone of variable breadth extends between the regions of the south-eastern and north-eastern trade-winds, wherein calms and rains generally

From thursday 12 to friday 12 we made but 12 L. and found ourselves in 7 D. and 20 min: our water being also neere spent, we were forst to come to half allowance, friday about 3 att afternoone the winde came altogether southerly and rather to the westward so as we could lye but west southerly and make but a W.N.W. way and in the Eveninge we saw a winde gall in the est. The winde increasing towards night, and the sky fearfully overcast we lay att hull and so continewed all night with violent raines and much winde. Oct. 24.

Saterday morning it clered up in the S. and we lay est S.E. Octo. 25. the other way to keip ourselves vp, but being able to lye but E.S.E. and E. by S., the sea also heaving us to the northward we made but a leeward way, att 3 in the afternoone in a gust the winde came N. and then hoped to recover our hight but it calmed agayne in the raines and so it continew[ed] in effect all night, and the morning that little winde which we had was butt att S. esterly so as betweene saterday 12 and sunday 12 we Oct. 26. made not above 9 L. and raysed not 10 min: towards the South.

From Sunday 12 a clock to munday 12 we had the winde Oct. 27. no better then S. and by E. and S.S.E. and made but 10 L. att most.

From Munday to twesday 12 a clock we had little winde with Oct. 28. faire weather, only at 5 in the morning we had a little gale, first

prevail, and which is visited only by striking vicissitudes, namely by terrible thunder and lightning, by waterspouts, and rains so heavy that the whole zone itself has been called by mariners "the Rains." The limits of this region reach in August to 15° of north latitude; and although Ralegh gives us no intimation of his longitude, we doubt not from his description that he was engulphed in that zone. M. de la Perouse observes, "The trade-wind left us in 14° north latitude, and the wind then constantly blew between west and west-south-west, till we reached the Line. We were not a day without wind, and once only had rain, when indeed it was so abundant as to fill twenty-five casks." (See the Editor's 'History of Barbados,' p. 21, for detailed remarks on this subject, to which would have been added Ralegh's illustration of these regions had he been acquainted with this journal at the period when those remarks were penned.)

at E.N.E. and then att E. and by S. and we made not above 8 Leg: and found ourselves in 7 D. stering away S. to recover our hight. Here we found the cumpas to vary 7 deg.[1]

Octo. 29. From Twesday to wensday 12 we had the winde large but so gentle a winde, as we made not above 10 leg. and found ourselves by an obscure observation in 6 Deg. 2 rainebowes we had in the morning but faire weather hath hitherto followed, and so we hoped that the raines had bine past, but the cirkle about the moone the twesday night and the duble rainebow on wensday morning payd vs towards the evening with raine and winde, in which gust we made shift to save some 3 hogseds of water, besyds that the companie having byne many dayes scanted and prest with drough dranck vp whole quarter canns of the bitter raine water. The wensday night was also calme with thunder and lightninge.

Oct. 30. Thursday morning we had agayne a duble rainebow which putt us in feare that the raines would never end, from Wensday

[1] It is much to be regretted that Sir Walter does not state whether that variation, or rather declination of the compass, was to the east or to the west of the true magnetic meridian. It would have formed a base upon which to build our conclusions in regard to the changes of the declination since that period; and it would have proved of the more value, since we possess so few observations with respect to the declination in those regions during the seventeenth century. A reference to Hansteen's 'Magnetismus der Erde' leaves however no doubt that Ralegh's variation was east of the true magnetic meridian. The line of *no variation* which passed through London about 1660 has since been progressively moving towards the east, namely towards Siberia; but the line of *no variation* from Ralegh's position to the high southern latitudes moves to the west, and is now, and has been for years, to the west of Ralegh's position. According to his observations at noon, he was in 7° north latitude, and from what follows hereafter, we suppose him to have been about $48\frac{1}{2}°$ west of Greenwich, which would place him in the geographical meridian of Para, and, according to Gauss's Karte of the present state of terrestrial magnetism, in about 3° + declination. Gauss assumes that the magnetic meridian of *no variation* passes the eastern group of the West India islands and touches the South American continent near Surinam. We observed in 1846 that the declination in Barbados, the most eastern island of the group, amounted to 1° 27′ east.

12 to Thursday 12 we made not above 6 L. having allwayes uncomfortable raines and dead calmes.

The last of October att night rising out of bedd, being in a great sweat by reason of a suddayne gust and much clamor in the shipp before they could gett downe the sailes, I tooke a violent cold which cast me into a burning fever then which never man indured any more violent nor never man suffered a more furious heat and an unquenchable drough, for the first 20 dayes I never receaved any sustenance but now and then a stewed prune but dranck every houre day and night, and sweat so strongly as I changed my shirts thrise every day and thrise every night.

The 11 of November we made the North Cape of Wiapoco[1] the cape then bearing S.W. and by W. as they told mee for I was not yet able to move out of my bedd we rode in 6 fadome 5 leauges of the shore, I sent in my skiff to enquire for my old sarvant Leonard the Indien who bine with me in Ingland 3 or 4 yeers, the same man that tooke Mr. Harcorts brother and 50 of his men when they came uppon that coast and were in extreame distress, having neither meat to carry them home nor meanes to liue ther but by the help of this Indien whom they made belieue that they were my men[2]. but I could not here of

11 of November.

[1] The Cape of Wiapoco, now Cape Orange, was called by Captain Keymis in 1596 Cape Cecyl. It forms the south-eastern point of the great bay into which the river Oyapoco (formerly Wiapoco) discharges itself. Captain Charles Leigh arrived on the 22nd of May 1604 at the mouth of the Oyapoco, which he called Caroleigh, and took possession of it in the name of King James. He settled a colony on the first heights on ascending, named by him Mount Howard. The death of Captain Leigh caused the colonists to abandon their settlement, and they returned to England. (Purchas, vol. iv. lib. vi. cap. 12.

[2] Robert Harcourt followed Leigh's enterprize, and arrived on the 17th of May 1608 in the river Oyapoco. The natives came on board, and were much disappointed in not seeing Sir Walter Ralegh, who had sent to some of them the year previous a message and some European clothing as a remembrance, in which they presented themselves on board of Harcourt's vessel. Harcourt desired his cousin Captain Fisher to visit Leonard Regapo, who, as mentioned in the text, had been with Ralegh in England,

him by my boat that I sent in for he was removed 30 mile into the country, and because I had an ill rode and 5 leages of, I durst not stay his sending for, but stood away for Caliana[1] wher the Cassique was also my sarvant and had lived with mee in the tower 2 yeers.

12 November. Yet the 12 day wee wayd and stood somewhat neerer the land some 3 leages of, my bote going and returning brought vs some of the country frutes, and left in the port two Hollanders for Onotto, gums, and spekeld wood[2].

13 Novemb. The 13 I sett saile alongst the coast and ancored that night in aleven fathom neere an Ilande wher there were so many burds as they kild them with staves; ther growes vppon it those trees which beare the great codds of hereculla silke. This Iland is

and was now residing on the river Conawini, which falls south of the river Cassipouri into the sea. Leonard accompanied Captain Fisher on his return to Oyapoco, although distant above a hundred miles from his country, and Harcourt attests the great affection which he seemed to have for Ralegh. (See the 'Relation of a Voyage to Guiana, performed by Robert Harcourt,' edition of 1626, pp. 10–11, and 18–19.)

[1] Caliana, or rather Caiana, as called by Keymis, is the river Cayenne. He reports of the harbour, "On all that coast we found not any like it; we therefore honoured this place by the name of Port Howard." The bar has become shallower, since Ralegh crossed it in the Destiny; it admits at present scarcely any vessel of a larger draught than fourteen or fifteen feet. (Plan de l'Embouchure de la Rivière de Cayenne, levé en 1820, par M. Gressier.)

[2] The Arnotto is an orange dye prepared from the pulp, or rather pellicle, which surrounds the seed of the *Bixa Orellana*, Linn., a shrub which grows wild in Guiana. The speckled wood here alluded to is the beautiful Letter- or Snake-wood, called by the French, Bois de lettres moucheté, and by the Dutch, Letter-hout. It comes from a tree (*Piratinera Guianensis* Aublet) which is now very scarce, and is only to be met with far in the interior, where we found it near the Canucu mountains, and likewise on the banks of the Upper Essequibo, between the first and second parallel of latitude. Robert Harcourt says of it: "There is a hard, heavy, red-speckled wood in that country, called Paira timinere, which is worth twenty or thirty pounds a tun." (Harcourt, p. 48.) It is called by the Caribs and the Macusis, Paira; and timinere, signifies 'painted' to distinguish it from a species which is not speckled. Aublet has made his generic name for the tree by corrupting it into Piratinera.

but littell and is from the maine land some 4. leag:[1] the same afternoone we wayed and stood alongst the coast towards Caliana W.S.W. and S.W. and by West; and ancored againe in the evening some 5 leauges S.W. from the Iland of byrds, in five fatome within a kinde of bay.

The 14th day we stood out of the bay, and passed by 3 or 4 Ilands[2] wher ther grew many trees of those that bere the coddes of silke also, by the Ilands we had 10 fathom, from whence we stood alongst into 6 fathom, and came to an ankor, thence I sent my barge ashore to enquire for my servant Harry the Indien, who [sent] his brother vnto mee with 2 other Cassiques promising to come to me with provisions if I came not into the river within a day or two. These Indiens stayd with mee that night, offring their service and all they had. Myne owne weaknes which still continewed, and the desire I had to be caried ashore to change the eare, and out of an vnsavory shipp, pestered with many sick men which being vnable to move, poysoned vs with a most filthy stench, perswaded me to adventer my shipp over a barr wher never any vessel of burden had past. In the rode my barge found one Ianson of Flushing, who had traded that place about a dussen yeares who came to me wher I ridd without, offring me his service for the bringing in of my shipp, and assuring mee that on the topp of a full sea ther was 3 14 Novemb.

[1] The island Sir Walter speaks of is at present called "Le Grand Connétable," being a corruption of the Dutch word Constapel, or Cannonier. It has a pyramidical shape, and is a great resort for sea-birds, the dung of which has given it quite a white appearance. The captains of Dutch vessels on passing by formerly amused themselves by firing a few shots at the rock to see the immense number of birds which frightened arose in the air, and from which circumstance it received its name.

The "codds of Herculla Silk" are the fruit capsules of the Silk-cotton Tree (*Bombax Ceiba* Linn., or perhaps of *B. globosa* Aublet). The seeds are enveloped in long silky hairs somewhat like the true cotton, but as there is no adhesion between the hairs, they cannot be used in the manufacture of stuffs.

[2] Several small islands along the coast are now called la Mère et les Filles, le Père, le Malingre, and l'Enfant perdu.

fathom, wherupon the rest of my fleet went into the river and ancored within in 4 and 5 fathom. It flowes ther N.E. and S.W., here I stayd att ancor from the 14th day to the 17 day, when
17 Novemb. by the help of Janson I gott over the barr in 3 fathom a quarter less, when I drew 17 foot water.

After I had stayd in Caliana a day or two my sarvant Harry came to me, who had almost forgotten his Inglish, and brought mee great store of very good Casavi bread, with which I fedd my company some 7 or 8 dayes, and putt vp a hogsed full for store, he brought great plenty of rosted mulletts which were very good meat, great store of plantens and piones with divers other sorts of frutes and pistaches[1], but as yet I durst not adventer to eat of the pione which tempted me exceedingly, but after a day or two being carried ashore and sitting vnder a tent, I began to eat of the pione, which greatly refresht me, and after that I fedd on the porck of the country[2], and of the Armadillios and began to gather a little strength.

Here I also sett all my sick men ashore, and made cleane my shipp and wher they all recovered and here wee buried Cap:
Cap: Pigott. Hastings, who died 10 dayes or more before and with him my sergent maiors Hart, and Captayne Henrie Snedall, giving the charge of Snedalls shipp to my Sarvant Captayne Robert Smith of Cornwale. We also in this river sett vp our barges, and made

[1] The fruits mentioned by Ralegh are the plantains (*Musa paradisiaca* Linn.), pine-apples (*Ananas sativus* Mill.), and ground-nut (*Arachis hypogæa* Linn.).

[2] The animal of which Sir Walter speaks is the Peccary. It resembles in its general appearance a European hog; but there are so many differences in its structure, that it forms a separate genus. The peccaries possess on their back a gland which contains a fluid matter of a musky smell, which organ is cut out as soon as they are killed. There are two species; one with a white oblique line in the form of a collar round the neck, and the other of a uniform darker colour and of larger size. The first is the *Dicotyles torquatus*, the other *D. labiatus* of Cuvier. An occasional hunt of these animals has afforded us much amusement while in the forests of Guiana, which, as they are sometimes met in flocks of hundreds, is not entirely without danger. The meat is very good eating, though they are seldom fat.

cleane our shipps trimde vp our cask, and filled store of water, sett vp our smithes forge and made such yron work as the fleet neded. In this river we refresht our selves from the 17 day of November till the 4th of December. Decemb. 4.

Cap. Janson whom we found a very honest man, departed from Caliana towards Flushing the[1] and Captaine Peter Ally being still trobled with the Vertigo desirous therfore to returne because vnable to indure the roling of the shipp, I gott passage for him with Janson and for[1] who could not yet recover his health in this hott country.

The 4th of December I wayed and fell downe to the havens mouth not daring to loose the spring tyde, the rest of my Shipps had yet somewhat to do about their boates which they newly sett vp, to witt the fliing Hart, wherin was Sir John Fern, and the Chudley, all promised to follow within a day or two, and I told them that I would stay them att the triangel Ilands called Epinessarie[2], only the viceadmirall followed mee to witt Cap: Penington in the Jason and notwithstanding that I had sounded the barr twise or thrise before I durst putt over, yet I came aground in 16 foote, it being a quarter ebb ere I could gett over Decemb. 4.

[1] Similar blanks in the original. The letter which Sir Walter wrote to Lady Ralegh by this opportunity is dated "from Caliana in Guiana the 14th of November." (See Remains of Sir Walter Ralegh, edition of 1656, p. 161. Harleian Collection, No. 39 Plut. 4. C.) We cannot discover who accompanied Captain Alley; that officer arrived in January 1618 in England, and it is supposed that he was the bearer of the manuscript which was afterwards printed under the title of 'Newes of Sir Walter Rauleigh,' which is dated the 17th of November 1617.

[2] The Triangle islands received that name from their position: they were afterwards called "îles du Diable," from some Indian superstition, and are at present known as the "îles du Salut," or isles of health. The miserable remnant of the unfortunate emigrants who to the number of twelve thousand left France and arrived in Cayenne in 1713, for the purpose of settling near the mouth of the Kourou, were brought to these islands. An epidemic having broken out among them at the Kourou, some recovered here their health in order to fall victims to starvation, as famine soon commenced to prevail at these barren islets. They form a fine and well-sheltered harbour for the largest vessel.

by reason of the little winde which I found a sea borde, we vsed all the help we had by warping and otherwise being greatly assisted by the viceadmirall boates and warpps, but wee stuck two hole tydes and two nights, and afterward had fowle water in 3 fathom, but God favored vs with very faire weather, and the ground was all oase, and very soft, for had it bynn hard ground and any weather att all, we had left our bones ther.

5 & 6. of Decemb. In this melancolly toyle we spent the 5th and 6th day and then came to Anker att the triangle Ilands before spoken of in 6 fadom wher I stayd for the rest of the fleet till the 10 daye who neglecting the spring tyde though they drew by farr less water than I did, were like to have perished uppon the flattes wher I strock.

Decemb. The 10 day the rest of the fleet came to mee all but the Chudley and then I imbarked my men in five shipps for Orenoke, to witt 400 Soldiers, and Saylers, the shipps I sent of were the Incounter commanded by Cap: Whitney. The Supply of Cap: King, the Pink of Robert Smith, Cap: Oleston, and Cap: Hall.

Sr Warran Sentleger to whom as to my Leiuctenant I gave the charge of those companies, fell extrame sicke att Caliana, and in his place as Sergent Maior I appointed my nephew George Ralegh, the land companies were commanded by Cap: Parker, Cap: North, my sonn W. Ralegh, Captaine Thornehurst, Capt: Hall, and Cap: Chudles, Levetenant; Captaine Kemish having the cheife charge for their landing within the river.

The 10 day they parted from vs with a moneth vittles or somewhat more, I gave them order to stay a day or two in Shurinamo[1], to gett pilotts and to bring some of our great barges a ground who were weake and leeke by twoing them from Caliana. I also gave them order to send into Dessekebe[2] for I assured them that they could not want Pilotts ther for Orenoke,

[1] The river Surinam.

[2] The river Essequibo. The Dutch were here established as early as 1580–90. They were however driven from their settlements by the Spaniards, assisted by the Indians.

being the next great river adioyning vnto it, and to which the Spaniards of Orenoke had dayly recourse.

The 15 of December we made the land neere Pvncto Anegada at the mouth of Orenoke[1], and that night we saw the northest part of Trinidado, and came to ancor in 30 fathom 6. L. of the shore, from thence we coasted the Iland neere the south syde in 15 fathom and neere the shore in 10. and 11 fathom and coming close abord the poynt of the rode att the west end of the Iland which poynt they naturally call Curiapan, and the Spaniards Puncto de gallo we had 5. fathom. It floweth on this south coast E.N.E. and W.S.W. it is needfull to saile neere the poynt of Gallo which you may do boldly because ther lyeth a dangerous legg of rock so half a mile of the rode to the westward, a most forcible current that setts of the poynt, a greater current can no wher be found the currant of Bahama excepted. Decem: 15.

The 17 we came to Ancor at Puncto Gallo wher wee stayd (taking water fish and some Armadellias, refreshing our men with palmeto, Guiavas[2], piniorellas and other frute of the country) till the last of December. In sayling by the south coast of Trinidado I say in one day to witt the 16 of December 15 raine- 17 Dec.

[1] In a manuscript map of the world, to which we have had opportunity to allude on a former occasion, the right bank of the Caño Manamo near its embouchure is called Anegada (from *anegar* in Spanish, to immerse or cover with water). From Sir Walter Ralegh's account it is evident that he alludes to a more eastern point, probably the present Point Barima, which is called Terra basse in the old manuscript map. This conclusion is rendered more probable by some observations in his Apology. (See Cayley, vol. ii. p. 124.)

[2] The Guiavas, or rather Guavas, are the fruits of *Psidium pomiferum* and *P. pyriferum* Linn., trees about eighteen feet high. They are as large as a middle-sized apple, which they resemble in shape, of a bright yellow outside, and the pulp of a reddish colour, intermixed with very small hard seeds. The second kind (*P. pyriferum*) is considered by many to be merely a variety of the first, improved by cultivation. They have a pleasant subacid and aromatic taste, and, prepared with sugar and milk, may be compared to strawberries. A rich jelly or marmalade is likewise made of them. We do not know what fruit Ralegh calls Piniorellas.

bowes, and 2 wind galls, and one of the rainebowes brought both ends together att the sterne of the shipp making a perfait cirkell which I never saw before nor any man in my shipp had seene the like[1].

Decemb. the last. The last of December we wayed ancor and turned up north est towards Conquerabo, otherwise called the port of Spayne being new yeers eve, and wee came to Ancor at Terra de Bri, short of the Spanish port some 10 leagues. This Terra de Bri is a peece of land of some 2 leagues longe and a league brode, all of ston pich or bitumen which riseth out of the ground in little springs or fountaynes and so running a little way, it hardneth in the aire, and covereth all the playne; ther are also many springs of water and in and among them fresh water fishe[2]. Here rode att ancor, and trymd our boates, we had here some fishe, and many of the country fesants somewhat bigger then ours[3], and many of the henns exceeding fatt and delicate meat.

Jan: the 19. The 19 of Januarie we sent vp Sir J. Ferns shipp to the Spanish port, to try if they would trade for Tobacco and other things, but when her boate was neere the shore while they on the land were in parle with Cap: Giles who had charge of the boat, the Spaniards gave them a volley of some 20 musketts att 40 paces distant, and yet hurt never a man, as our bote putt of they called our men theeves and traytors with all manner of opprobrious speeches[4].

[1] In the spray of the sea or a cascade a circular rainbow is often seen, and if it were not for the interruption of the earth a circular spectrum would be seen at all times when the conditions are favourable for forming a rainbow.

[2] See *ante*, p. 2, note 4.

[3] Several species of birds from Guiana and other parts of South America have been compared with the pheasants of the Old World, but chiefly *Penelope cristatus* Gmel., *P. pipile* Jacq. and *Phasianus Mamot* Gmel., the Catraca of Buffon. The first is the most common, and is called Marudi in British Guiana; the flesh is tasteful, though sometimes (as we know by experience) very tough.

[4] Fray Simon, in his 'Noticias historiales,' asserts that Ralegh intended to disembark his men for the purpose of assaulting St. Joseph. Lieutenant Benito de Baena, informed of his project, posted his people so advantage-

The[1] of Januarie we sent back the Viceadmirall Cap: Penington to puncto Gallo to attend the returne of our companies in Orenoke.

The 29 of Jan: we lost one of Sir Jo: Ferns men, who being ashore boyling of the country pich was shott by a Spaniard who lay in the woods all night with five other Spanierds, our shipps taking the alarm we waied out our boates, I tooke my barge with six shott, Capt: Chudley tooke his skiff, and Sir W. Sentleger his, wee pursued them with all hast possible and forst them to forsacke their canoas and run into the thick woods, leaving behinde them their cloakes, and all other their implements but their arms. Ther were of Sir J: Fern's men three, and one boy, one of them was slayne, one swam abord, and third hidd himself in the woods till my barge came ashore, the boy we suppose was caried with them alive. Jan. 29.

The last of Jan: we returned from the pich land to Puncto Gallo, hoping to meet our men which we sent into Orenoke. Jan. the last.

The first of Februarie the sentenell which we had layd to the eastward of Puncto Gallo to discouer if any shipps or boates cam from the east alongst the coast, for we could not discouer any thing wher we rode till they were within a mile of vs by that the poynct lay out so farr; these of the sentenell discovered 7 Indiens and brought them vnto vs. They had a village some 16 mile from vs to the eastward, and as it proued afterward came but as spies to discouer our forces, they were two dayes abord and would be acknown, that they could speake any word of Spanish, but by signes they made vs know that they dwelt but one dayes jurney towards the east. I keipt 3 of them abord and sent 12 of my men with the other 4 to see their towne and Feb. the 1.

ously at Port of Spain, that the attack of the English was repulsed with the loss of several men, one being taken prisoner, who informed De Baena of the departure of a part of the fleet for the Orinoco. Ralegh's simple account of this affair is more probable; the prisoner of whom De Baena speaks was doubtless the boy lost during the affair of the 29th of January.

[1] A similar blank in the original.

to trade with them, but in ther way thitherward one of the Viceadmiralls men espied an Indien, one of the 4 who two yeere before he had seene in Orenoke, and taking him by the arme told him that he knew him, and that he could speake Spanish, in the end after many threates, he spake, and confest, that one of the three abord my shipp could also speake Spanishe; wher-vppon the Viceadmiralls man returning abord mee, and I threat-ing the cheif of these which I had keipt, one of them spake Spa-nish, and told mee that certayne Indiens of the dround lands inhabited by a nation called Tibitivas ariving in a Canoa att his port, told him that the Inglish in Orenoke had taken S[t] Thome, slaine Diego de Palmita the Governour, slayne Cap: Erenetta, and Cap: John Rues, and that the rest of the Spanierds (their Captaynes slayne) fledd into the mountaynes and that two Ing-lish Captaynes were also slayne. This tale was also confirmed by another Indien which my men brought from the Indien towne with divers other particularities, which I forbeare to sett downe till I know the trewth, for the 6 of this moneth I sent the viceadmirall skiff from Puncto Gallo towards Orenoke man'd with 10 musketiers to understand what my men had don their, and the cause of their longe stay, having received no newse from them since they entred Orenoke but by these Indiens since the 10 of December, other then that they were att the rivers mouth, which newse Cap: Chudley (who accompanied them so farr) brought mee.

Jan: the 3.[1] The 3 of January my men returned from the Indien town and brought with them some Casavi bread with other frutes, and very faire Orenges.

Jan: the 4. The forth of January a boat that I had sent over to the south

[1] We have copied the date literally from the original manuscript, though it is evident that Ralegh meant the month of February. The great sus-pense about the fate of the Orinoco expedition, which at that period must have been much increased by the reports brought to him by the Indians, doubtless caused an error, which gives us a picture of the anxiety of his mind.

syde wher I saw a great fier returned not finding any people ther.

The 6. day I sent a skiff over toward Orenoke man'd with 10 musketiers, to here what was become of my men their. The same day came into this port Cap: Giner of the Ile of Waight and his pinnes. Jan. 6.

The 8 day I sent 16 musketiers by land to the Indien towne to bring away some of the Indiens which spake Spanish and to separate them from those two which I keipt abord mee because I found them so divers in their reports as towching Orenoke, and because one of them had confest the day before that himself with the pilott which I sent into Orenoke in the skiff, and one of them in the Indien towne, were in St Thome when it was taken by the Inglish. I was desirus by taking 2 or 3 of the rest to know the trewth but so careless were the mariners I sent as they suffered all to go loose and to escape: but I had yet 2 Indiens abord mee, and a third went pilot for Orenoke, one of these I sent away with knives to trade with a nation inhabiting the est part of Trinidado called the Nepoyios, with this charge that if he came not agayne after 4 dayes (which was the time by him required) that I would then hange his brother which was the pilot as aforesayd, and this other Indien abord, to which the Indien abord condiscented. Jan. 8.

But the 12. of Februarie, I went ashore and tooke the Indien with mee fastned and well bound to one of my men, so caried him with me to shew me the trees which yeild balsemum of which I had recouered a nuttfull of that kinde which smells like Angolica and is very rare and pretious[1], and after it was 10 Feb. 12.

[1] Ralegh's observation, that the balsam resembled Angolica, by which he alludes to the violet-scented Orris-root (*Iris florentina*), causes us to conjecture that it is the balsam of Tolu, which is yielded by a tree called *Myrospermum toluiferum*, Rich. We have found that useful tree near the Saerere mountains, between the rivers Rupununi and Takutu, and the natives of these regions wear the seeds, which are equally fragrant with the resin, as ornaments round their body. If we are correct in our supposition, this tree is no longer to be met with in Trinidad.

a clock and very hott, the wood also being full of musketos, I returned and left my Indien in charge with one of my masters mates and 3 others, but I was no sooner gonn but they untyde him and he att the instant tooke the wood and escaped, notwithstanding that I had told them that if the Indien gatt but a tree betweene him and them and were loose that all the Inglish in the fleet could not fetch him agayne. I had now none left but the pilott sent to Orenoke and I feare me that he also will slipp away by the negligence of the mariners who (I meane the common sort) are dilligent in nothing but pillaging and stealing.

13 Feb. The 13 day Cap: Giner and I made an agrement that he shoulde follow me with his small shipp and pinnes for 6 moneths after this 13 day.

The same Evening I sent Sir W. Sentleger Cap: Chudley and Cap: Giles with 60 men to the Indien towne to try if I could recover any of them.

Here closes Sir Walter Ralegh's journal. It is very probable that the next day brought him the letter which Keymis had written on the 8th of January from the Orinoco, containing the information of his son's death. We may well conceive that this bereavement, and the total failure of his plans rendered him incapable of chronicling the subsequent events. In his letter to Sir Ralph Winwood, in speaking of the death of his son, he says, "with whom, to say truth, all the respects of this world have taken end in me;" and what could better depict the state of his mind than the request to Sir Ralph, "to give a copy of this letter to my Lord Carew; for to a broken mind, a sick body, and weak eyes, it is a torment to write many letters [1]."

The events connected with the expedition up the Orinoco, as

[1] Sir Walter Ralegh's Remains, and Harleian Coll. No. 39, Plut. 4. C. fols. 351, 355.

far as they are known to us from his letters addressed to Lady Ralegh, Sir Ralph Winwood, Lord Carew, and from the Apology for his last voyage, are vague and unsatisfactory; it may be of interest therefore to relate briefly the account which the Spanish historians give of the assault of Santo Thomè or St. Thomas[1]. It will however be requisite to take a retrospective view of some occurrences which preceded this event.

After the death of Antonio de Berreo, the Governor of Trinidad, Guiana and El Dorado, as he pompously styled himself, his son Don Fernando succeeded him, who at the commencement gave general satisfaction. He however changed his conduct towards the colonists, and their complaints having reached the court of Madrid, Captain Don Sancho Alguiza received orders to proceed from Venezuela to Guiana to investigate the matter. Alguiza considered the complaints well-founded, and Don Fernando was suspended from his governorship, while his chief accuser received a command, by virtue of the decision of the Supreme Council, ratified by Philip the Third, to administer the government. Don Fernando de Berreo lost no time in proceeding to Madrid, where he pleaded his defence and the services of his late father with great success; and although Philip had already nominated Don Diego Palomeque de Acuña (a relative of Don Diego Sarmiento de Acuña, afterwards Count de Gondomar[2]) as Governor, and had actually signed the requisite documents for that purpose on the 8th of November, 1615, Berreo nevertheless won the good graces of the Duke of Lerma, the virtual ruler of Spain, of which Philip was but nominal sovereign; and that powerful favourite induced the monarch to bestow upon Berreo for life the Governor-generalship of New Granada, including the inferior government of Guiana and Trinidad, for which Palomeque had already received a commission. Palomeque and Berreo left Spain together for their government, and the former

[1] The name of this town is variously spelt; besides the above, it is sometimes written San Tomè, Santo Tomas, and Santo Thomè.

[2] Dr. Lingard erroneously says that Palomeque was Gondomar's brother.

had only arrived a few months in Guiana when he received a royal cedula, dated the 19th of March, 1617, in which he was desired to guard himself against the contemplated attack of Gualtero Reali, who it was alleged was preparing an expedition consisting of several frigates and vessels, well-armed and manned, for the purpose of invading Guiana. Palomeque was likewise informed that a report had reached Madrid by way of England, that five or six vessels were being equipped by adventurers in Holland with the intention of descending upon the coast of Guiana[1].

The complaint of Sir Walter Ralegh, that he had been betrayed by his own royal master long ere he departed from England, is therefore fully authenticated by the Spanish historian Fray Simon.

We have seen from Ralegh's journal that the expedition intended for the Orinoco left the Triangle Isles on the 10th of December[2]. While crossing the bar off the "Puncto Anegado" (probably Point Barima), the Encounter, commanded by Captain Whitney, and the Confidence by Captain Wollaston, got aground, and lay fast for three days. The expedition arrived off the island of Yaya (Assapana of Ralegh's first voyage) according to the English accounts on the 1st of January, 1618[3]; according to the Spanish historian, on the 12th of January[4]. An Indian fisherman saw the fleet approaching and hastened to give the Governor Palomeque information of it, who did not lose a moment to make the necessary preparation for the defence of Santo Thomè, which town had been removed from the mouth of the Caroni since Keymis's voyage in 1596, and consisted now of one hundred and forty houses, a church, and two convents. He assembled the principal colonists, and called together all the people labouring in the fields, among whom he distributed

[1] Fray Simon, Setima Noticia Histor. cap. xxiii. p. 636.

[2] See *ante*, p. 202.

[3] Keymis's letter to Sir Walter is dated "this 8th of January, 1617–18." See Manuscript copy in Sir Hans Sloane's Collection.

[4] Fray Simon, *l. c.* p. 637.

arms and ammunition. Their number amounted to fifty-seven, of whom more than a fourth were invalids. Two pieces of artillery were posted on the banks of the Orinoco, and thus prepared the Governor awaited the arrival of the English. At eleven o'clock three vessels hove in sight near Punta Araya, some leagues above the mouth of the river Guarguapo. Soon after the Carvel and the five launches followed, and five hundred men[1] were disembarked near the Narrows (Ensenado) of Arugo or Aramaya. Under the supposition that the forces which had been landed were to make a diversion by land, while the vessels were to attack the town by water, Don Diego despatched Captain Geronimo de Grados with ten men to occupy an ambuscade on some rising ground about "three musket shots" from Santo Thomè[2]. The English soon forced him to abandon this post and to fall back upon the town, which during the night of the 1st to the 2nd of January (in the ninth hour of Friday the 12th of January, according to the Spanish account) was attacked on two points. The Spaniards, overpowered by numbers, were obliged to retreat, after having offered a most valiant resistance. It appears the English considered themselves already victorious, and one of their number advanced before the rest, shouting victory, but Grados gave him such a sword-stroke on the left side of the neck, "that he sent the heretic to have the cry answered in hell[3]."

Though the guard-house was taken, the Spaniards rallied

[1] This number is according to the Spanish account; Sir Walter says however that soldiers and sailors together amounted only to four hundred men, while Simon asserts that the whole equipment of Ralegh amounted to more than a thousand men. (Fray Simon, *l. c.* p. 637.)

[2] Grados used a stratagem to make the number of his men appear much larger than it was, by cutting a match-cord in pieces, which he lighted and placed at intervals.

[3] "Que embio el herege a que le respontieran a su canto en el infierno." (Fray Simon, *l. c.* p. 640.) This was most probably young Ralegh, though Simon thinks he was slain by Don Diego, or rather that they fell by each other's hands.

again in the public square or Plaza, and threw themselves into some houses adjoining, in which loop-holes had been cut; from thence they successfully fired at the English with "their murderers" and muskets, till the assailants set fire to the houses. The Governor Don Diego de Palomeque and Captain Monge were missing, and another captain wounded; the Spaniards resolved therefore to retreat to the convent of San Francisco, which was on the opposite side of the town from that where the English had entered: this was however stormed, and they fled into the adjacent forests[1]. On the first alarm that the enemy was entering Santo Thomè, the women with their children and the invalids had taken flight, without provisions of any kind, towards the Caroni[2]. Garcia de Aguilar and Juan de Lazama, the two alcaldes upon whom the command devolved after the death of the Governor, sent Grados with a few soldiers to escort the women and children across the river, from whence he con-

[1] The fate of Father Francesco de Leuro, the Curate of the city, gives an instance of the faithful attachment of the Indians. The poor Padre had lost the use of his limbs for the last six months, and was confined to his bed. In the confusion which arose when the English entered the town, he had been forgotten by every one except an Indian woman, Luysa de Fonseca (Simon calls her "una India ladina," namely one who was able to speak the Spanish language), who carried the poor priest out of his house to an adjacent pit. Here he was found by the English, who treated him with humanity and kindness. When the English evacuated Santo Thomè they set the few remaining houses on fire, and the poor paralytic priest was again forgotten, and, less fortunate than on the former occasion, was burnt with the house in which he was lying.

[2] Fray Simon says, "Dandoles fuerças el miedo una legua hasta la boca del rio que llaman Caroni, y entra en el Orinoco arriba de la ciudad." (Cap. xxiv. p. 641.) This historian no doubt errs in naming the Caroni. The site of Santo Thomè was formerly near the confluence of the Caroni with the Orinoco; but we learn that it had been removed further down, and was now at least ten leagues to the east of that river. The river here alluded to is probably the Guanapo, which flows into the Orinoco a short distance to the west of the present Guayana vieja, the site of the town destroyed by Keymis, and a small laguna is called to this day Seiba; it must however be observed, that there is likewise an island of that name in the Orinoco, about six leagues above the mouth of the Caroni.

ducted them afterwards to the island of Seiba, where it was thought they would be more secure. Here he shared a little Indian corn or maize and some dried meat among them.

Young Ralegh and four others, who were among the fallen, were put in shrouds in the guard-house, and conveyed into the church, accompanied by all the soldiers under arms, with muffled drums beating, pikes trailing, and five banners carried before them, as the fallen men were all Captains[1]. The son of the General and another were buried near the high altar, and the three others in the body of the church. On the day of the funeral, continues Father Simon, arrived two vessels, one of them larger than the others, which was taken for the "Capitana de la armada[2]."

The English left no stone in the town unturned in search of gold, silver or precious stones. Disappointed in their expectation, they sent one hundred and fifty men armed with pikes and other instruments to scour and ransack the neighbouring plantations and to drive away the cattle. The Spaniards laid several ambuscades, and attacked them with such success, when divided, that they quickly fell back upon the town, which they continued to occupy[3].

[1] Captain Parker states that they lost only two captains, namely Ralegh and Cosmor, both of whom were probably buried near the high altar.

[2] Keymis in his letter to Sir Walter Ralegh, dated January 8th, observes, "Captains Whitney and Wollaston are but now come to us." The greatest confusion prevails in all the dates between the English and the Spanish accounts. Gumilla in his 'Orinoco Illustrado', places Ralegh's first expedition in 1545.

[3] The conflict which took place at the taking of Santo Thomè is related by Ralegh in his Apology in the following words: "It seemes that the Sergeant major Keymis and the rest were by accident forced to change their first resolution, and that finding a Spanish towne or rather village, set up twenty miles distant from the place where Antonio Berreo (the first Governour by me taken in my first discovery) who had attempted to plant, viz. some two Leagues to the westward of the mine: They agreed to land and encamp between the myne and the Towne, which they did not suspect to be so neer them as it was, and meaning to rest themselves on the River's side till the next day, they were in the night set upon

The English afterwards sent two launches manned with forty men up the river to the Caño Seiba, where the women and children would probably have been taken if Captain Grados had not removed them. This officer posted ten Spaniards and ten Indian archers advantageously near the entrance of the Caño, who opened such a well-directed fire against the first launch, that nine men out of the ten in the boat were killed[1]; the other boat made no further advance, and returned towards Santo

and charged by the Spaniards, which being unlooked for, the Common sort of them were so amazed, as had not the Captaines and some other valiant Gentlemen made a Head and encouraged the rest, they had all been broken and cut in pieces. To repell this force putting themselves in order, they charged the Spaniards and following them upon their retreat they were ready to enter the Town, ere they knew where they were, and being then charged againe by the Governour and foure or five Captaines, which led their companies, my sonne not tarrying for my musketiers, run up in the head of a company of pikes, where he was first shot, and pressing upon a Spanish Captaine called Erinetta with his sword, Erinetta taking the small end of his musket in his hand, strucke him on the head with the stock and feld him, whom againe John Plesington my sonnes Serjeant, thrust through with his Halbert, at which time also the Governour Diego Palmeque and the rest of the Spanish Captaines being slaine, and their companies divided, they betooke themselves into a house, or hold adjoyning to the market place, whence with their murderers and muskets (the houses having loopholes cut out toward the market place) they slew and wounded the English at their pleasure, so as we had no way to save ourselves but by firing those houses adjoyning, which done all the Spaniards ran into the bordering woods and hills, keeping the English still waking with perpetual alarums.

"The town such as it was being in this sort possessd, Keymis prepared to discover the myne, which at this time he was resolved to doe, as appeareth by his letter to me of his owne handwriting hereafter inserted; he tooke with him Captaine Thornhurst, Master William Herbert, Sir John Hambden, and others, but at his first approach neer the banke where he meant to land, he received from the wood a vollew of shot which slew two of his company, hurt six others, and wounded Captain Thornhurst in the head, of the which he languished three months after." (Sir Walter Rawleigh his Apologie in the Select Essayes and Observations, &c., London, 1650, p. 29.)

[1] According to the description which Sir Walter Ralegh gives of this affair, Captain Keymis lost two men, six were hurt, and Captain Thornhurst received a wound in his head.

Thomè. The English commander, incensed at this failure, now armed three boats, and having embarked a larger force, they explored the river as high up as the Guarico, which falls into the Orinoco near the village of Cabruta, about one hundred and ten leagues from Santo Thomè [1]. They were twenty days absent upon this expedition, during which the English sounded the river at different points, established communications with the Caribs, the inveterate enemies of the Spaniards, and showed every disposition to establish themselves permanently on the Orinoco. The Spaniards resolved to oppose such a design by all the means in their power; and having consulted with their Indian allies, the latter placed sixty archers at their command, who with twenty-three Spaniards well-armed entered the town, then in possession of the English, intending to approach the guard-house secretly during the night, where the enemy had the strongest force, and to fall unexpectedly upon them, after having set the neighbouring houses on fire. Their plan did not succeed, in consequence of heavy rains, which had rendered the roofs of the houses so moist that they could not fire them: they contented themselves therefore with pouring at daybreak a shower of balls and arrows upon their enemies, after which they retreated. The English had been twenty-six days in possession of the town, when the Spaniards, who still secreted themselves in the neighbourhood, sent four soldiers with a letter containing information of these occurrences to the Real Audiença of Santa Fé, requesting that troops and ammunition might be speedily despatched to the Orinoco for their protection. They likewise demanded a supply of clothing, as in their retreat from the town they had no time to carry off any besides what they had upon them. They further requested the Audiença to nominate an officer to govern them, and to send some spiritual assistance, as Fray Juan de Maya, the guardian of the convent of San Francisco, was the only priest who had escaped. The president

[1] The ascent of the expedition so high up the river is not mentioned by Ralegh, nor in any other English account.

of the Audiença received the letter on the 9th of April, and consulting the archbishop, Don Hernando de Arias, and other influential men, it was resolved to send Don Fernando de Berreo with Diego Martin de Baena to the Orinoco, to assist the Spaniards. The latter arrived before Santo Thomè on the 19th of August. The English, whose numbers had been meanwhile much weakened by disease and the attacks of the Spaniards and Indians, had abandoned the town, carrying with them all objects of any value, pilfering the church and the cabildo, and embarking some hundred and fifty quintals of tobacco: five hundred more had been destroyed by the fire[1]. On their departure they set the town on fire, which consumed the church, the convent, and the few houses that had escaped the former conflagration. They carried away with them a number of sick and wounded, and had suffered a loss of at least two hundred and fifty men. We possess no data in the English letters respecting this unfortunate expedition when Keymis's party left Santo Thomè; but according to the Spanish historians[2], Fray Simon and Caulin, the English re-embarked on the 29th of January, 1618.

[1] Fray Simon gives a detailed account of the booty. The amount of gold which they found in the treasury was 600 reales in money, a gold bar ("una barra de oro de cabo y cola"), an ingot and some other pieces, which together amounted to about 2000 reales, besides a weighty gold chain, a large silver hand-basin (*aguamanil*), and some golden trinkets which had been deposited there. Simon accuses them of having taken away some of their guns and the bells from the church and the two convents of San Domingo and San Francisco, with all the church ornaments. He estimates the whole private loss at 40,000 reales. They likewise carried away three negro slaves (two the property of a widow) and two Indians, one of whom returned ultimately from England to his native country.

[2] The Spanish account agrees in general with the chief events made known by Keymis and Parker, but Fray Simon is silent on the existence of mines at that period. He observes towards the conclusion of his relation of the attack on Santo Thomè, that it was reported, that "Gualtero Reali was a great pirate, and that he had formerly navigated the coasts of Terra-firma and the Islands 'de Barlobento,' and that there was a rich gold mine on the banks of the Orinoco, from which he carried to London some

It is not known when the expedition under Keymis reached Trinidad. On joining Ralegh he endeavoured to justify his proceedings, alleging that he had neither a sufficient force to defend his position against the attacks of the Spaniards, nor people to work the mine; and that young Ralegh being slain, Sir Walter himself unpardoned, and as he supposed not likely to live, he had no reason to open the mine either for the Spaniards or the King. Ralegh indignantly rejected his excuses, and reproached him as the sole cause of the ruin which he considered unavoidable; and this appears to have made such an impression upon Keymis's mind, that he shortly after attempted to shoot himself in the breast. The pistol was small, and the ball having struck upon a rib did not immediately take effect; and, determined upon self-destruction, he plunged a knife into his side. "His boy going into his cabin, found him lying upon his bed with much blood by him, and looking in his face saw him dead[1]."

A letter, of which merely an extract has hitherto been published[2], alludes to Keymis's suicide in most uncharitable expressions. This document is also of interest, as giving some more details of the Orinoco expedition.

"A Letter written by Captaine Charles Parker, one of Sr Walter Raleighs companie at Guiana; to Captain Alley. Ano 1617[3].

"CAPTAIN ALLEY,

"Your goinge from vs was verie fortunate in that you prevented the vndergoinge vnspekable miseryes for wee disimboged

casks full of the earth, as already mentioned." (Setima Noticia, cap. xxix. p. 663.) This observation contradicts Dr. Southey's assertion, that none of the Spanish historians mentioned Ralegh's former visit to Guiana. (Southey's Lives of the Admirals, vol. iv. note at p. 310.)

[1] Ralegh's letter to Sir Ralph Winwood.

[2] Edinburgh Review, No. cxliii. p. 85.

[3] Brit. Mus. MSS. Harl. 39. fol. 351. Several of the old MS. copies of

from Caliana towards Orenoco Captaine Witnes shipe Captaine Wouliston the flieboat and karvill, the Admirall vizadmirall with the other great shipes went from Trinidadoe to harbor tyll owr returne, wee were a month going vpe Orinocoe at laste we landed within a league of St. Thome, and about one of the clocke at nighte we made an assaulte, wher we loste Captaine Ralegh and Captain Cosmor, but Captaine Raleghe lost him selfe with his vnaduised daringnes as you shall heare, for I will acquinte you, how we were ordered. Captain Cosmor led the forlorne hope with some 50 men, after him I brought upe the first devission of shotte, next brought vp Captaine Raleigh a devission of Pikes who no sooner hearde vs charged but indiscreetely came from his commaunde to vs, wher he was vnfortunatly welcomed with a bullett, which gave him no tyme to call for mercye to our hevenly father for his sinfull lyfe he had ledde; we presently tooke the Towne without lose of any more then two wherof on was M[r] Harington the Countise of Bedfords kinsman. The Spanyard was not stronge, and mistrustynge our potencie fled, and lefte their Gouernor with some other 2 Captaines, which bravely dyed: The Gouernor Don de Jego Palmeko de Acuna, Captain Santo, Captaine Alisnetto when wee were possessed of the Towne Captaine Kemish tooke diveres gentlmen with him to fynde the myne, and trifeled vpe and downe some 20 dayes keepinge vs in hope still of findinge it, but at laste we found his delayes meere illusiones and him selfe a mear machevill, for he was false to all men and moste odious to him selfe, for moste vngodly he butchered himselfe lothinge to live since he could doe no mor villany; I will speke no more of this hatefull fellow to God and man; But I informe you as neere as I canne what we that staye

letters written from the island of St. Christopher's bear, like Parker's, the year 1617. There can be no doubt that, chronologically, 1618 is meant. The confusion has arisen from the great inconvenience, until the altering of the style in 1752, that the civil or legal year commenced on the 25th of March, while the historical began on the 1st of January, and it was customary to affix to events which occurred during the first three months of the year two dates, *e.g.* 1617–18, &c.

shall truste to, we have devided our selves alredy, Witney and Woulaston are consorted to looke for homward bound men, the Admyrall, vizadmirall Sr John Ferne will for new-found lande to revittuall, and aftere to the western Ilands to looke for homward bounde men, for my parte by the permissyon of God I will make a voyadge or burie my selfe in the sea so I pray you make knowne to my frends; Aboute the latter end of Auguste I hope wee shall have fethered our neste and beinge in Harbur more I cannot write, onely this I desire God that you may prosperously live that wee may fortunatly meet.

"I rest yor affectionate frend

"CHARLES PARKER."

"The xxij^th of March
1617."

The report which was spread by Ralegh's enemies, that he had treacherously slain Keymis, has not the slightest probability, and is the foulest slander upon his memory. The reasons given, that if dead he could not divulge Ralegh's previous knowledge of the non-existence of mines, and his determination of committing piracy, are too shallow to deserve any credence. Ralegh was sincerely attached to Keymis, and when he contemplated committing suicide in the Tower, he wrote in his letter to Lady Ralegh, "Be good to Keymis, for he is a perfect honest man and hath much wrong for my sake[1]." Only the poignancy of his grief can excuse Ralegh's bitter reproaches of Keymis, which no doubt hastened his commission of self-destruction.

We observe from Captain Parker's letter that dissatisfaction had already broken out at this period among the commanders and crew of the squadron, and Ralegh mentions in his letters to Sir Ralph Winwood and to his wife, dated St. Christopher's, March 21st and 22nd respectively, that he had sent home, under the charge of his cousin Herbert, several of the disaffected per-

[1] See Ralegh's letter to his wife in Bishop Goodman's 'The Court of King James,' vol. ii. p. 93.

sons. It was ultimately determined to proceed to Newfoundland, for the purpose of refitting; at this place the crew of his ship, the Destiny, became mutinous, and the vessels which had hitherto remained with the squadron were on the point of separating, when Ralegh and Ferne held out to them the hope that combined they might succeed in interrupting and vanquishing the Mexican treasure-fleet[1]. It is asserted that this was merely a stratagem to keep them together; and having succeeded in quelling the mutiny, Ralegh insisted on returning directly to England[2]. They made in the first instance Kingssale in Ireland, and arrived in Plymouth in the beginning of July, 1618. The unfortunate result of Ralegh's expedition, and the news of his attack upon Santo Thomè, had reached England before him, and it is reported that Captain North communicated the melancholy news to King James with much caution and feeling on the 13th of May. Gondomar being informed of it demanded an audience of the King, promising that all he had to say should be included in one word. When he came into the royal presence, he cried out vehemently, "Piratas, piratas, piratas!" and left the audience.

It is said that Ralegh, as soon as he learned (even before he landed) of the royal proclamation, resolved to surrender himself. Whether he placed too fatal a reliance upon the expediency of his proceedings, or whether it was an additional proof of that

[1] A minute of the proceedings of the Commission, in the handwriting of Sir Julius Cæsar, one of its members, says, "On being confronted with Captains St. Leger and Pennington he confessed that he proposed the taking of the Mexico fleet if the mine failed." (Brit. Mus. Lansdowne MSS. No. 142, fol. 412.

[2] Fray Simon reports erroneously that Ralegh proceeded from Trinidad to Virginia, and that he landed afterwards at the harbour "de Plemna en Inglaterra," from whence he went to London, where his wife received him with great lamentations in consequence of the death of her son. This information was brought by the servant whom Ralegh took with him from Santo Thomè, and who ultimately returned to Guiana after having witnessed the execution of the knight,—a circumstance upon which the Spanish historian dwells with undisguised satisfaction.

despondency in his character to which we have had occasion to allude several times, cannot now be determined; but Captain King, his faithful companion in so many of his adventures and expeditions, asserts that he instantly resolved to surrender himself; and, to prevent any misconstruction of his plans, he moored his ship and sent his sails ashore on entering the harbour.

The subsequent events are of sufficient notoriety. It is asserted by Oldys, that the commissioners who had been appointed to examine Ralegh, were unable, even in the strictest exercise of their duty, to extract from the depositions of his late companions in the Guiana voyage any evidence of treasonable designs or piratical practices. This assertion of his too lenient biographers is directly contradicted by the minutes of Sir Julius Cæsar[1]; moreover the allusions contained in Captain Parker's letter, and Ralegh's own observation in the letter to his lady from St. Christopher's[2], leave no doubt that it was his intention, if he should fall in with the "Plate fleet," to attack it. "This day," says Sir Thomas Wilson, who acted as spy upon Ralegh, in his report, "he told me what discourse he and my Lord Chancellor had had about taking the Plate fleet, which he confessed he would have taken had he lighted upon it. To which my Lord Chancellor said, 'Why you would have been a pirate.' 'Oh,' quoth he, 'did you ever know of any that were pirates for millions? they only that work for small things are pirates.'"

The commissioners did not venture to hazard a fresh trial, founded either upon the attack of Santo Thomè or the unsupported evidence of Stuckley and Mannourie, of treasonable designs; and as Ralegh was to fall a victim to Gondomar's vengeance, for the sake of the desired Spanish alliance, the old

[1] Brit. Mus. Lansdowne MSS., No. 142, fol. 412. These minutes are very loosely penned, and almost require a commentary to be intelligible.

[2] "I have cleaned my ship of sick men and sent them home, and hope that God will send us somewhat before we return."

sentence for high-treason, passed in November 1603, was now to be executed. On Wednesday the 28th of October he was taken out of his bed, though suffering from fever, and conveyed from the Tower by writ of Habeas-corpus to the King's Bench bar at Westminster, where his plea of a pardon implied by his subsequent commission was overruled, and execution ordered. Sir Walter was delivered into the custody of the sheriffs of Middlesex, and conveyed to the Gatehouse near the Palace-yard. The warrant for his execution had evidently been signed beforehand: as soon as the sentence was passed, it was produced already signed. The pusillanimous King had gone to Hertfordshire, to be out of the way. Between Ralegh's return from the King's Bench and his execution, which took place the next morning, the 29th of October, 1618, he is supposed to have written the pathetic verses which we quote further on. We learn from Aubrey that "the time of his execution was contrived to be on my Lord Mayor's Day (viz. the day after St. Simon and St. Jude), that the pageants and fine shewes might drawe away the people from beholding the tragedie of one of the gallantest worthies that ever England bred[1]."

Ralegh's mind rallied wonderfully from the moment that his fate was decided, and we are told by Dr. Tounson, Dean of Westminster, who attended Sir Walter in his last hours, that "he was the most fearless of death that ever was known; and the most resolute and confident, yet with reverence and conscience." "The world," Ralegh calmly observed, "is itself but a larger prison, out of which some are daily selected for execution." His courage did not leave him to his last moment, and having given the signal that he was ready, by lifting up his hand, he was beheaded at two strokes, without the least convulsion or motion of his body. Thus died one of the bravest and most distinguished ornaments of Queen Elizabeth's reign.

[1] Aubrey's Letters, London edition, vol. ii. p. 520.

On the Snuff of a Candle.

" Cowards may fear to die; but courage stout
Rather than live in snuff, will be put out."

Verses found in his Bible, in the Gatehouse at Westminster.

" Even such is time, that takes on trust
Our youth, our joys, our all we have,
And pays us but with age and dust,
Who in the dark and silent grave,
When we have wander'd all our ways,
Shuts up the story of our days!
But from this earth, this grave, this dust,
The Lord shall raise me up, I trust." [1]

We have already observed that the exact day of this great man's birth is not known; Camden and others state that he was sixty-six years of age at his death, according to which he must have been born in the year 1552. We have likewise alluded to the statement of his former biographers, that Walter (who fell in his twenty-fourth year at Santo Thomè) and Carew were his only children; but contrary to this assertion is a passage in the remarkable letter addressed to his wife, when he contemplated committing suicide in the Tower, in which he expressly states, "To my poor daughter, to whom I have given nothing," &c. It is much to be regretted that such scanty notices of his daily and familiar life have been preserved, and that such a question should remain undecided. If the letter be genuine (which we doubt not), the fact is proved that Sir Walter had besides his two sons, Walter and Carew, a daughter; and the question only remains to be determined, whether she was the offspring of his marriage with Lady Ralegh; but as we have already stated our opinion on this subject in the Introduction to this volume, we refer to those pages.

Sir Robert Naunton and Sir John Harrington, who knew

[1] Numerous versions exist of these verses, which Archbishop Sancroft, who transcribed the lines, calls "Ralegh's Epitaph made by himself and given to one of his [attendants] the night before his suffering." The above has been copied from Ralegh's Works, Oxford edition, vol. viii. p. 729.

Ralegh personally, describe him as of good appearance. "He had in the outward man," says Naunton, "a good presence in a handsome and well-compacted person, a strong natural wit, and a better judgement, with a bold and plausible tongue, whereby he could set out his parts to the best advantage[1]." And Aubrey, speaking of his picture, says, "In the great parlour of Downton at Mr. Ralegh's is a good piece (an original of Sir W.) in a white satin doublet all embroidered with rich pearles, and a mighty rich chaine of great pearles about his neck[2].... He had a most remarkable aspect, an exceeding high forehead, long-faced and sour-eielidded, a kind of pigge-eie[3]." Though this description seems rather equivocal, Aubrey soon after asserts that Sir Walter's graceful presence was no mean recommendation to him[4].

Ralegh dressed with taste and magnificence; the splendid silver armour in which, as Captain of the Guard, he rode abroad with Queen Elizabeth was famed even in that age, so remarkable for profusion in dress. The engraving of Sir Walter by Vertue, executed in 1735 from an original portrait then in the possession of his descendants the Elwes family, is considered the best.

The character of this great man presents one of the enigmas which the study of human nature occasionally offers to the scrutinizing eye of posterity. While we cannot refrain from regarding with admiration most of his actions, his life furnishes likewise evidences of lamentable inconsistencies. It has been observed by Hallam, that "he never showed a discretion bearing the least proportion to his genius;" and we willingly avail ourselves of the observation of this historian, to cover with charity so many moral deflections in Ralegh's history, which would otherwise be stains upon his character.

[1] Fragmenta Regalia, Art. Ralegh.

[2] As we are not aware that the custom of wearing chains of pearls was followed by any other but by Ralegh at that period, we are almost inclined to believe it was in imitation of the Indian fashion, where men and women alike to this day wear necklaces of glass beads, since they are no longer able to procure real pearls.

[3] Aubrey's Letters, vol. ii. p. 511.

[4] Ibid. p. 516.

An unbiased view of the great events of Sir Walter's life proves that he was naturally ambitious, and that to attain his object he was not always scrupulous as to the means he employed. Many of his errors were the offspring of visionary ideas and chimerical plans—a striking feature of the period in which he lived. What greater proof of this assertion can we require, than his grave disquisition whether there was a crystalline heaven, a *primum mobile,* whether the tree of knowledge was the *Ficus indicus,* and other questions of a similarly ludicrous nature[1]?

We have already stated our opinion that Ralegh believed firmly in the riches of Guiana, and we do not impute to him excessive credulity for having given full faith to the fallacious accounts which existed at that period of the metallic wealth of Guiana; but we blame him for the means which he used to procure converts to his opinions and contributions to the execution of his schemes[2]. His gross flattery to Queen Elizabeth, and his exaggerated style in representing his belief in the wealth of Guiana as resting upon personal examination, are likewise censurable. It is evident that he entertained ulterior plans greater than merely the working of gold-mines, namely the acquisition and colonization of Guiana; but his views in this great undertaking were liable to question. Ralegh was looked on by his contemporaries with distrust; by his theatrical deportment during his first imprisonment in the Tower, he had forfeited the good opinion of many of his fellow-courtiers, and the belief

[1] History of the World, First Book, cap. i. iii. iv. vii. &c.

[2] "In his youth his companions were boysterous blades, but generally those that had witt, except otherwise upon designe to gett them engaged for him e. gr. Sir Charles Snell of Kington Saint Michael in North Wilts, my good neighbour, an honest young gent. but kept a perpetual sott; he engaged him to build a ship (the Angel Gabriel) for the designe for Guiana which cost him the Manor of Yatton Keynell, the farme of Easton Piers, Thornhill, and the Churchlease of Bps. Cannings, which ship upon Sir Walter Ralegh's attainder was forfeited." (Aubrey's Letters, etc. vol. ii. p. 514.)

that he was not over-scrupulous in his assertions gained ground rapidly. Ben Jonson says of him, that he esteemed fame more than conscience.

A haughty and proud demeanour, and an utter contempt for the lower classes, were not qualified to procure him popularity; and the share which he was thought to have had in the tragical fate of Essex, the idol of the people, materially contributed to this popular aversion. Aubrey observes, that "he had an awfulness and ascendancy in his aspect over other mortals," which is not always a gift to be coveted, as it frequently leads to personal enmity; nevertheless no man was more beloved than Ralegh by his immediate attendants and companions, several of whom accompanied him repeatedly on his adventurous expeditions.

Though we have not been able to go all lengths with Ralegh's admirers, in bestowing indiscriminate praise upon all his actions, we are fully impressed with the opinion that his defects were the offspring of the characteristic period in which he lived, and that those parts in which Ralegh shone far outweighed his weaknesses.

Richly endowed with natural gifts, his indefatigable industry procured him a surprising knowledge, not only in military and maritime science, in geography and history, but likewise in the mechanical arts. Whatever object occupied his mind, he devoted to it the whole power of his genius, assisted by an energy almost unparalleled. Cecil remarks of him, "he can toil terribly[1]." This quality may lessen the amazement so frequently expressed by his contemporaries, from whence he got his ac-

[1] We have rather been surprised to find an incidental remark which speaks to the contrary. In a letter, written probably by one of the secretaries of the Earl of Essex, making some apologies why he had not heard from the court, occurs the following passage: "And for good Mr. Ralegh, who wonders at his owne diligence (because diligence and he are not familiars)" etc. The writer of this epistle gives another instance of our assertion, that Ralegh was not in repute for a strict adherence to truth; he continues, "Thus do you see that a man whose fortune scants him of

quirements. Ralegh's early life was passed in full activity during his military career in Ireland, France and Portugal; and when at home (we learn from Aubrey), he frequented taverns and other places of amusement[1]. Under such circumstances, which are not conducive to the acquisition of learning, the development of the powers of his mind, and the extent of knowledge which he displays in his writings, are truly miraculous. With this were united a polite address, a strong natural wit, and great powers of conversation; what wonder therefore that he captivated Elizabeth, "who was much taken with his elocution, loved to hear his reasons, and took him for a kind of oracle!" Sir Arthur Georges assures us, in his 'Relation of the Island Voyage,' that even Essex preferred Ralegh's conversation to that of most of his friends.

His inclinations seemed to direct him to a sea-faring life and maritime exploits, which he followed with a greater zeal than any other pursuit. His voyages were not undertaken upon hazard; the publication of his Guiana expedition gives sufficient evidence of his knowledge of the works of authors who had written on the New World, in which he was greatly assisted by his acquaintance with foreign languages.

The charge of atheism, which Father Parsons brought against Ralegh, deserves so little credit that we have passed it over. The poetry and prose writings of Ralegh alike breathe "a strong and genuine spirit of piety," and none more so than his epitaph written during the last hours of his life.

Though Ralegh acted a distinguished part in his military, naval and civil life, he was chiefly illustrious in maritime affairs,

meanes to do you service will not bear coales to be accused of dulness, especially by your Rereadmirall who making haste but once in a year to write a letter in post, gave date from Weymouth to his last dispatche, which by the circumstances I knew was written from Plymouth." (Brit. Mus. Lansdowne MSS. 85, No. 19.) It needs scarcely be observed, that the circumstances here alluded to refer to the expedition to Cadiz in 1596.

[1] "Ralegh instituted a club or meeting of *beaux esprits* at the Mermaid, a celebrated tavern in Friday Street." (Gifford's Life of Jonson, p. 65.)

and shines most conspicuously as a founder of colonies and promoter of commerce. His naval exploits were conducted with boldness and determination, and we have few examples of more active patriotism in a private individual than in Ralegh. The phantom to which he sacrificed his reputation, his fortune, and his life, namely the gold-mines of Guiana, haunted him to his last moments. His Apology expresses a continued assurance in the existence of gold-mines near the banks of the Orinoco; and in "the inventory of such things as were found on the body of Sir Walter Rawleigh, Knight, the 15th day of August, 1618," which document was sent to Sir Thomas Wilson by Sir Robert Naunton, Secretary of State, occur the following objects:

"A Guiana idol of Gold.

"A Spleenstone, (left with him for his own use).

"One wedge of fine gold at 22 carratts.

"An other stob of coarser gold.

"Item one plott of Guiana and Nova (R—)[1] and another of the river of Orenoque.

"The description of the river Orenoque.

"A plott of Panama.

"A tryal of Guiana ore with a description thereof.

"A Sprig jewel.

"Five assays of the Silver myne[2]."

These articles were probably taken from him after his recommittal to the Tower, when in the act of making his escape.

It appears from this inventory that Sir Walter had written some accounts of the Orinoco, in addition to what are contained in his 'Discovery of Guiana;' and the manuscript here alluded to may have been part of "the particular treatise of the West Indies," &c. which, with a map of the Orinoco, he mentions several times in the description of his first Guiana voyage[3].

[1] The omitted words are probably Reyno de Granada.

[2] See 'Life of Sir Walter Raleigh,' by Patrick Fraser Tytler, pp. 466, 467. Edinburgh, 1833.

[3] Amongst the MSS. of Sir Joseph Jekyll, Master of the Rolls, which

We learn from a letter which Lady Ralegh wrote after her husband's death to Lady Carew, that Sir Thomas Wilson ("the spy," as he has been called by Ralegh's biographers) continued his persecution against the family, and seized his books, manuscripts and mathematical instruments[1]. We have therefore a clue to the fate of the numerous manuscripts which Ralegh is said to have left behind, and we think with Mr. Tytler, that, "as Wilson was at the time Keeper of the State Paper Office, there is still a hope that Ralegh's manuscripts may be found amongst some of the unexplored treasures of the great national collections."

were sold by auction in London in 1739, was a volume containing "Several letters wrote by Sir Walter Rawleigh in relation to Guiana, subscribed by his own hand." It is not known what became of this volume, nor whether the letters were autographs or only transcripts. They were marked Lot 312.

[1] This letter is printed entire in Tytler's 'Life of Sir Walter Ralegh,' p. 464. "I beseech your Ladyship," writes Lady Ralegh, "that you will do me the favour to intreat Sir Thomas Wilson to surcease the pursuit of my husband's books and library; they being all the land and living which he left to his poor child; hoping that he would inherit him in these only, and that he would apply himself to learning to be fit for them; which request I hope I shall fulfil as far as in me lieth. Sir Thomas Wilson has already fetched away all his mathematical instruments, one of which cost £100 when it was made; I was promised them all again, but I have not received one back."

ERRATA.

Page xv, *for* remainder *read* unexpired term.

— 55 (note), *for* Cairina moshata *read* Cairina moschata.

— 118 (note), line 10 from bottom, *for* mercantile house *read* India House.

INDEX.

[The Roman Numbers refer to the pages of the Editor's Introduction.]

THE END.

PRINTED BY RICHARD AND JOHN E. TAYLOR,
RED LION COURT, FLEET STREET.